MARTA BREEN is an author of nonfiction works with a number of publications to her name. Among other things, she has written *Girls, Wine, and Song: 50 Years of Girls in Norwegian Rock and Pop, Born Feminist,* and the bestseller *60 Women You Should Know About* in collaboration with illustrator Jenny Jordahl. They have also worked together on the book *The F Word,* which won the Norwegian Ministry of Culture's textbook prize for young people.

JENNY JORDAHL is a prizewinning illustrator and cartoonist who runs the comic strip blog Livet blant dyrene (Life Among the Animals). She has illustrated several books with Marta Breen, among others. Jordahl debuted as an author with the picture book *Hannemone and Hulda* in 2017.

YELLOW JACKET
an imprint of Bonnier Publishing USA

251 Park Avenue South, New York, NY 10010
Copyright © 2018 by Cappelen Damm AS
This Yellow Jacket edition, 2019.
Manufactured in China HH 1118
First U.S. Edition
10 9 8 7 6 5 4 3 2 1
Library of Congress Cataloging-in-Publication Data
is available upon request.
ISBN 978-1-4998-0874-2
yellowjacketbooks.com
bonnierpublishingusa.com

FEARLESS FEMALES

THE FIGHT FOR FREEDOM, EQUALITY, AND SISTERHOOD

by MARTA BREEN

illustrated by JENNY JORDAHL

YELLOW JACKET

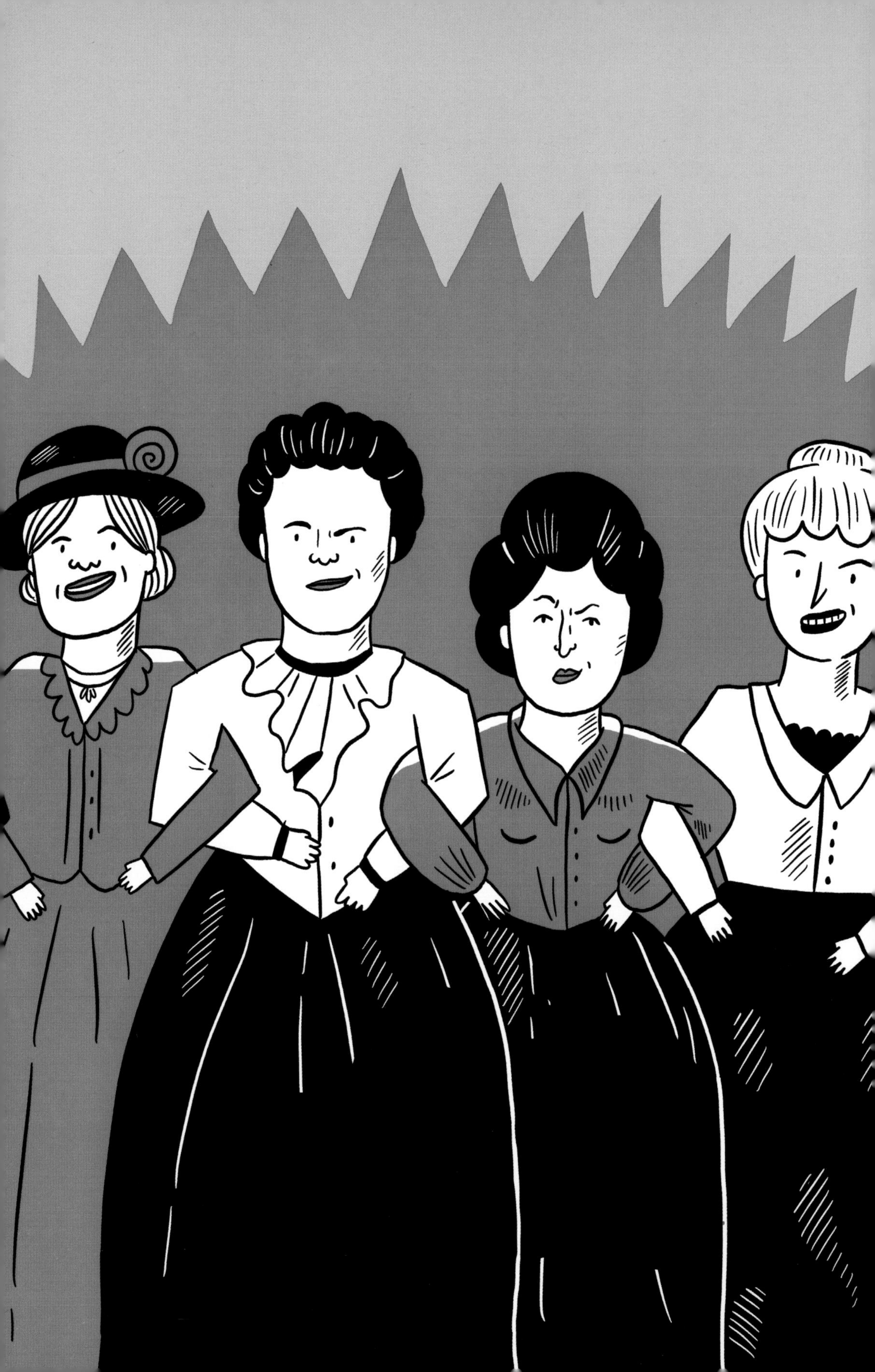

Dear Readers,

We grew up in an era where many people thought gender equality had come far enough. Some even claimed it had "gone too far." It was unpopular to talk about feminism when we were teenagers.

But things have changed. Patriarchal leaders have seized power in a number of countries in recent years, and this is shaking people out of a stupor. Women and men all over the world are coming to understand that old victories are not carved in stone: Your rights can be taken from you again if you are not careful. This was why millions of women rallied for the Women's March in 2017. And this is why we are now in the middle of the fourth wave of feminism.

Feminism is the opposite of misogyny. And what is misogyny? Well, it's the notion that the opinions of women are less valid, that their work is less worthwhile, that they do not have the right to make decisions about their own lives and their own bodies, that they deserve less freedoms than men, and that they should obey men. This misogyny has long, historical roots and is still very widespread. And it means that millions of women are subjected to violence, sexual harassment, forced marriage, and other forms of oppression every single day.

The history of feminism often focuses on progress. It is about updating old norms, traditions, and ways of thinking. There will always be those who seek to resist this and to return things to the way they were. But these people rarely succeed in the long run. The world is slowly but surely making progress—with help from feminists and their allies.

With love,

Marta Breen and Jenny Jordahl

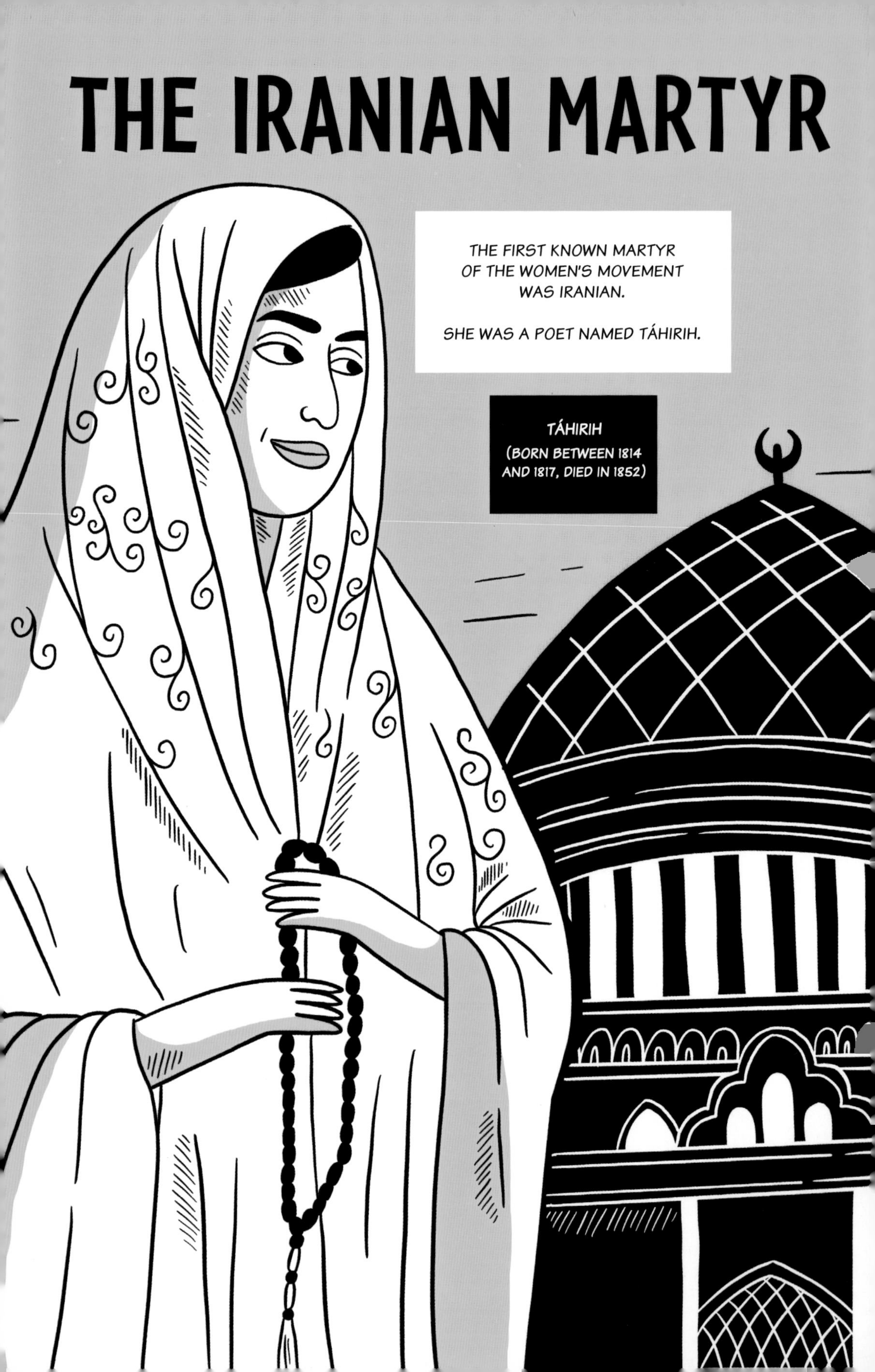
THE IRANIAN MARTYR
THE FIRST KNOWN MARTYR OF THE WOMEN'S MOVEMENT WAS IRANIAN.
SHE WAS A POET NAMED TÁHIRIH.
TÁHIRIH (BORN BETWEEN 1814 AND 1817, DIED IN 1852)

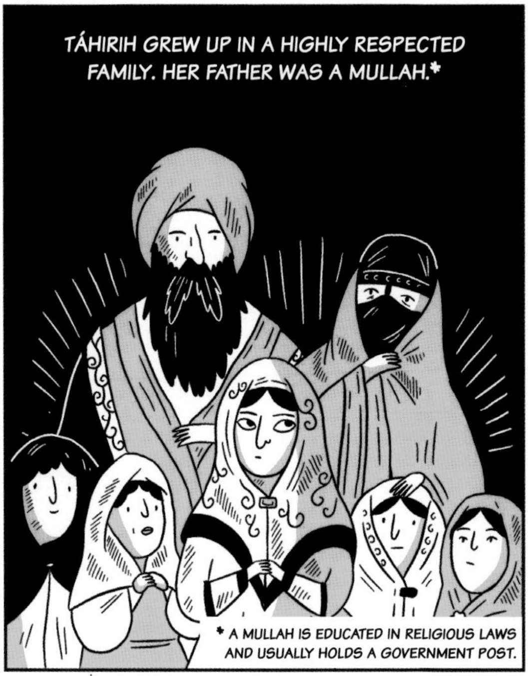
TÁHIRIH GREW UP IN A HIGHLY RESPECTED FAMILY. HER FATHER WAS A MULLAH.*
* A MULLAH IS EDUCATED IN RELIGIOUS LAWS AND USUALLY HOLDS A GOVERNMENT POST.

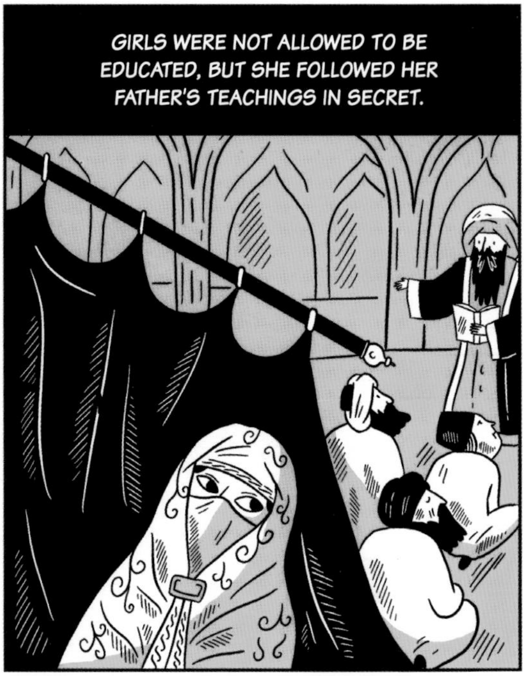
GIRLS WERE NOT ALLOWED TO BE EDUCATED, BUT SHE FOLLOWED HER FATHER'S TEACHINGS IN SECRET.

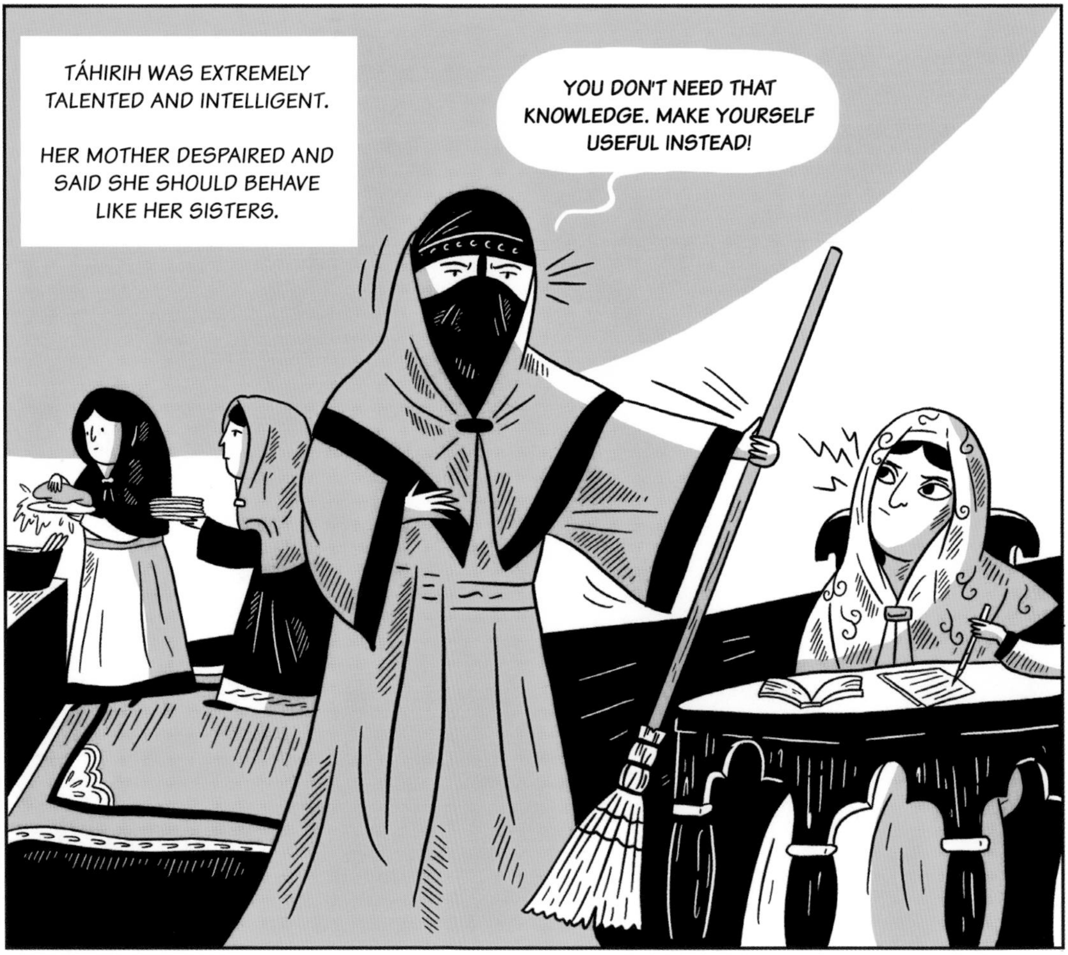
TÁHIRIH WAS EXTREMELY TALENTED AND INTELLIGENT.
HER MOTHER DESPAIRED AND SAID SHE SHOULD BEHAVE LIKE HER SISTERS.
YOU DON'T NEED THAT KNOWLEDGE. MAKE YOURSELF USEFUL INSTEAD!

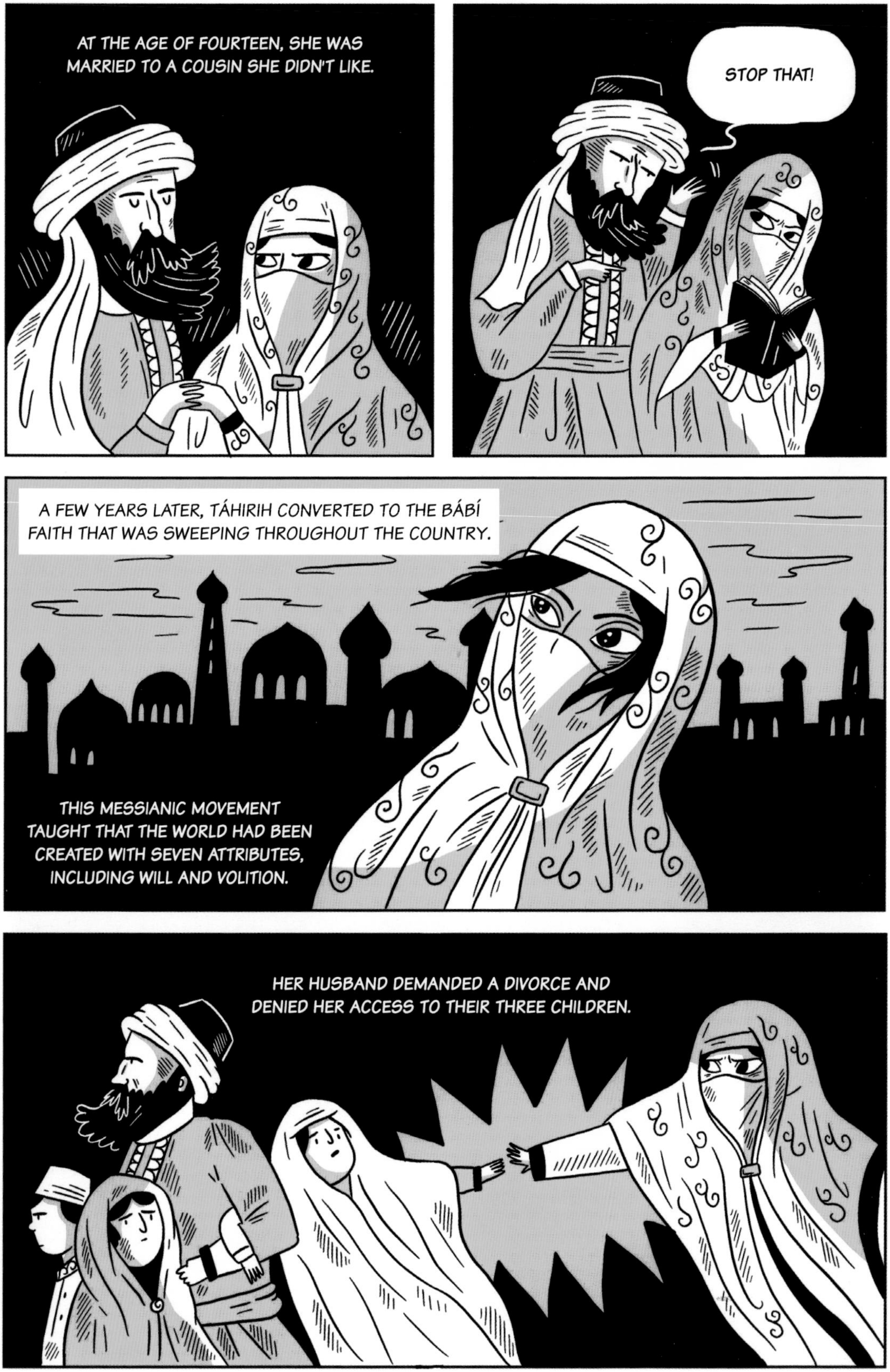
AT THE AGE OF FOURTEEN, SHE WAS MARRIED TO A COUSIN SHE DIDN'T LIKE.
STOP THAT!
A FEW YEARS LATER, TÁHIRIH CONVERTED TO THE BÁBÍ FAITH THAT WAS SWEEPING THROUGHOUT THE COUNTRY.
THIS MESSIANIC MOVEMENT TAUGHT THAT THE WORLD HAD BEEN CREATED WITH SEVEN ATTRIBUTES, INCLUDING WILL AND VOLITION.
HER HUSBAND DEMANDED A DIVORCE AND DENIED HER ACCESS TO THEIR THREE CHILDREN.

EVEN THOUGH WOMEN WERE FORBIDDEN FROM SPEAKING IN PUBLIC, TÁHIRIH NOW SPENT ALL HER TIME SPREADING HER MESSAGE OF EQUALITY.

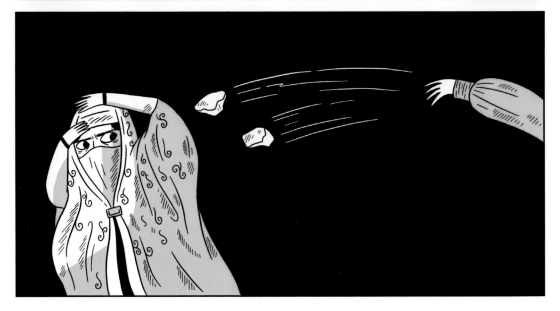

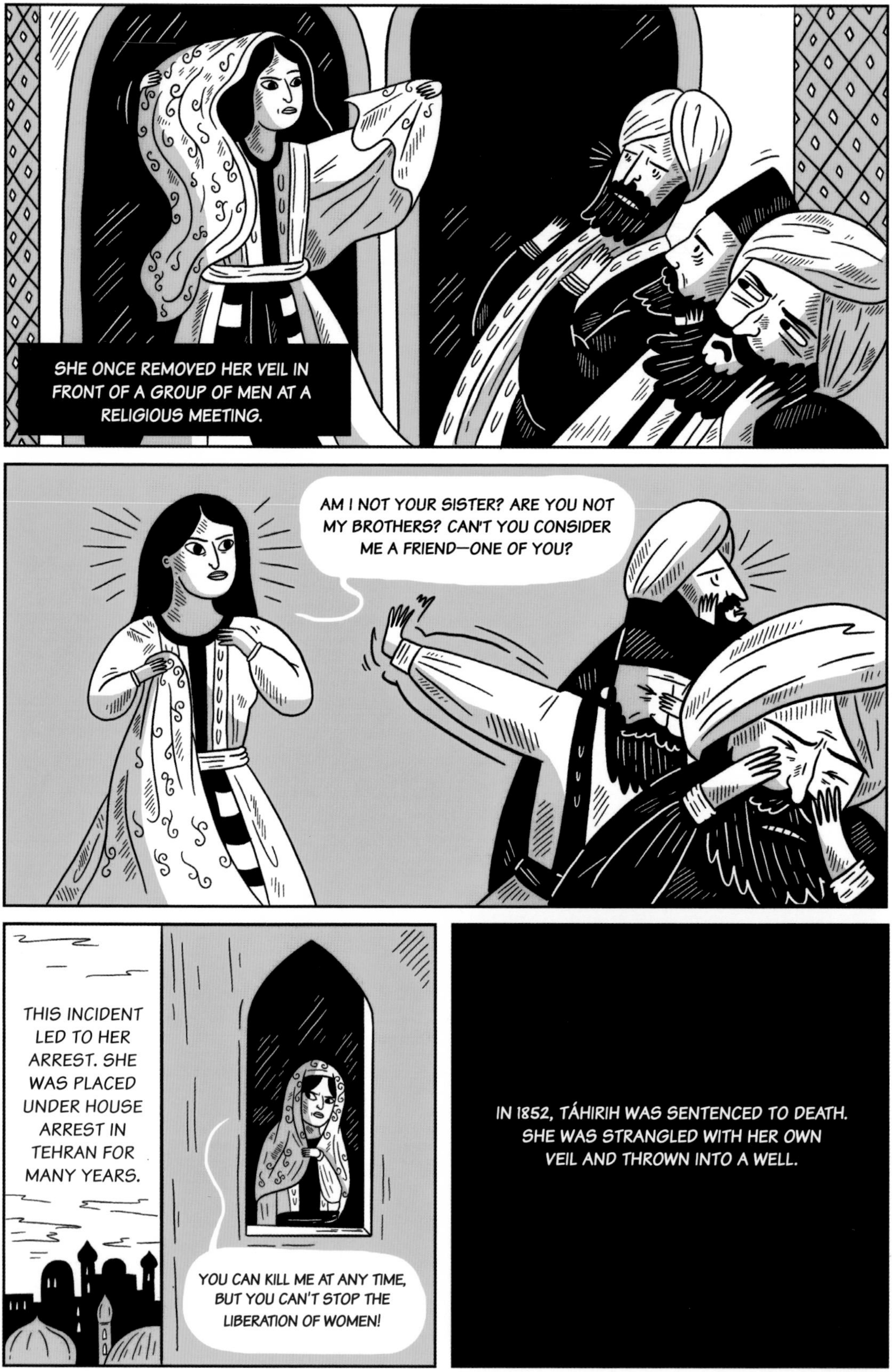
SHE ONCE REMOVED HER VEIL IN FRONT OF A GROUP OF MEN AT A RELIGIOUS MEETING.
AM I NOT YOUR SISTER? ARE YOU NOT MY BROTHERS? CAN'T YOU CONSIDER ME A FRIEND—ONE OF YOU?
THIS INCIDENT LED TO HER ARREST. SHE WAS PLACED UNDER HOUSE ARREST IN TEHRAN FOR MANY YEARS.
YOU CAN KILL ME AT ANY TIME, BUT YOU CAN'T STOP THE LIBERATION OF WOMEN!
IN 1852, TÁHIRIH WAS SENTENCED TO DEATH. SHE WAS STRANGLED WITH HER OWN VEIL AND THROWN INTO A WELL.

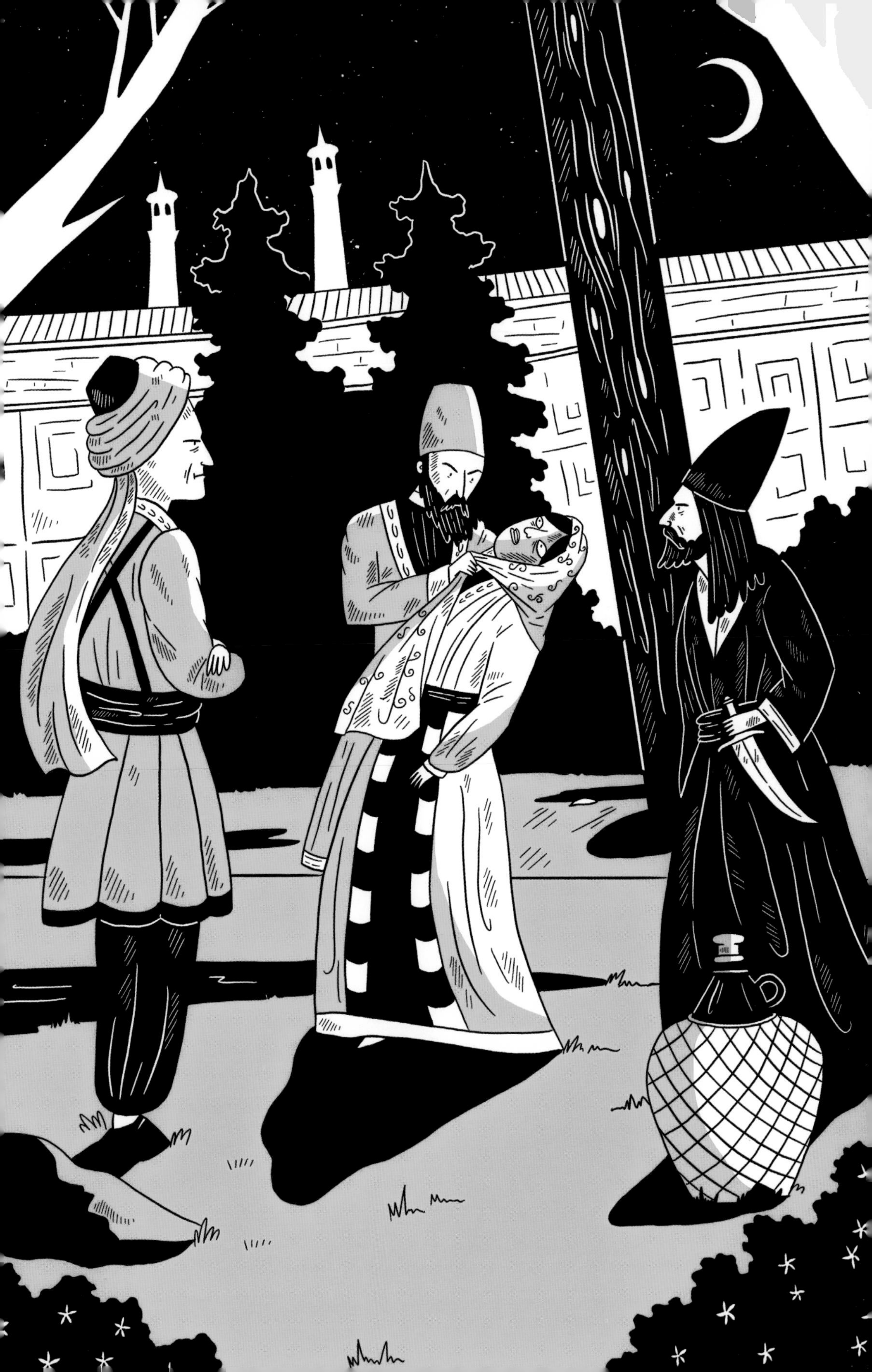

EUROPE IN
THE NINETEENTH
CENTURY

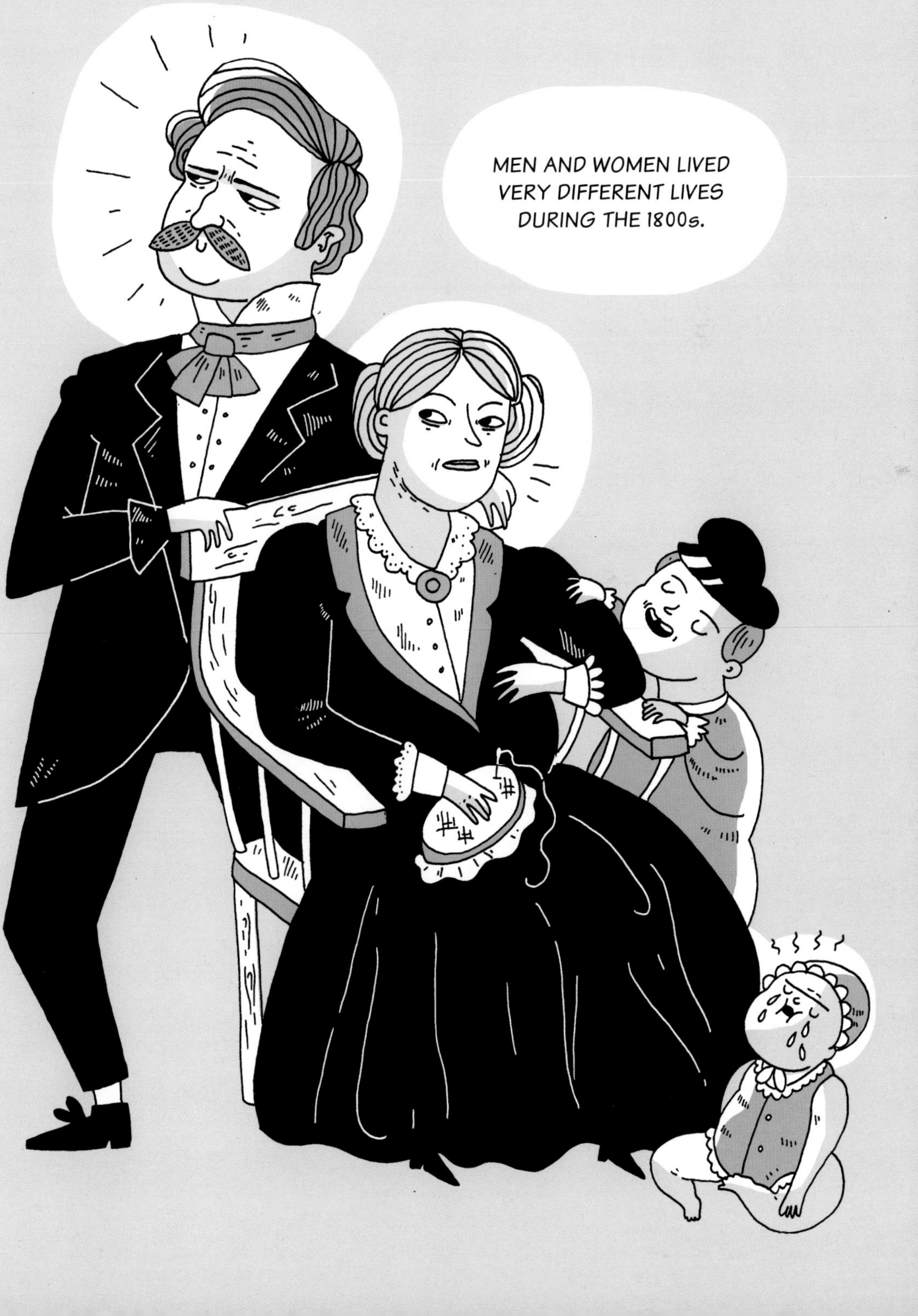
MEN AND WOMEN LIVED VERY DIFFERENT LIVES DURING THE 1800s.

EUROPEAN WHITE WOMEN HAD FAR FEWER RIGHTS THAN MEN. THEY WERE NOT ALLOWED TO BE EDUCATED, AND THEY WERE NOT ALLOWED TO OWN LAND.

THIS MEANT THAT WHITE WOMEN WERE LARGELY UNABLE TO EARN THEIR OWN MONEY.

THEY WERE NOT ALLOWED TO VOTE IN ELECTIONS, EITHER.

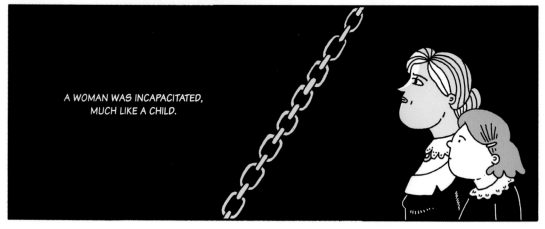

A WOMAN WAS INCAPACITATED, MUCH LIKE A CHILD.

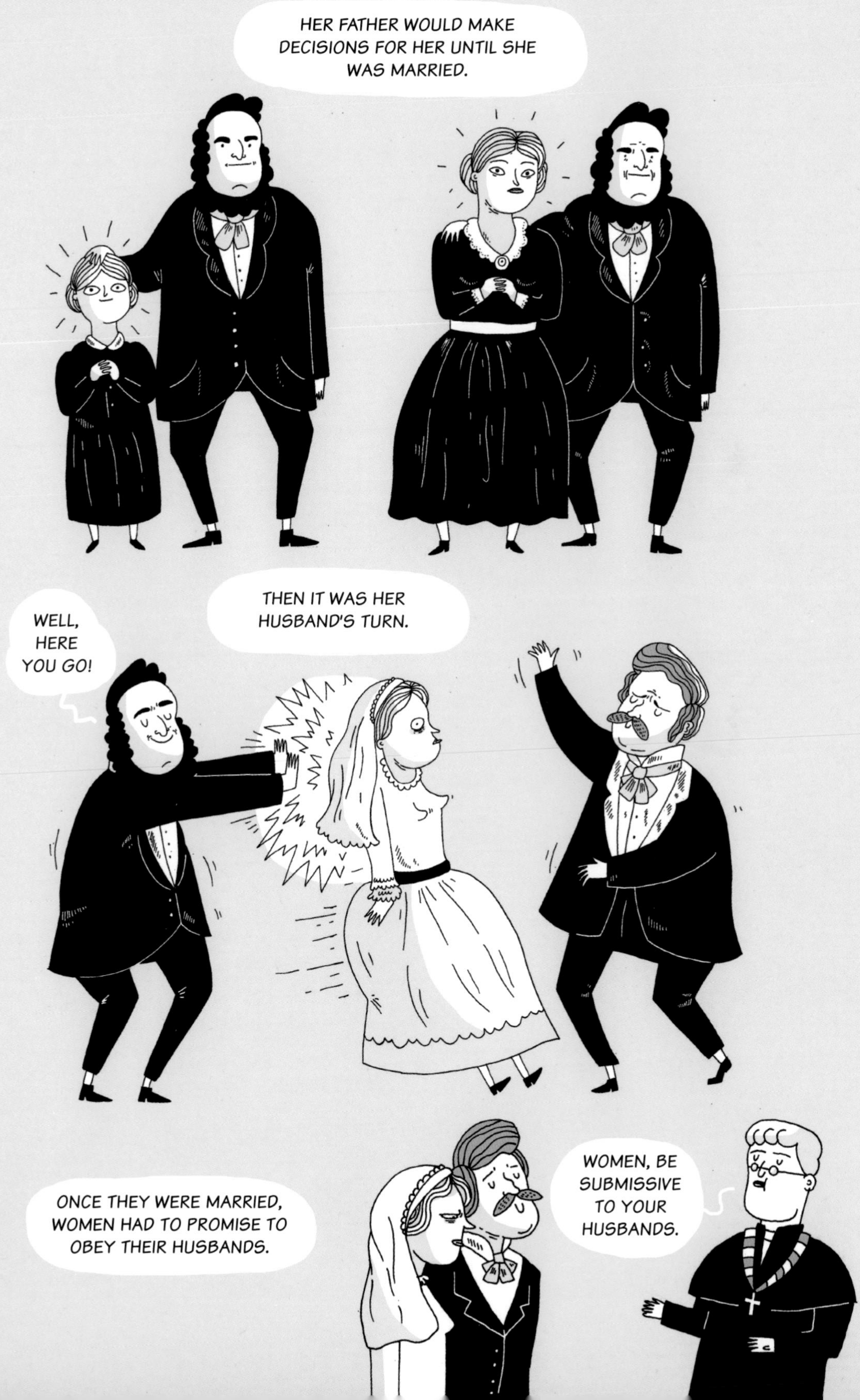
HER FATHER WOULD MAKE DECISIONS FOR HER UNTIL SHE WAS MARRIED.
THEN IT WAS HER HUSBAND'S TURN.
WELL, HERE YOU GO!
ONCE THEY WERE MARRIED, WOMEN HAD TO PROMISE TO OBEY THEIR HUSBANDS.
WOMEN, BE SUBMISSIVE TO YOUR HUSBANDS.

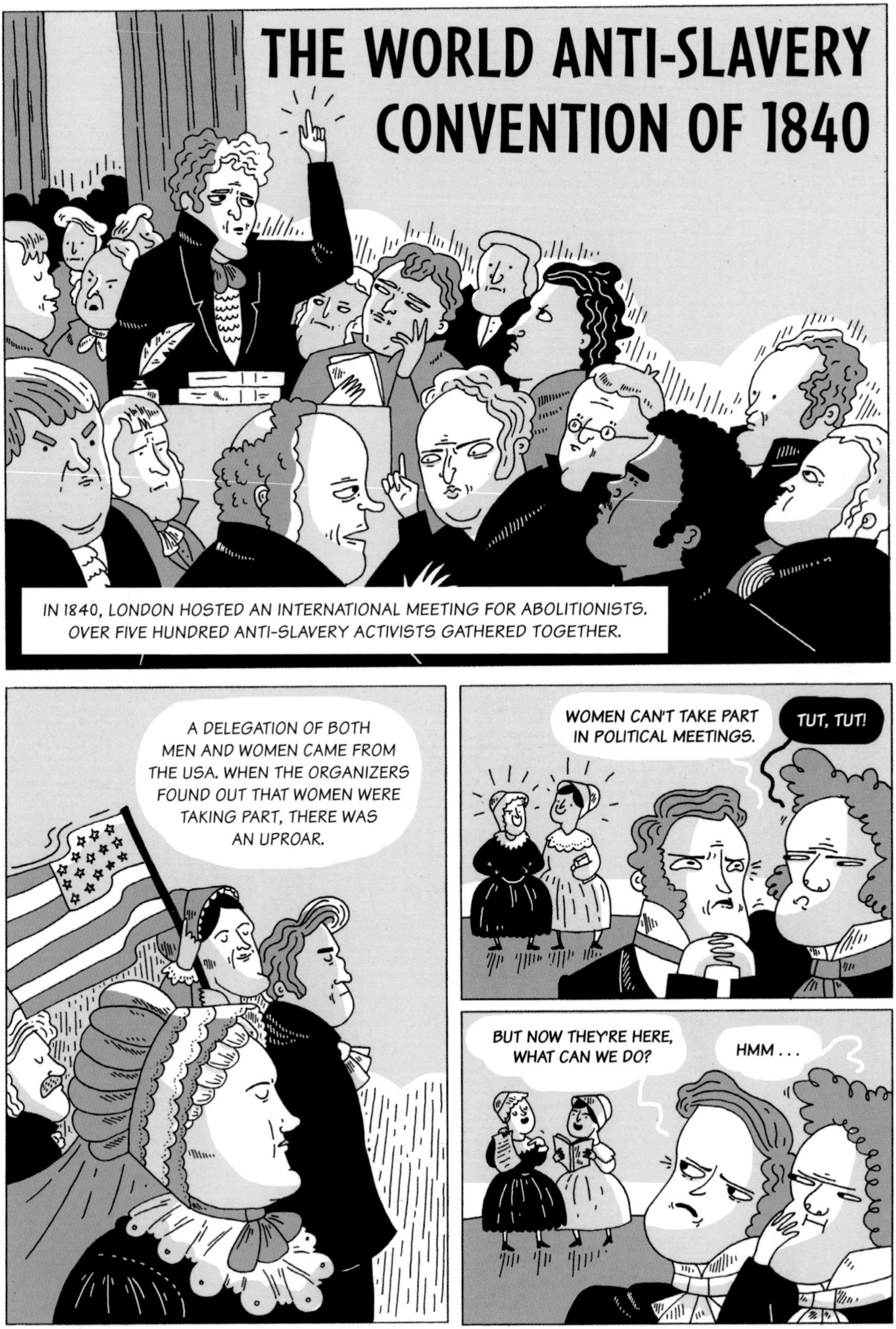
THE WORLD ANTI-SLAVERY CONVENTION OF 1840
IN 1840, LONDON HOSTED AN INTERNATIONAL MEETING FOR ABOLITIONISTS. OVER FIVE HUNDRED ANTI-SLAVERY ACTIVISTS GATHERED TOGETHER.
A DELEGATION OF BOTH MEN AND WOMEN CAME FROM THE USA. WHEN THE ORGANIZERS FOUND OUT THAT WOMEN WERE TAKING PART, THERE WAS AN UPROAR.
WOMEN CAN'T TAKE PART IN POLITICAL MEETINGS.
TUT, TUT!
BUT NOW THEY'RE HERE, WHAT CAN WE DO?
HMM . . .

THE AMERICAN WOMEN WERE NOT ALLOWED TO SPEAK AND HAD TO SIT QUIETLY AND LISTEN BEHIND A CURTAIN.

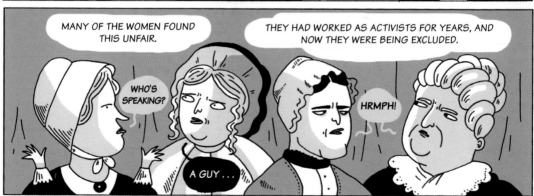

MANY OF THE WOMEN FOUND THIS UNFAIR.

THEY HAD WORKED AS ACTIVISTS FOR YEARS, AND NOW THEY WERE BEING EXCLUDED.

WHO'S SPEAKING?

HRMPH!

A GUY . . .

GAH!

BAH!

ARE YOU THINKING WHAT I'M THINKING?

OH, YES! DEFINITELY!

15

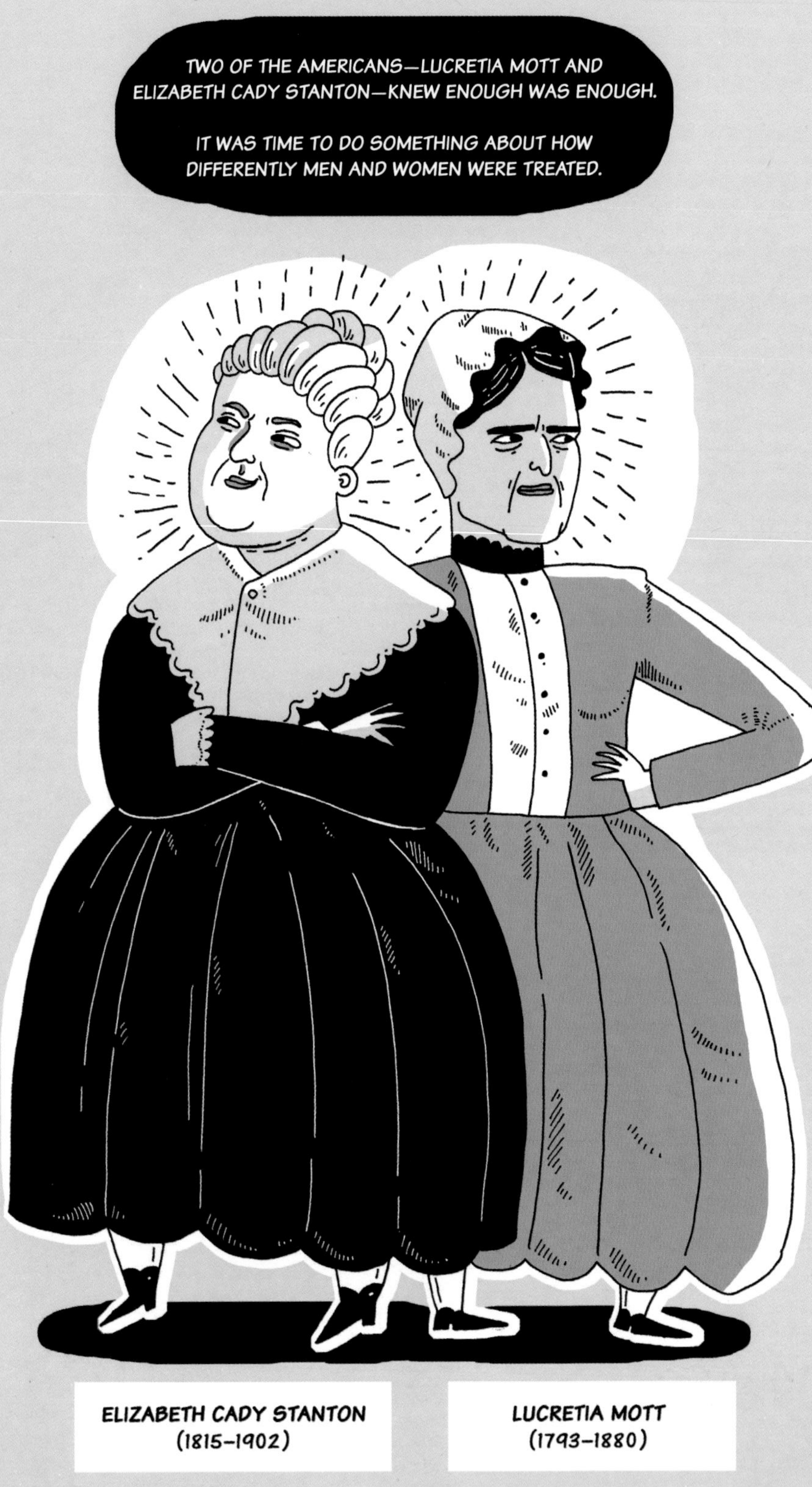
TWO OF THE AMERICANS—LUCRETIA MOTT AND ELIZABETH CADY STANTON—KNEW ENOUGH WAS ENOUGH.
IT WAS TIME TO DO SOMETHING ABOUT HOW DIFFERENTLY MEN AND WOMEN WERE TREATED.
ELIZABETH CADY STANTON (1815–1902)
LUCRETIA MOTT (1793–1880)

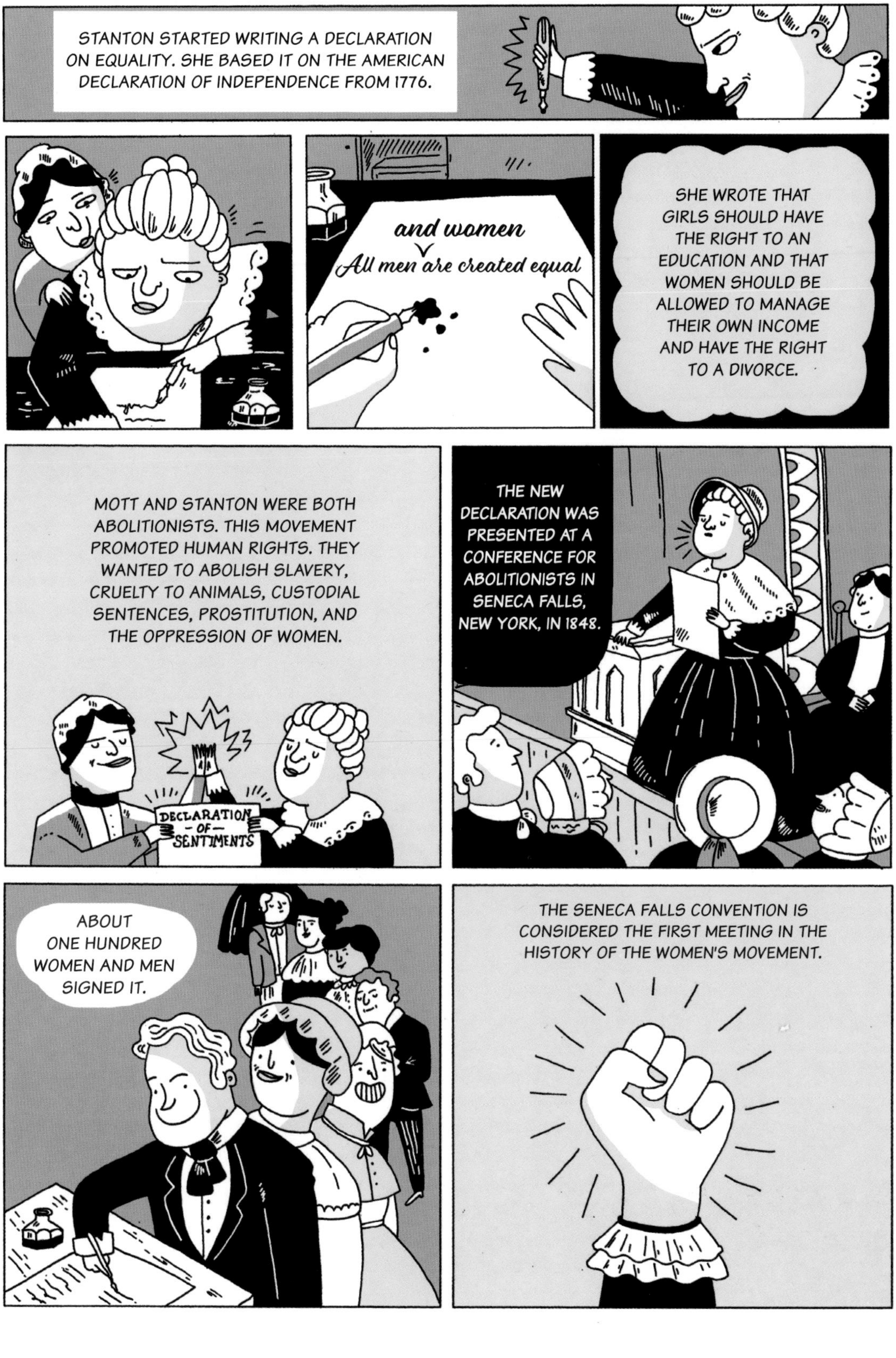
STANTON STARTED WRITING A DECLARATION ON EQUALITY. SHE BASED IT ON THE AMERICAN DECLARATION OF INDEPENDENCE FROM 1776.
and women
All men are created equal
SHE WROTE THAT GIRLS SHOULD HAVE THE RIGHT TO AN EDUCATION AND THAT WOMEN SHOULD BE ALLOWED TO MANAGE THEIR OWN INCOME AND HAVE THE RIGHT TO A DIVORCE.
MOTT AND STANTON WERE BOTH ABOLITIONISTS. THIS MOVEMENT PROMOTED HUMAN RIGHTS. THEY WANTED TO ABOLISH SLAVERY, CRUELTY TO ANIMALS, CUSTODIAL SENTENCES, PROSTITUTION, AND THE OPPRESSION OF WOMEN.
DECLARATION OF SENTIMENTS
THE NEW DECLARATION WAS PRESENTED AT A CONFERENCE FOR ABOLITIONISTS IN SENECA FALLS, NEW YORK, IN 1848.
ABOUT ONE HUNDRED WOMEN AND MEN SIGNED IT.
THE SENECA FALLS CONVENTION IS CONSIDERED THE FIRST MEETING IN THE HISTORY OF THE WOMEN'S MOVEMENT.

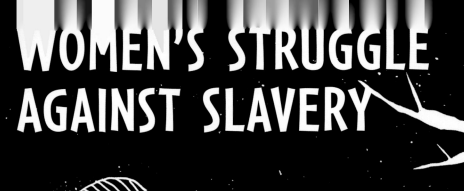

WOMEN'S STRUGGLE AGAINST SLAVERY

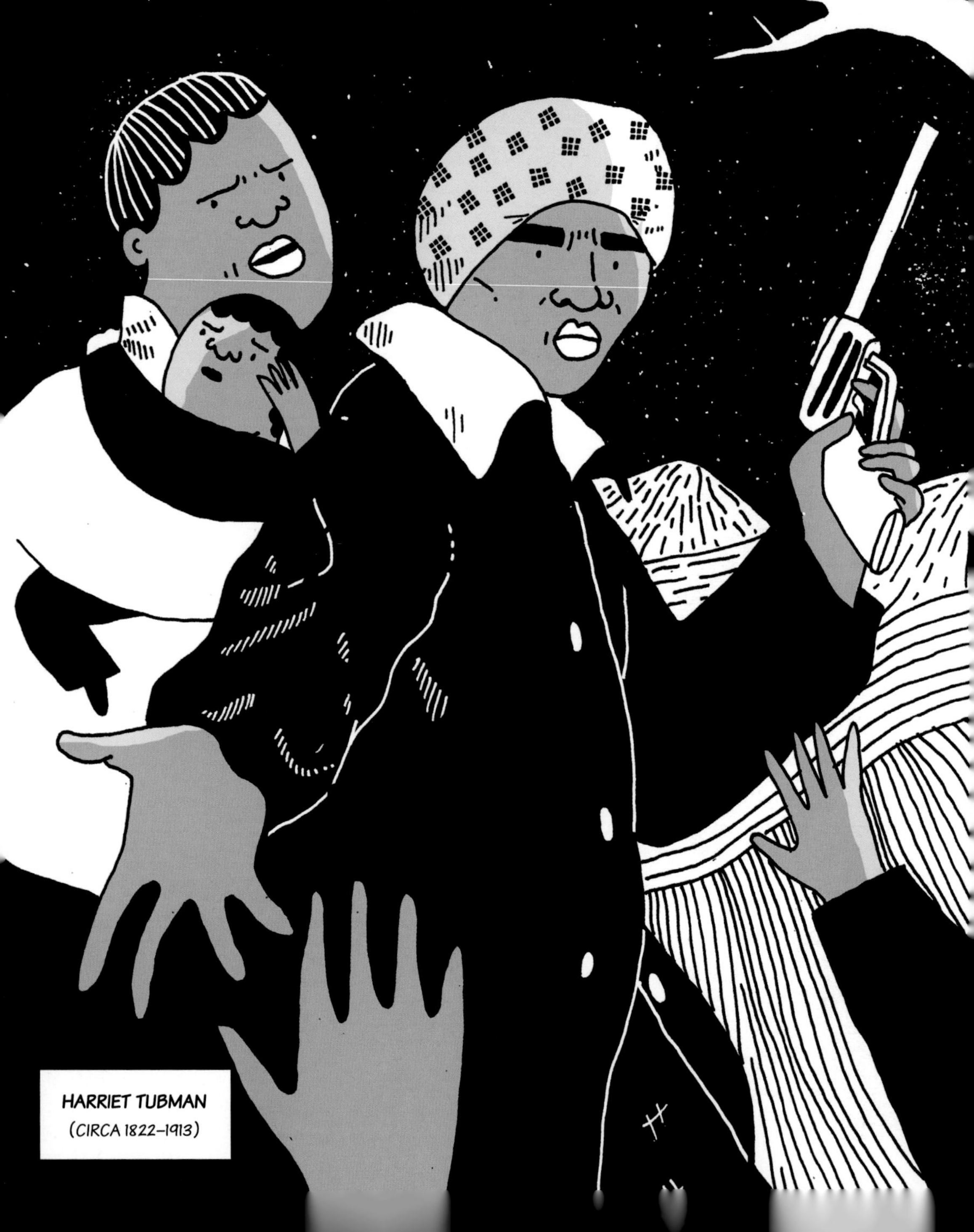

HARRIET TUBMAN
(CIRCA 1822–1913)

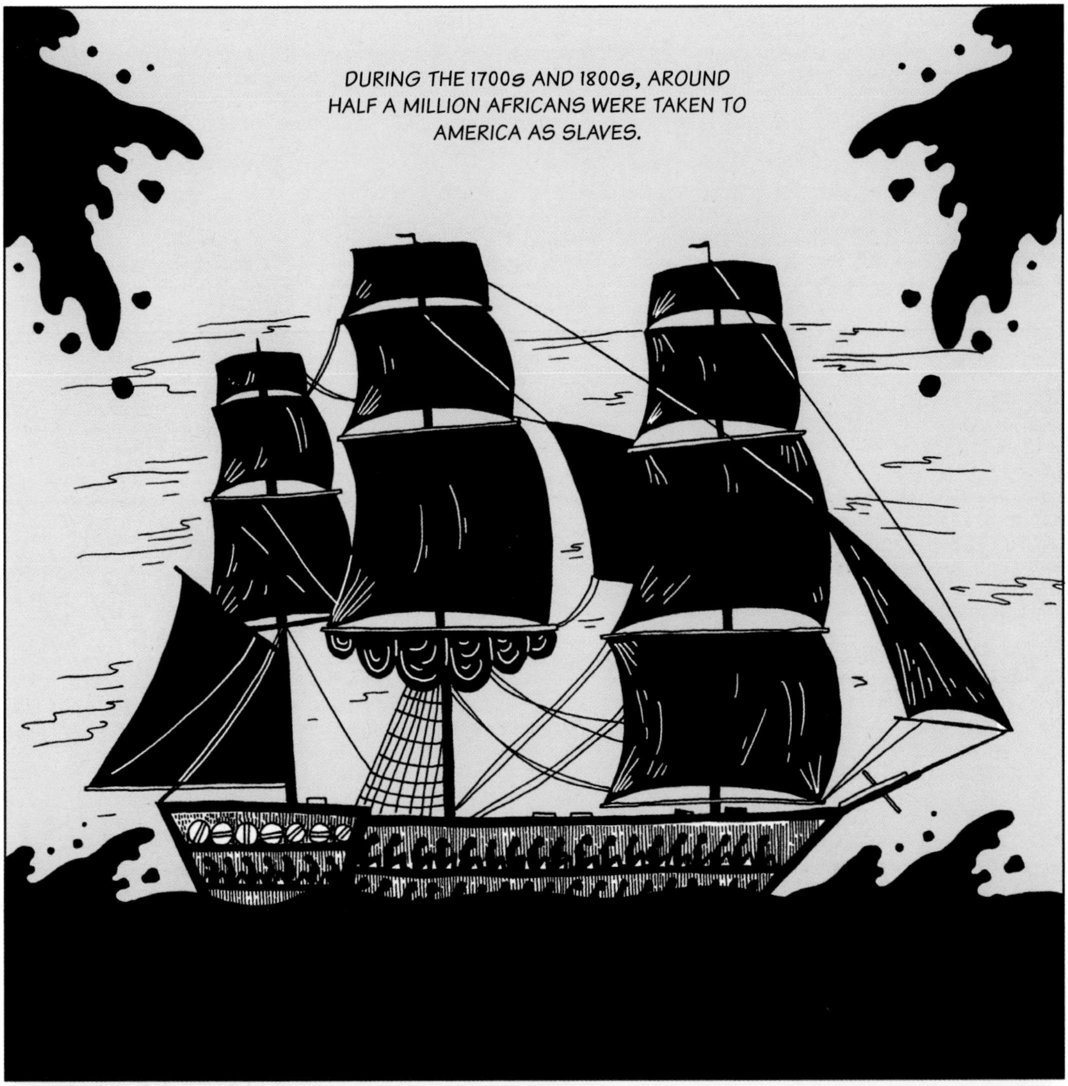
DURING THE 1700s AND 1800s, AROUND HALF A MILLION AFRICANS WERE TAKEN TO AMERICA AS SLAVES.

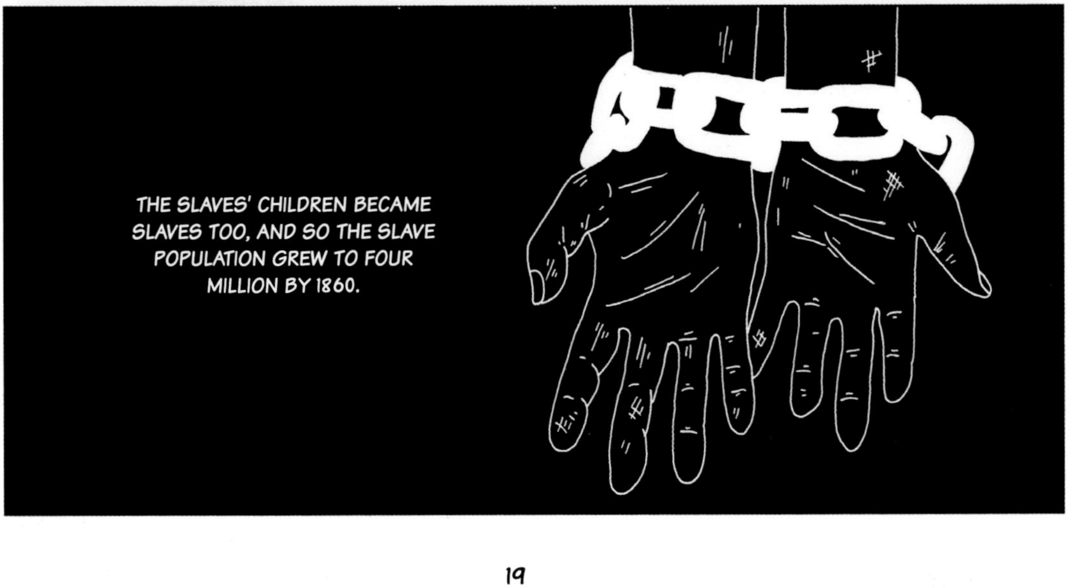
THE SLAVES' CHILDREN BECAME SLAVES TOO, AND SO THE SLAVE POPULATION GREW TO FOUR MILLION BY 1860.

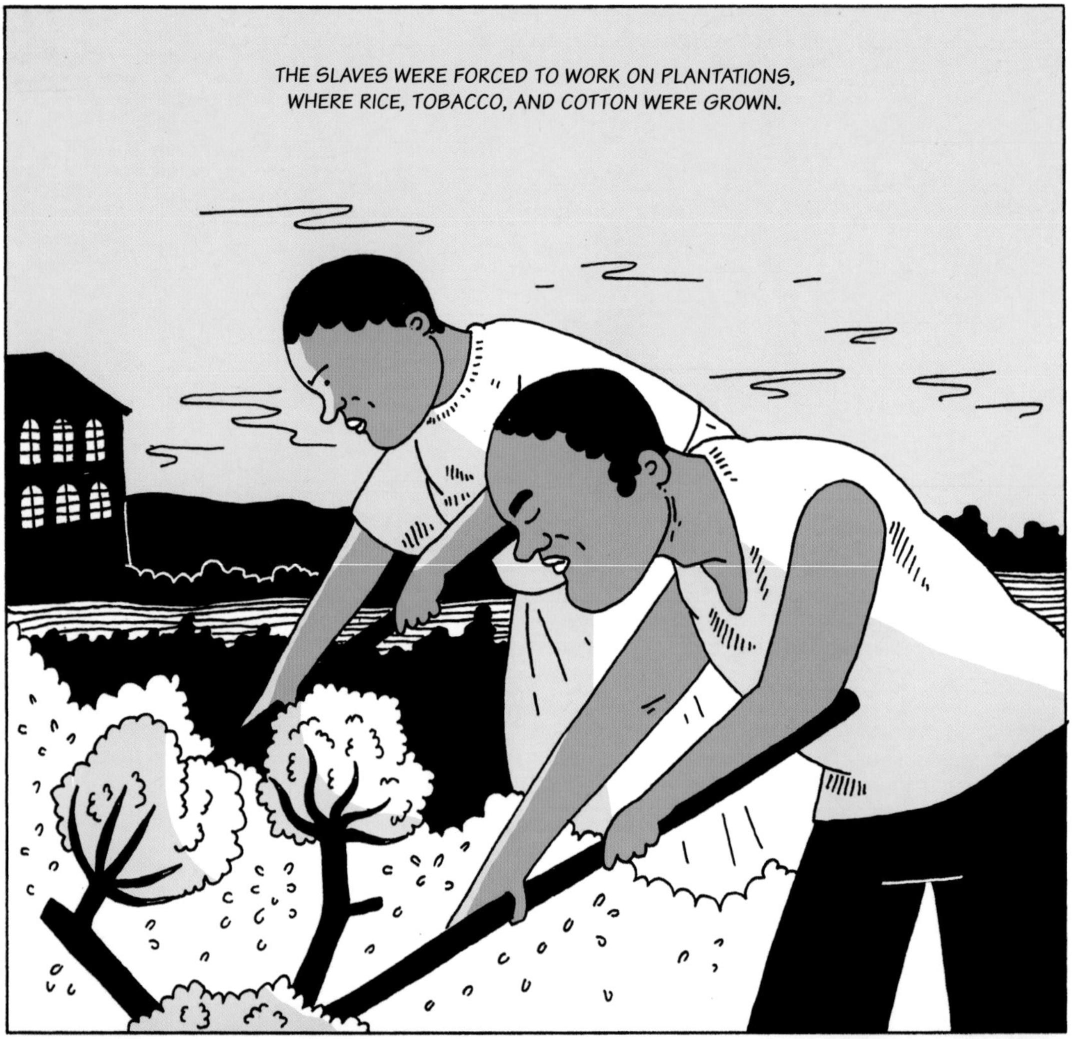
THE SLAVES WERE FORCED TO WORK ON PLANTATIONS, WHERE RICE, TOBACCO, AND COTTON WERE GROWN.

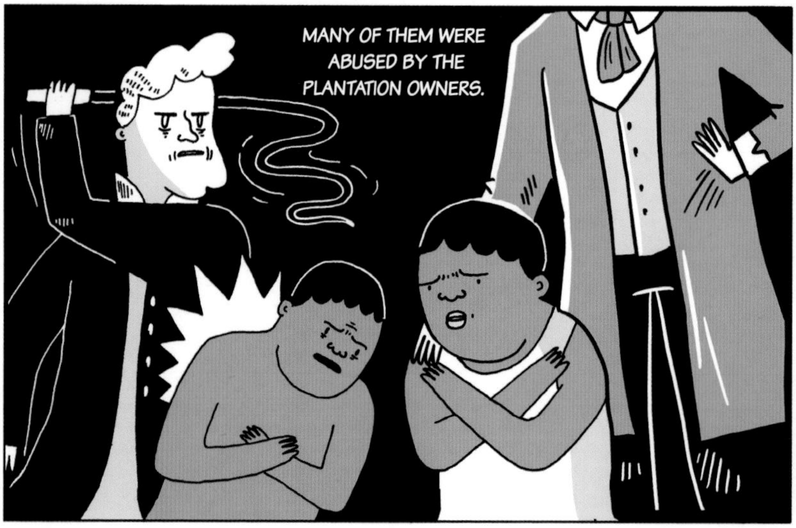
MANY OF THEM WERE ABUSED BY THE PLANTATION OWNERS.

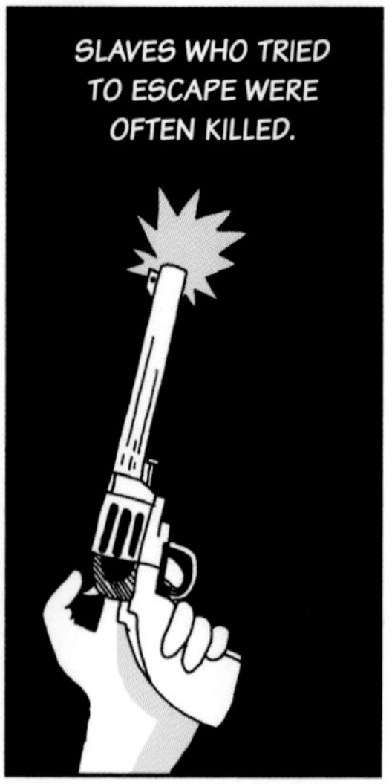
SLAVES WHO TRIED TO ESCAPE WERE OFTEN KILLED.

HARRIET TUBMAN WAS ONE OF THE MANY BORN INTO SLAVERY IN 1820.

WHEN SHE WAS SIX, SHE WAS TAKEN FROM HER PARENTS AND SENT TO WORK ON A DIFFERENT PLANTATION.

SHE WAS CONSTANTLY WHIPPED AND BEATEN.

ONE DAY, AN IRON WEIGHT WAS THROWN AT HER HEAD.

SHE WAS UNCONSCIOUS FOR TWO DAYS.

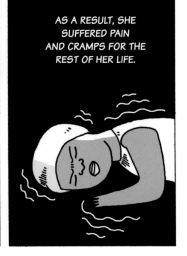

AS A RESULT, SHE SUFFERED PAIN AND CRAMPS FOR THE REST OF HER LIFE.

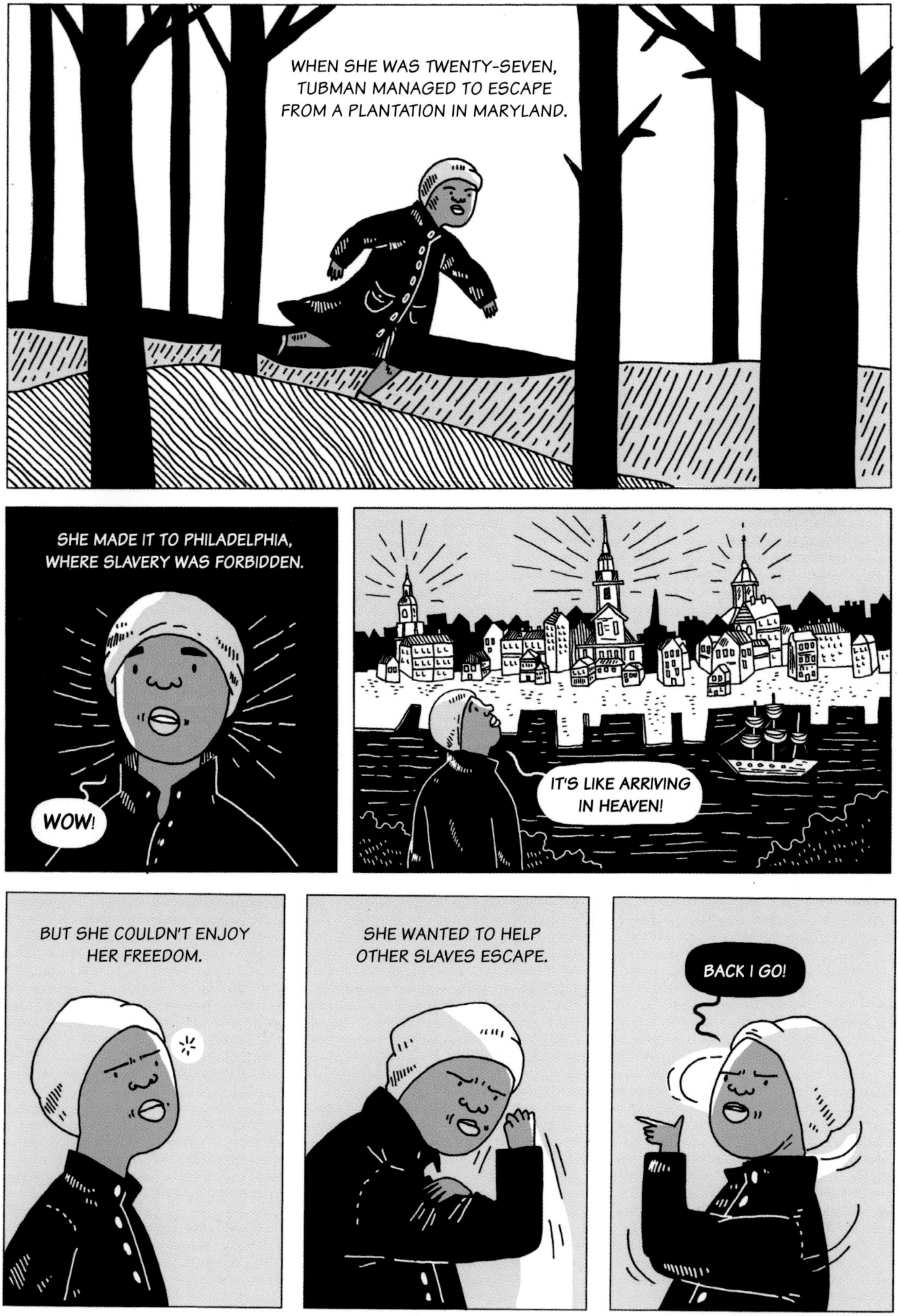
WHEN SHE WAS TWENTY-SEVEN, TUBMAN MANAGED TO ESCAPE FROM A PLANTATION IN MARYLAND.
SHE MADE IT TO PHILADELPHIA, WHERE SLAVERY WAS FORBIDDEN.
WOW!
IT'S LIKE ARRIVING IN HEAVEN!
BUT SHE COULDN'T ENJOY HER FREEDOM.
SHE WANTED TO HELP OTHER SLAVES ESCAPE.
BACK I GO!

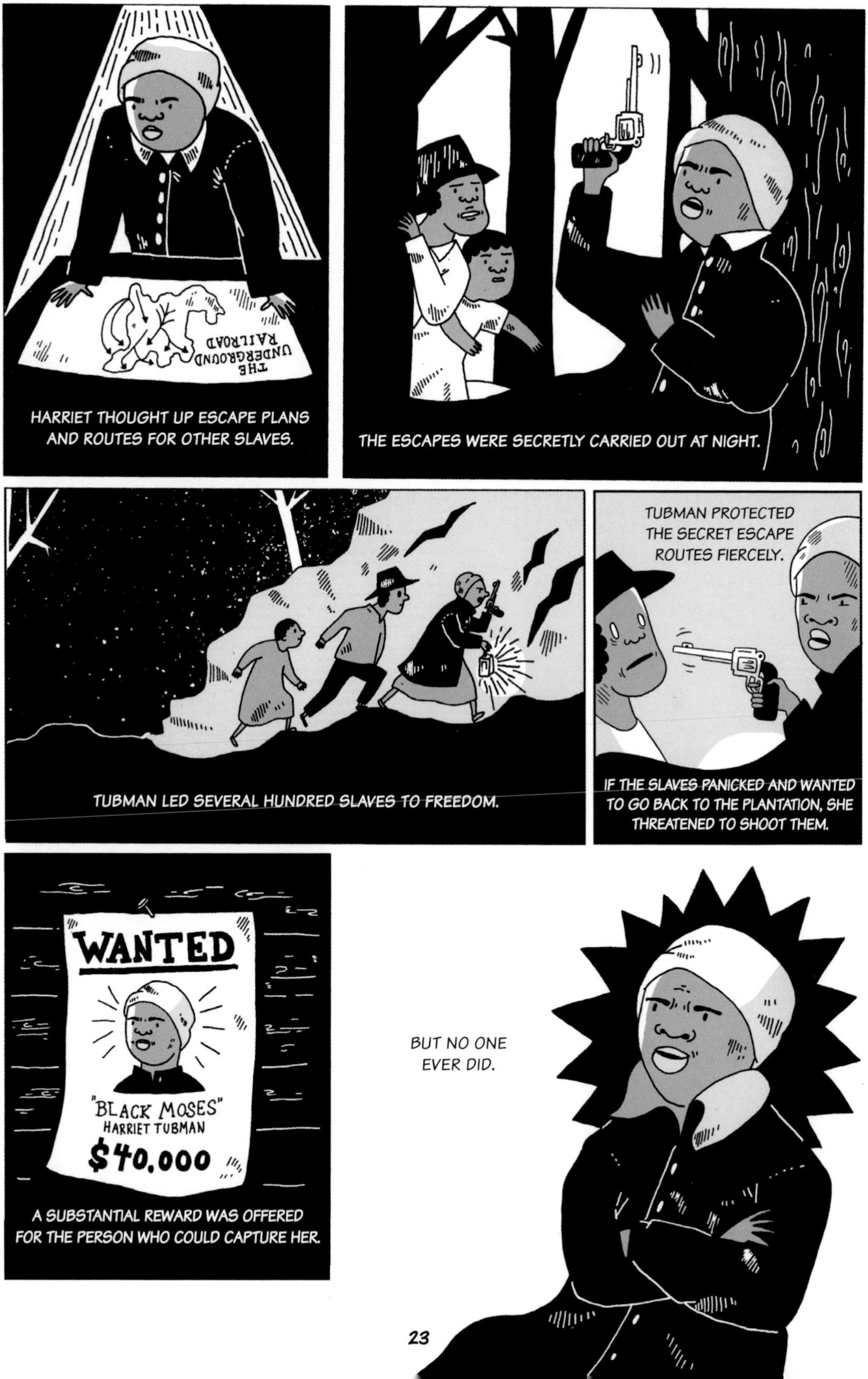
THE UNDERGROUND RAILROAD
HARRIET THOUGHT UP ESCAPE PLANS AND ROUTES FOR OTHER SLAVES.
THE ESCAPES WERE SECRETLY CARRIED OUT AT NIGHT.
TUBMAN LED SEVERAL HUNDRED SLAVES TO FREEDOM.
TUBMAN PROTECTED THE SECRET ESCAPE ROUTES FIERCELY.
IF THE SLAVES PANICKED AND WANTED TO GO BACK TO THE PLANTATION, SHE THREATENED TO SHOOT THEM.
WANTED
"BLACK MOSES"
HARRIET TUBMAN
$40,000
A SUBSTANTIAL REWARD WAS OFFERED FOR THE PERSON WHO COULD CAPTURE HER.
BUT NO ONE EVER DID.

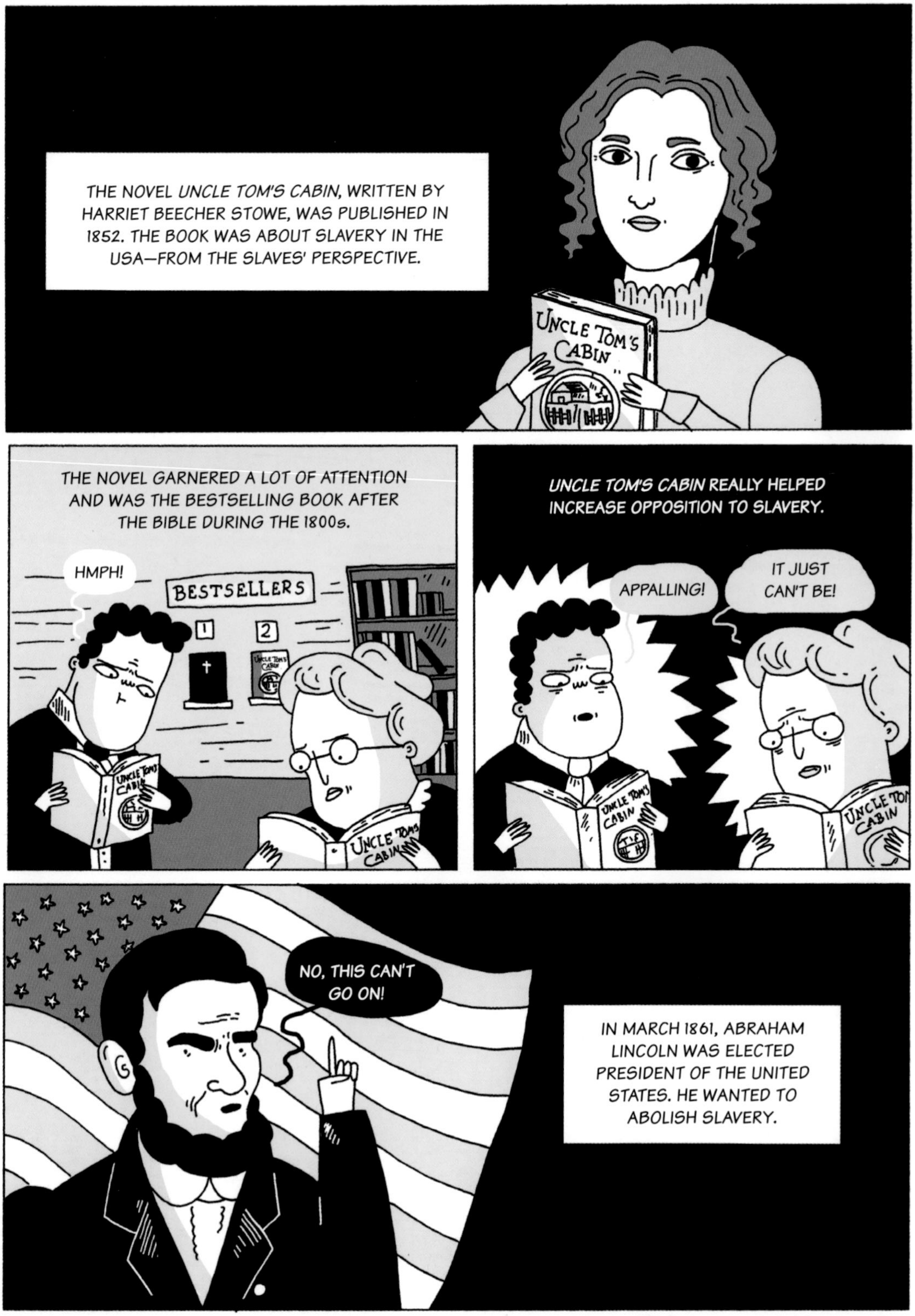
THE NOVEL *UNCLE TOM'S CABIN*, WRITTEN BY HARRIET BEECHER STOWE, WAS PUBLISHED IN 1852. THE BOOK WAS ABOUT SLAVERY IN THE USA—FROM THE SLAVES' PERSPECTIVE.
UNCLE TOM'S CABIN
THE NOVEL GARNERED A LOT OF ATTENTION AND WAS THE BESTSELLING BOOK AFTER THE BIBLE DURING THE 1800s.
HMPH!
BESTSELLERS
1
2
UNCLE TOM'S CABIN REALLY HELPED INCREASE OPPOSITION TO SLAVERY.
APPALLING!
IT JUST CAN'T BE!
NO, THIS CAN'T GO ON!
IN MARCH 1861, ABRAHAM LINCOLN WAS ELECTED PRESIDENT OF THE UNITED STATES. HE WANTED TO ABOLISH SLAVERY.

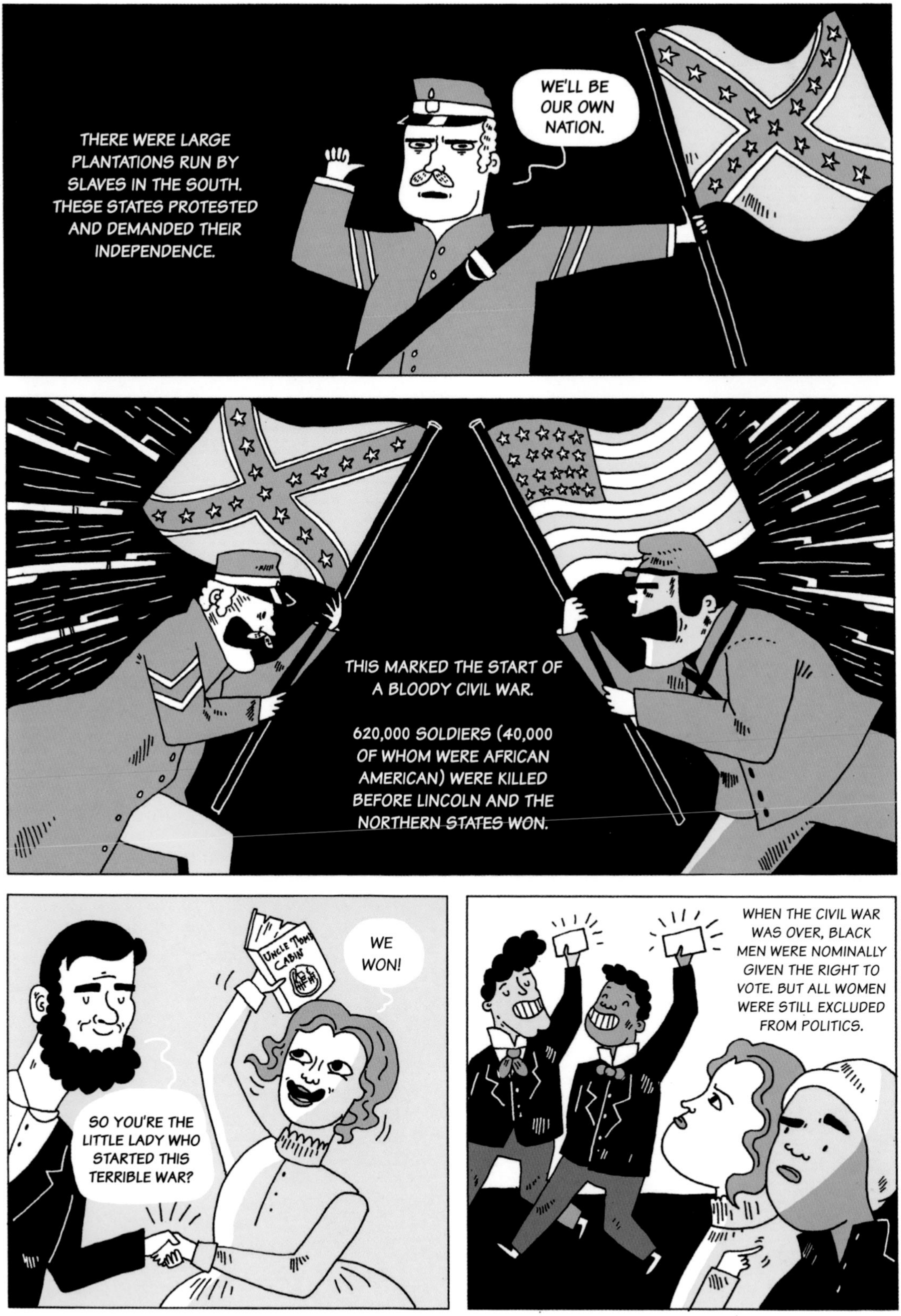
THERE WERE LARGE PLANTATIONS RUN BY SLAVES IN THE SOUTH. THESE STATES PROTESTED AND DEMANDED THEIR INDEPENDENCE.
WE'LL BE OUR OWN NATION.
THIS MARKED THE START OF A BLOODY CIVIL WAR.
620,000 SOLDIERS (40,000 OF WHOM WERE AFRICAN AMERICAN) WERE KILLED BEFORE LINCOLN AND THE NORTHERN STATES WON.
UNCLE TOM'S CABIN
WE WON!
SO YOU'RE THE LITTLE LADY WHO STARTED THIS TERRIBLE WAR?
WHEN THE CIVIL WAR WAS OVER, BLACK MEN WERE NOMINALLY GIVEN THE RIGHT TO VOTE. BUT ALL WOMEN WERE STILL EXCLUDED FROM POLITICS.

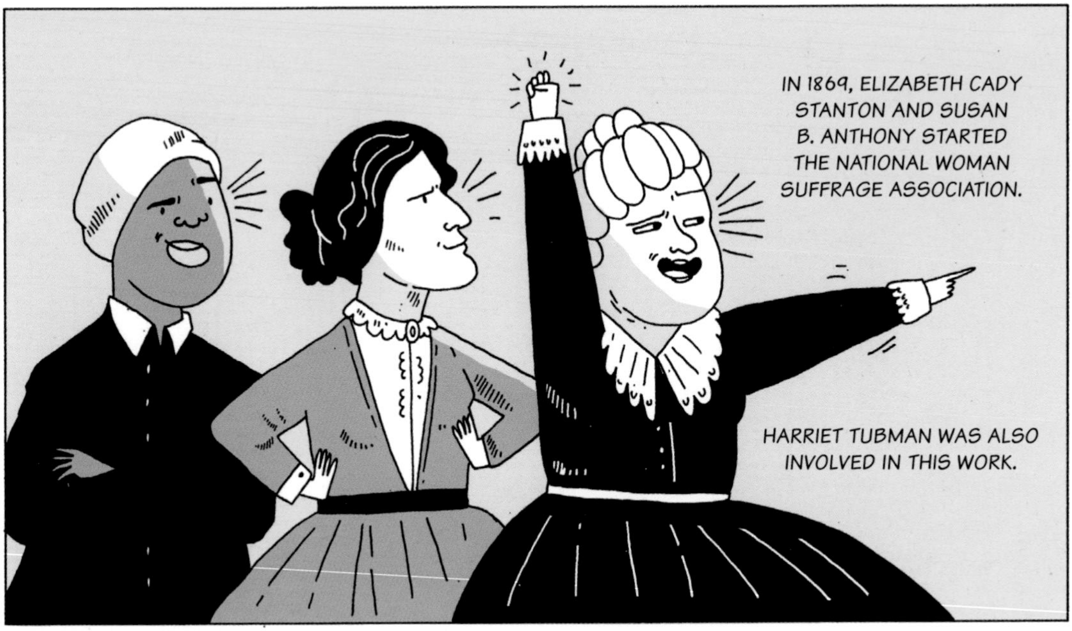
IN 1869, ELIZABETH CADY STANTON AND SUSAN B. ANTHONY STARTED THE NATIONAL WOMAN SUFFRAGE ASSOCIATION.
HARRIET TUBMAN WAS ALSO INVOLVED IN THIS WORK.

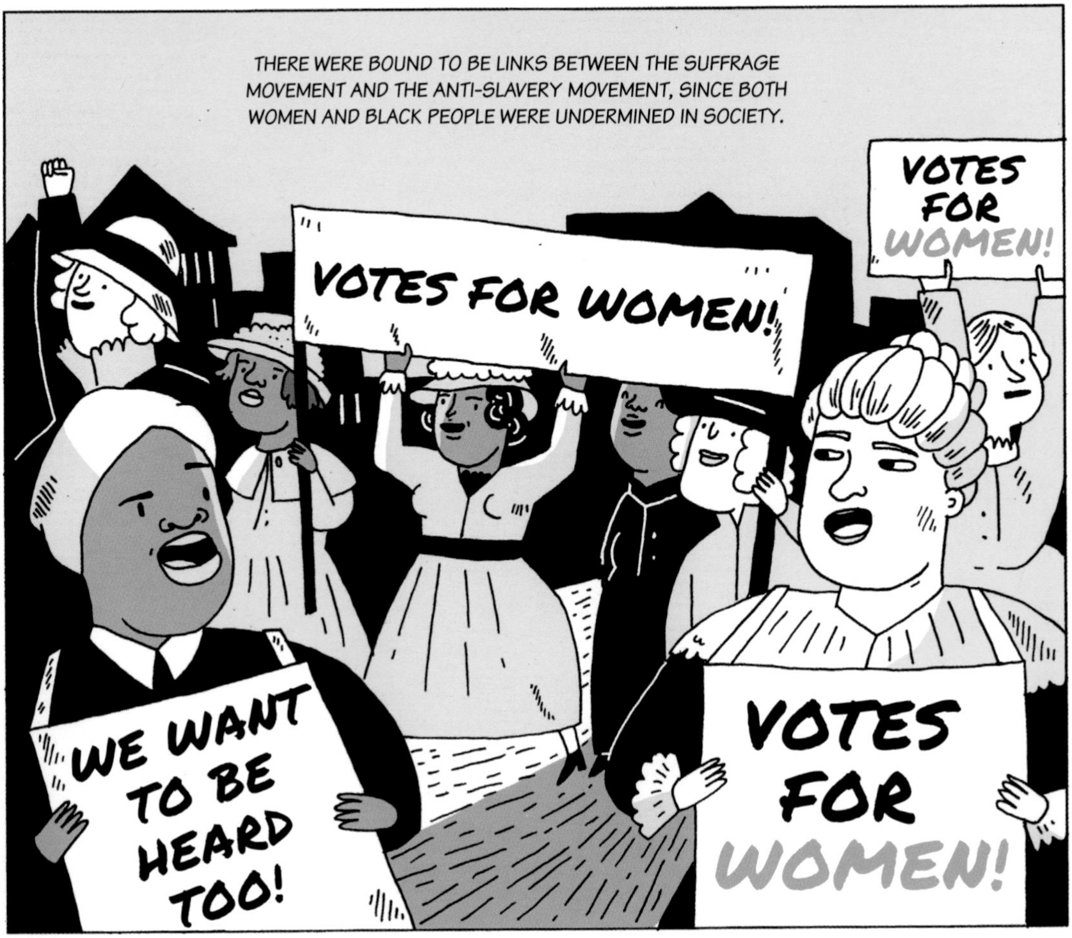
THERE WERE BOUND TO BE LINKS BETWEEN THE SUFFRAGE MOVEMENT AND THE ANTI-SLAVERY MOVEMENT, SINCE BOTH WOMEN AND BLACK PEOPLE WERE UNDERMINED IN SOCIETY.
VOTES FOR WOMEN!
VOTES FOR WOMEN!
WE WANT TO BE HEARD TOO!
VOTES FOR WOMEN!

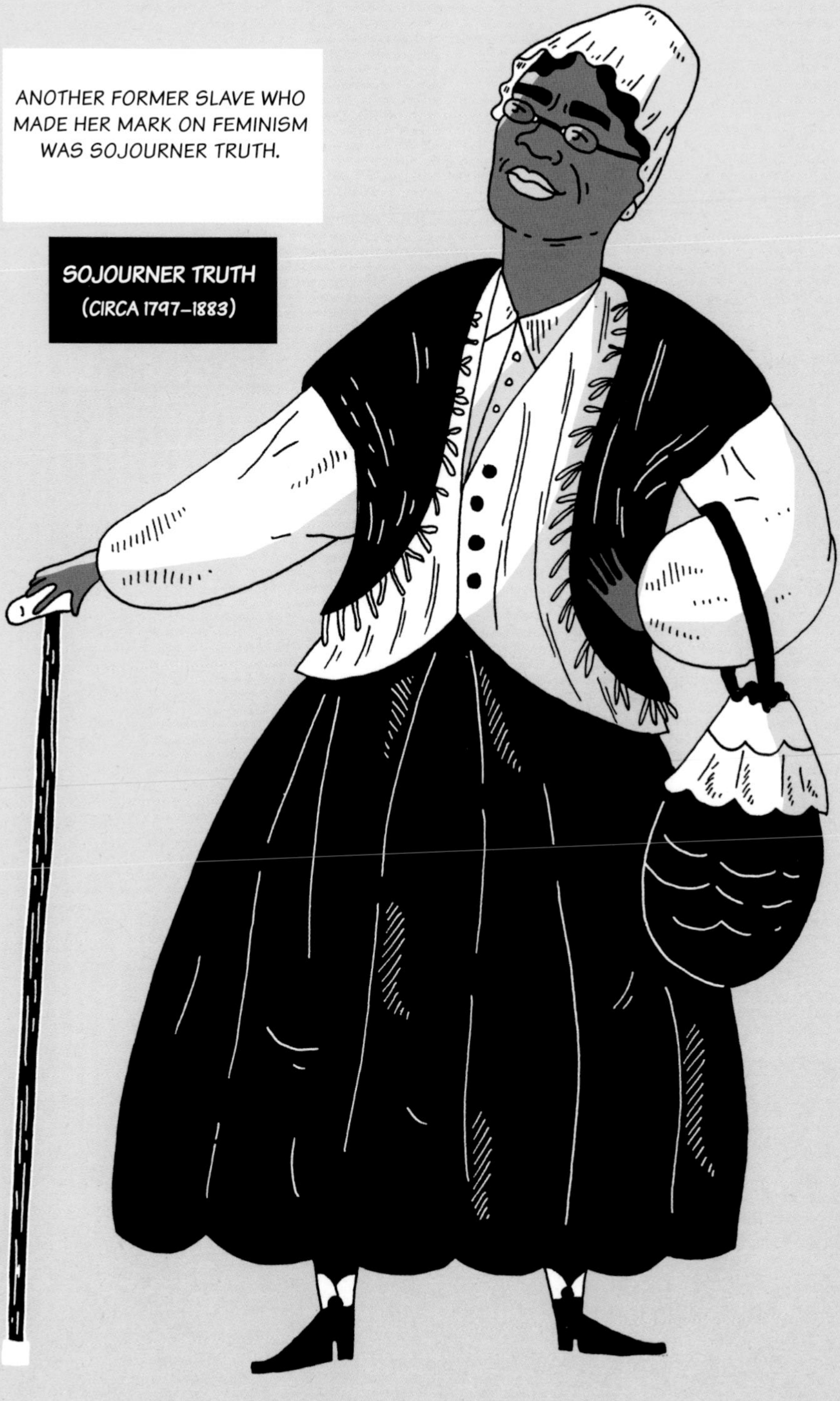
ANOTHER FORMER SLAVE WHO MADE HER MARK ON FEMINISM WAS SOJOURNER TRUTH.
SOJOURNER TRUTH
(CIRCA 1797–1883)

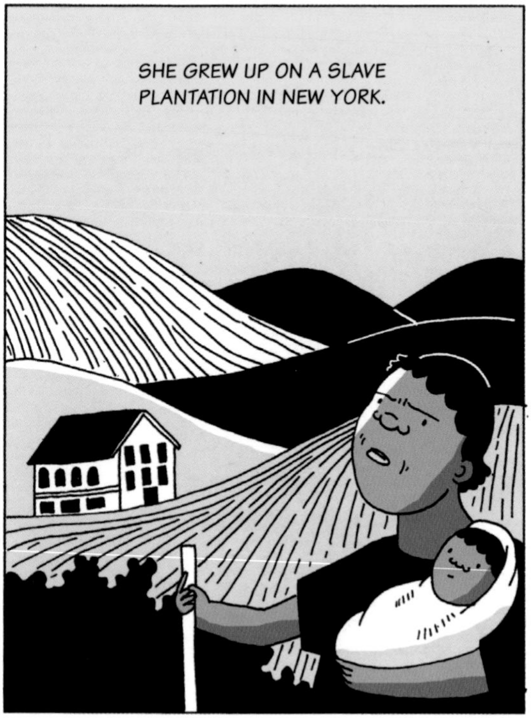
SHE GREW UP ON A SLAVE PLANTATION IN NEW YORK.

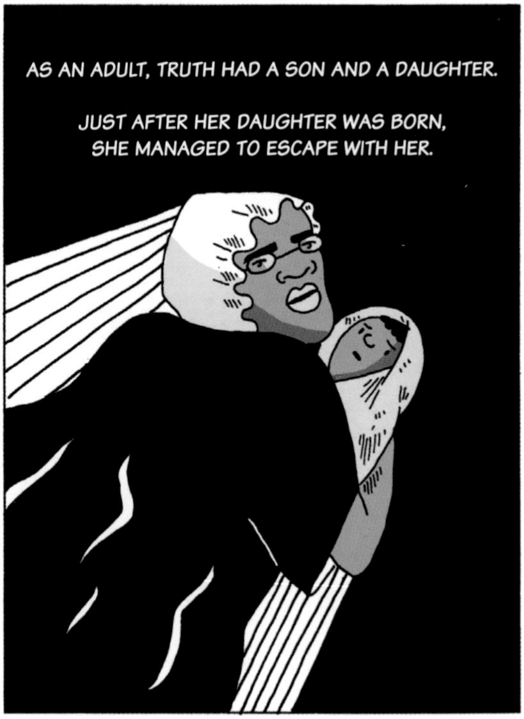
AS AN ADULT, TRUTH HAD A SON AND A DAUGHTER.
JUST AFTER HER DAUGHTER WAS BORN, SHE MANAGED TO ESCAPE WITH HER.

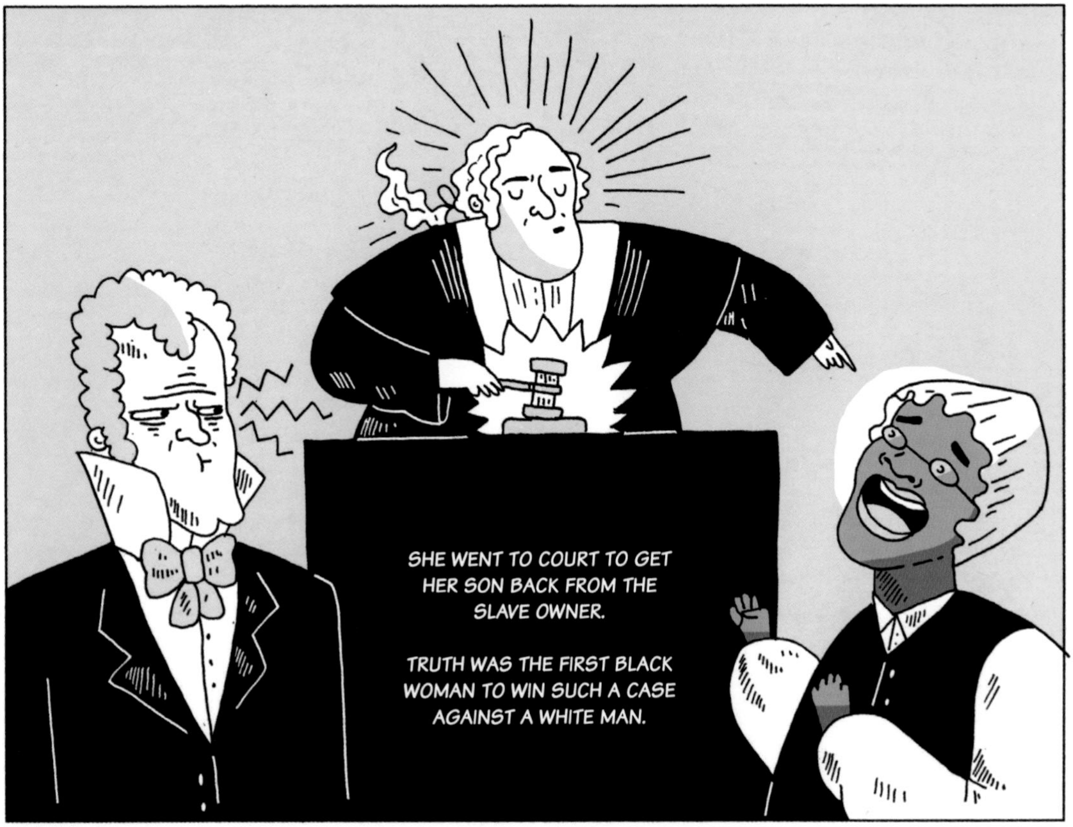
SHE WENT TO COURT TO GET HER SON BACK FROM THE SLAVE OWNER.
TRUTH WAS THE FIRST BLACK WOMAN TO WIN SUCH A CASE AGAINST A WHITE MAN.

AT THE AGE OF SEVENTY, SHE GAVE A FAMOUS SPEECH AT THE FIRST ANNUAL MEETING OF THE AMERICAN EQUAL RIGHTS ASSOCIATION.

MY FRIENDS!

HER SPEECH WAS AIMED AT THOSE FIGHTING FOR THE SUFFRAGE OF WHITE WOMEN WITHOUT REALIZING THAT BLACK WOMEN HAD NO RIGHTS AT ALL.

THERE IS A GREAT STIR ABOUT COLORED MEN GETTING THEIR RIGHTS.

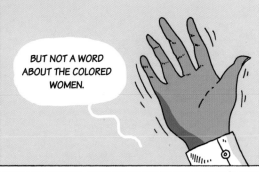

BUT NOT A WORD ABOUT THE COLORED WOMEN.

IF COLORED MEN GET THEIR RIGHTS AND NOT COLORED WOMEN THEIRS . . .

. . . YOU SEE THE MEN WILL BE MASTERS OVER THE WOMEN . . .

. . . AND IT WILL BE JUST AS BAD AS IT WAS BEFORE.*

* VERBATIM, 1867

29

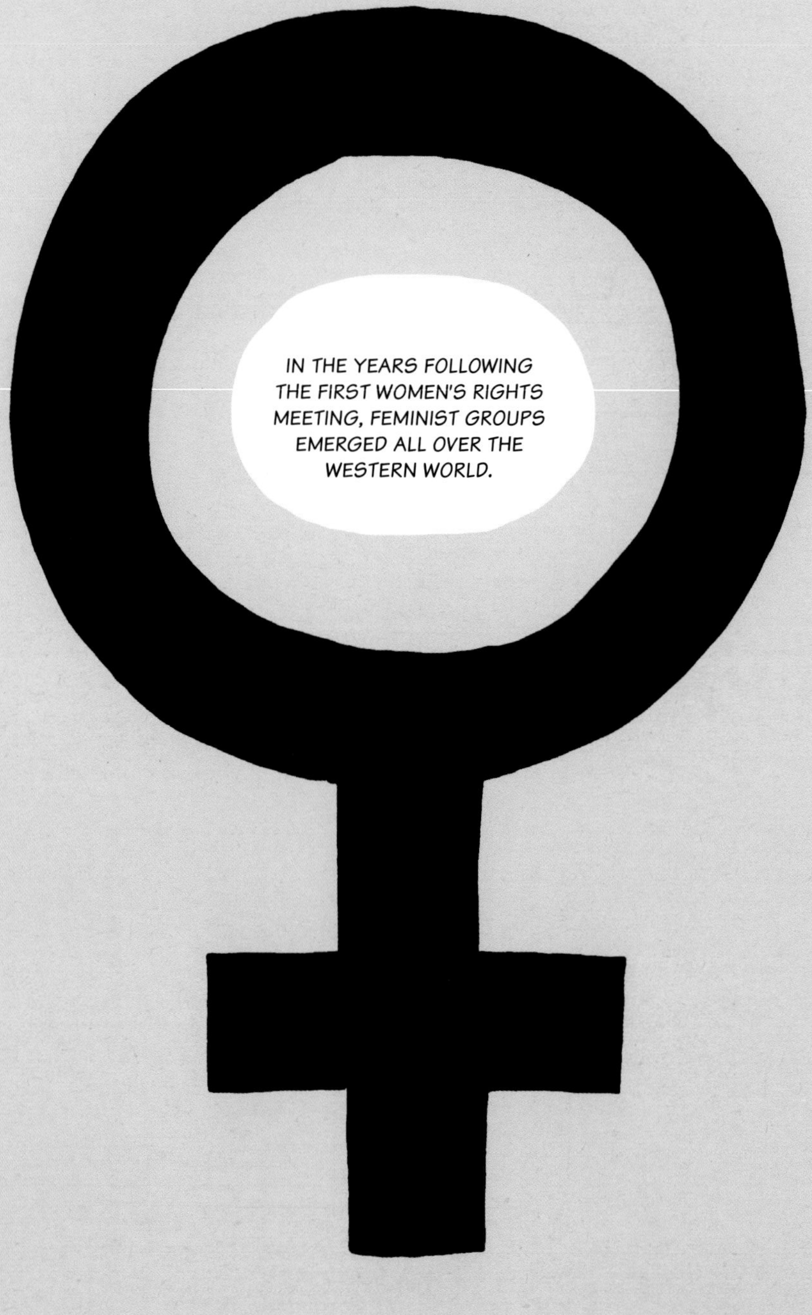
IN THE YEARS FOLLOWING THE FIRST WOMEN'S RIGHTS MEETING, FEMINIST GROUPS EMERGED ALL OVER THE WESTERN WORLD.

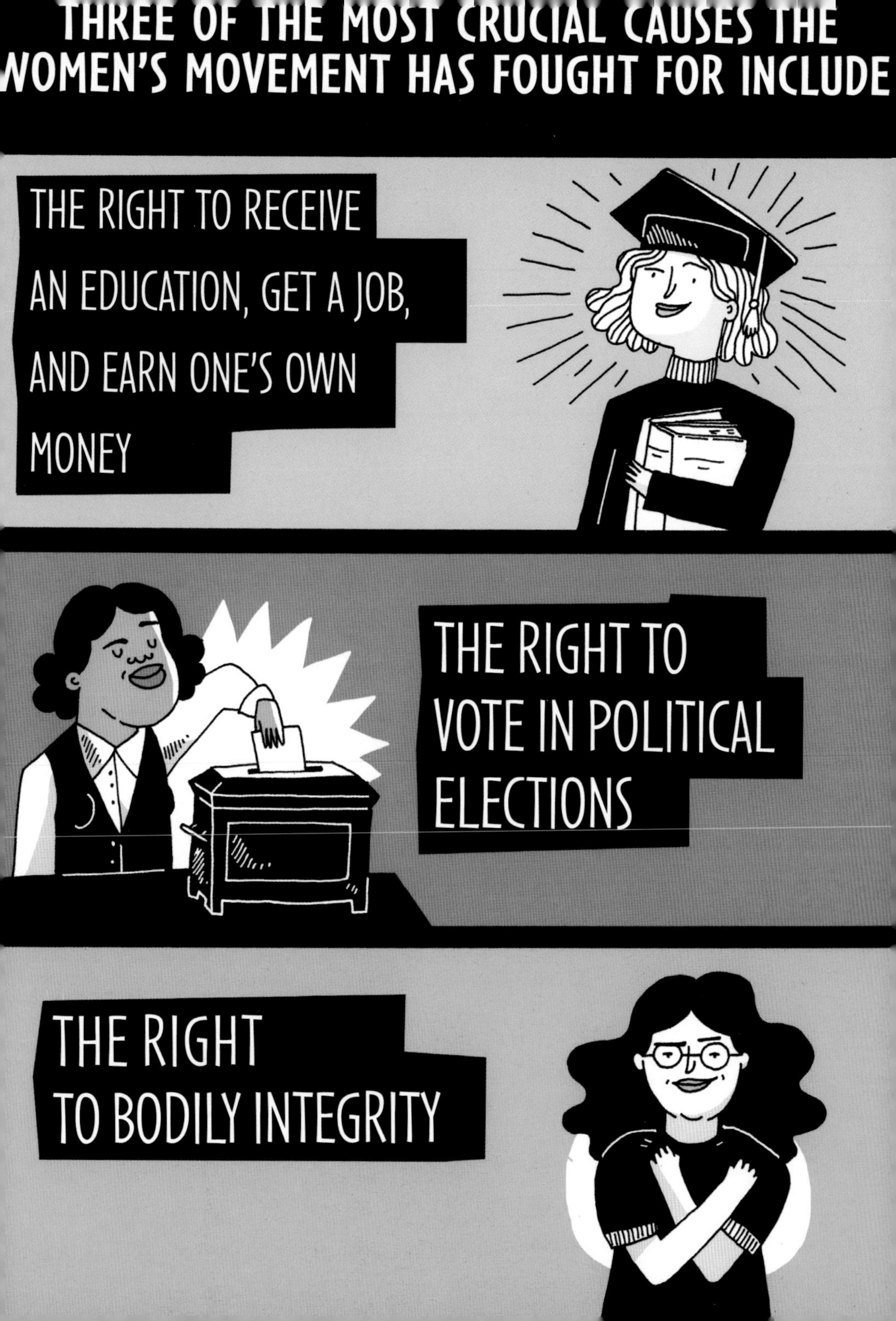

THREE OF THE MOST CRUCIAL CAUSES THE WOMEN'S MOVEMENT HAS FOUGHT FOR INCLUDE
THE RIGHT TO RECEIVE AN EDUCATION, GET A JOB, AND EARN ONE'S OWN MONEY
THE RIGHT TO VOTE IN POLITICAL ELECTIONS
THE RIGHT TO BODILY INTEGRITY

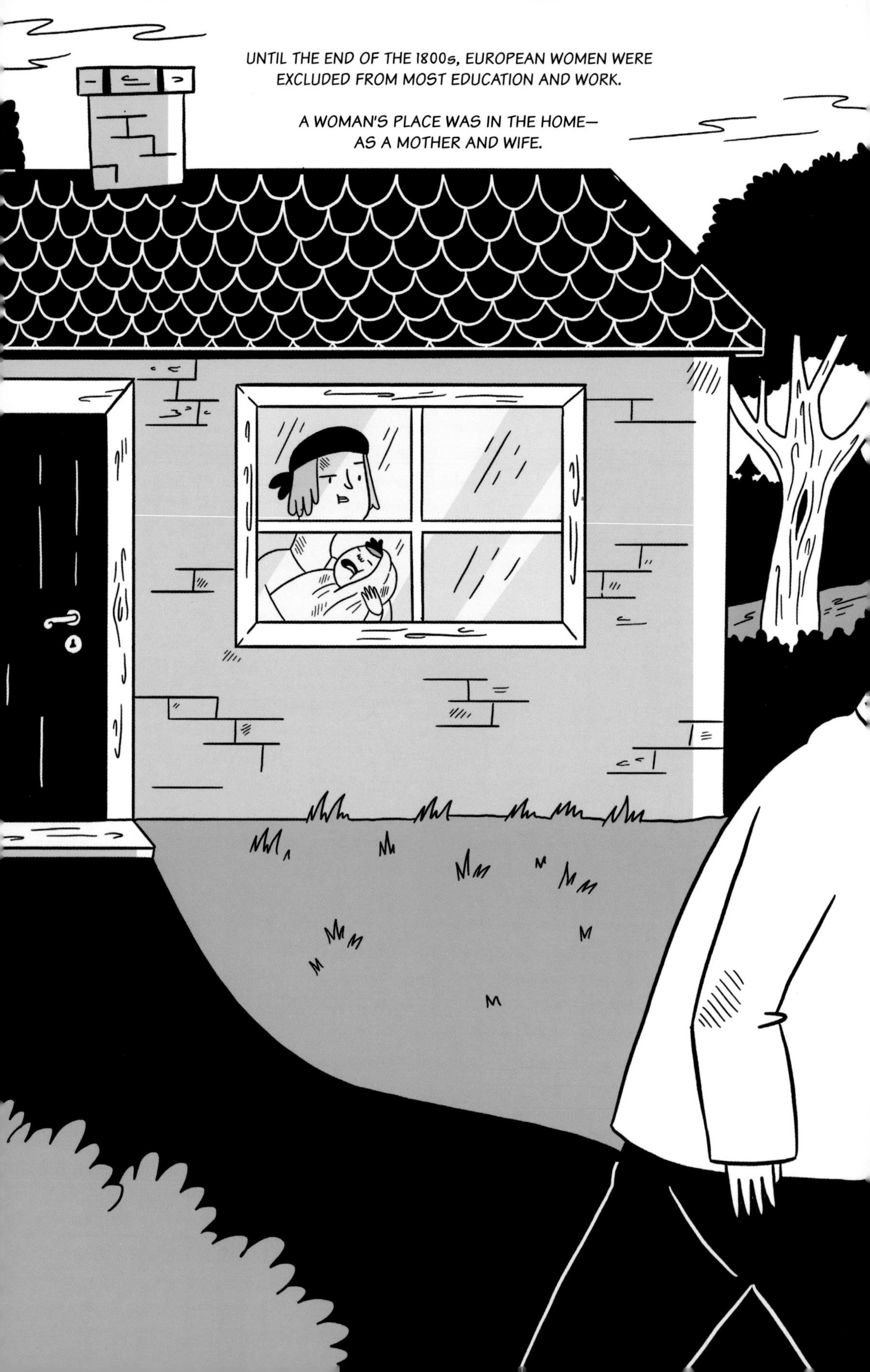
UNTIL THE END OF THE 1800s, EUROPEAN WOMEN WERE EXCLUDED FROM MOST EDUCATION AND WORK.
A WOMAN'S PLACE WAS IN THE HOME— AS A MOTHER AND WIFE.

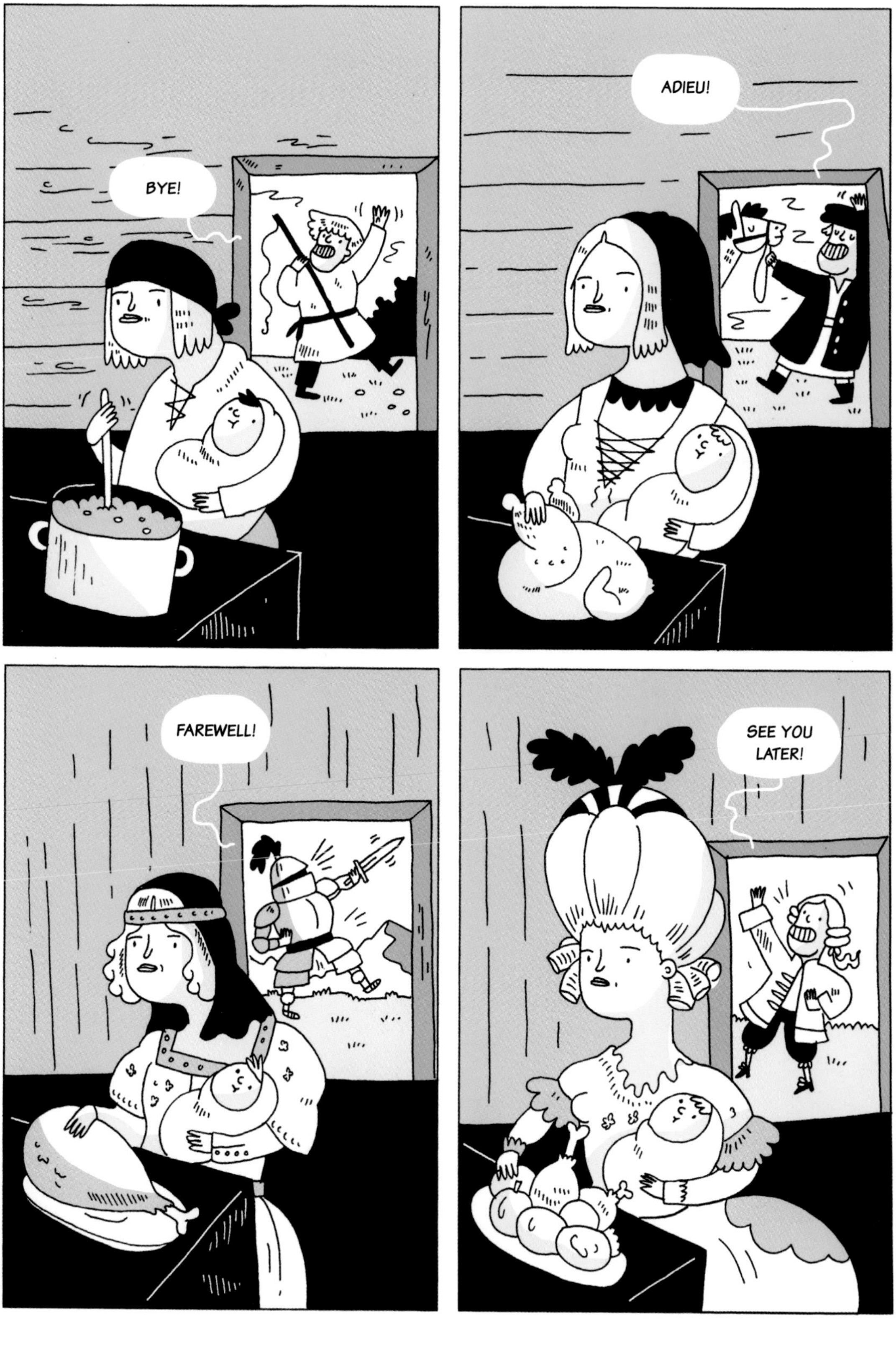
BYE!
ADIEU!
FAREWELL!
SEE YOU LATER!

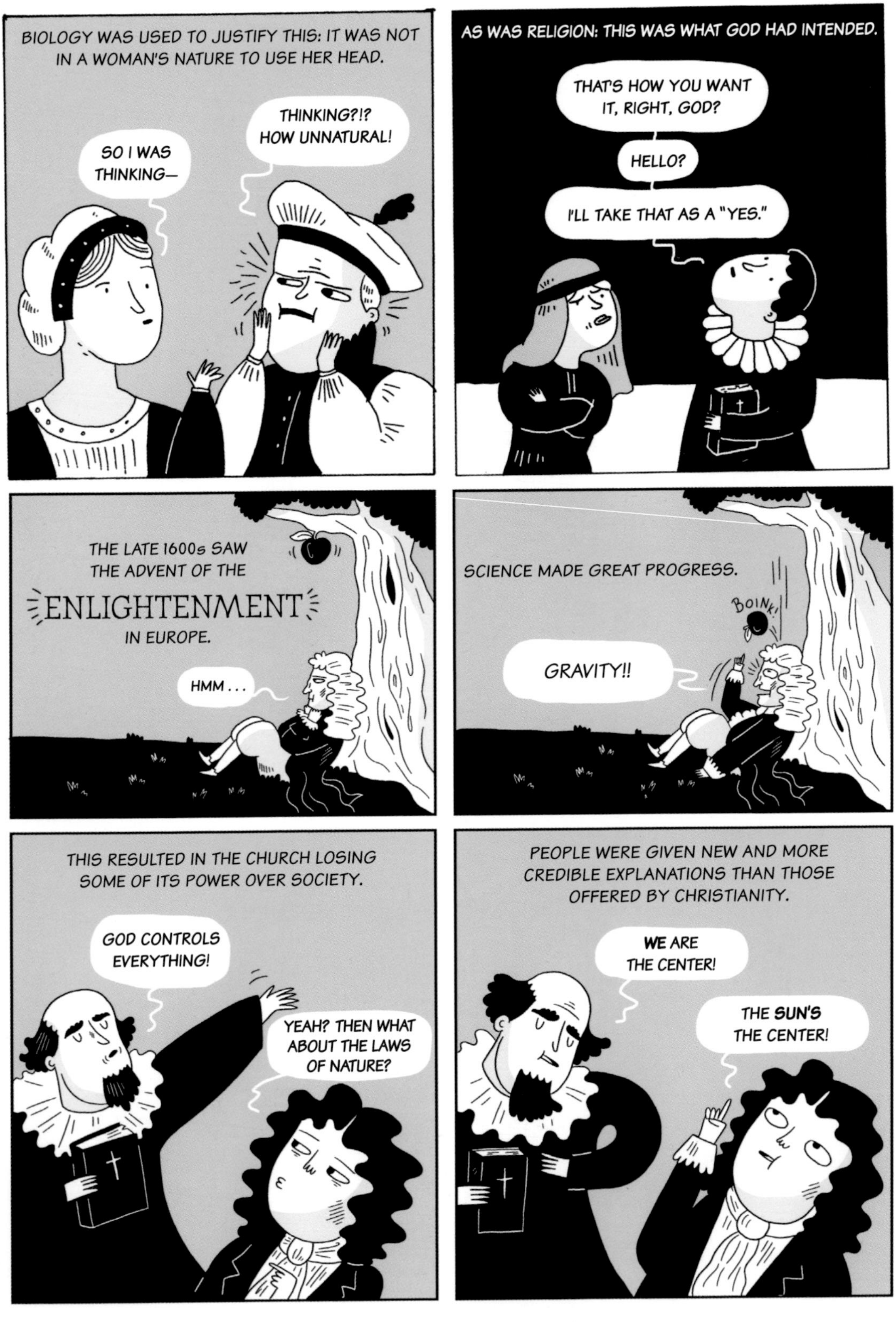
BIOLOGY WAS USED TO JUSTIFY THIS: IT WAS NOT IN A WOMAN'S NATURE TO USE HER HEAD.
SO I WAS THINKING—
THINKING?!? HOW UNNATURAL!
AS WAS RELIGION: THIS WAS WHAT GOD HAD INTENDED.
THAT'S HOW YOU WANT IT, RIGHT, GOD?
HELLO?
I'LL TAKE THAT AS A "YES."
THE LATE 1600s SAW THE ADVENT OF THE ENLIGHTENMENT IN EUROPE.
HMM . . .
SCIENCE MADE GREAT PROGRESS.
BOINK!
GRAVITY!!
THIS RESULTED IN THE CHURCH LOSING SOME OF ITS POWER OVER SOCIETY.
GOD CONTROLS EVERYTHING!
YEAH? THEN WHAT ABOUT THE LAWS OF NATURE?
PEOPLE WERE GIVEN NEW AND MORE CREDIBLE EXPLANATIONS THAN THOSE OFFERED BY CHRISTIANITY.
WE ARE THE CENTER!
THE SUN'S THE CENTER!

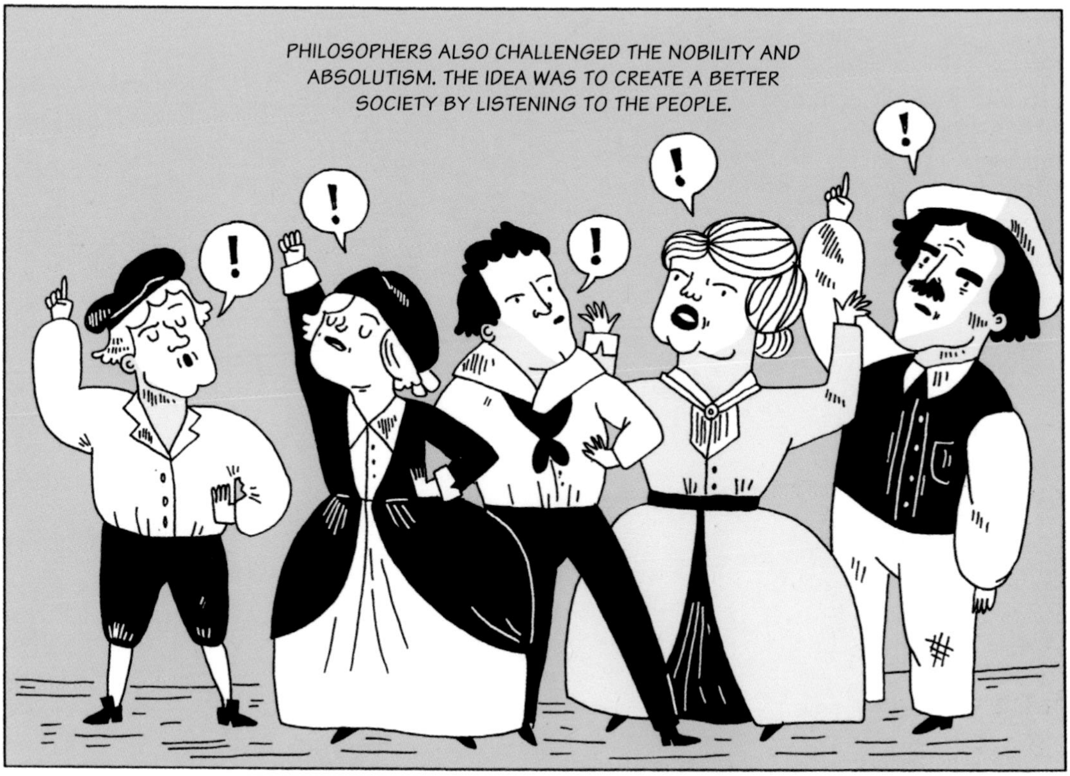
PHILOSOPHERS ALSO CHALLENGED THE NOBILITY AND ABSOLUTISM. THE IDEA WAS TO CREATE A BETTER SOCIETY BY LISTENING TO THE PEOPLE.
!
!
!
!
!

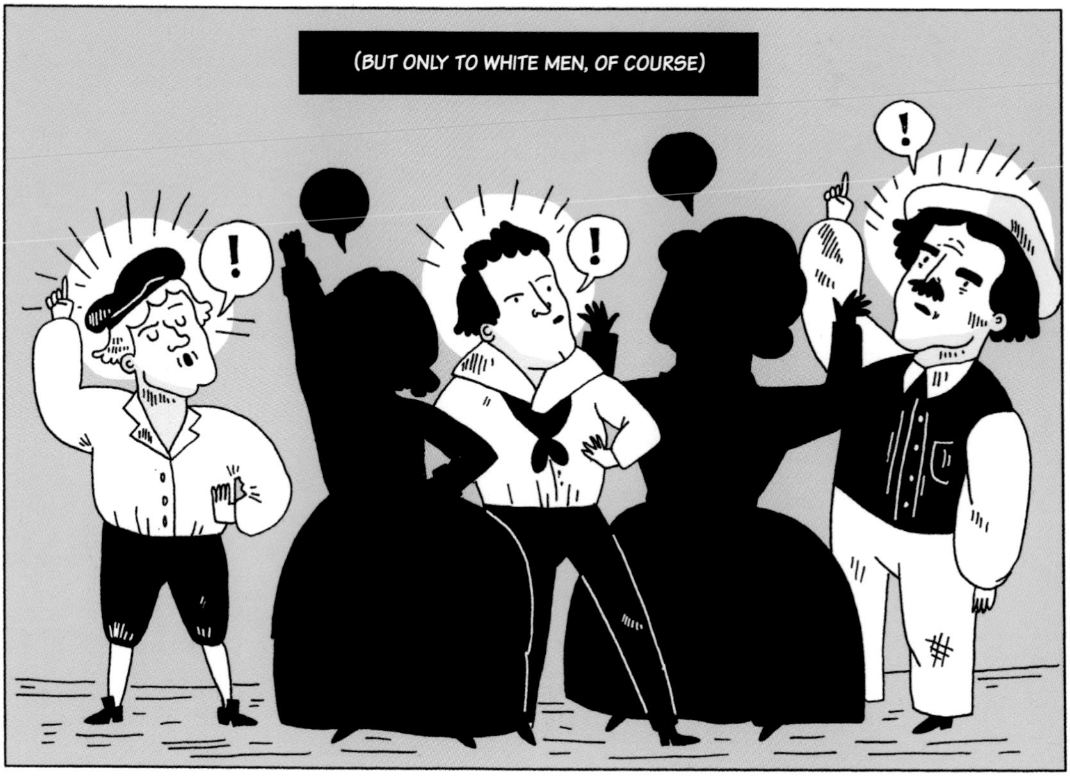
(BUT ONLY TO WHITE MEN, OF COURSE)
!
!
!

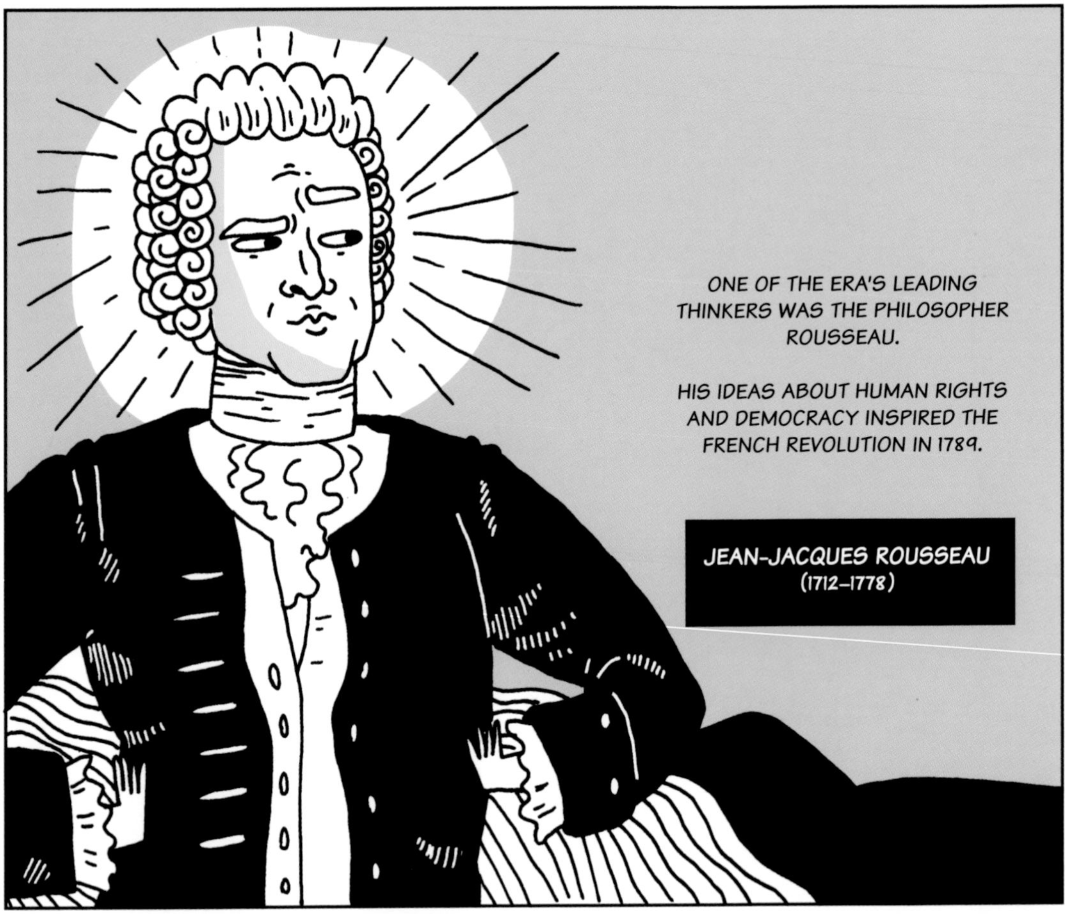
ONE OF THE ERA'S LEADING THINKERS WAS THE PHILOSOPHER ROUSSEAU.
HIS IDEAS ABOUT HUMAN RIGHTS AND DEMOCRACY INSPIRED THE FRENCH REVOLUTION IN 1789.
JEAN-JACQUES ROUSSEAU (1712–1778)

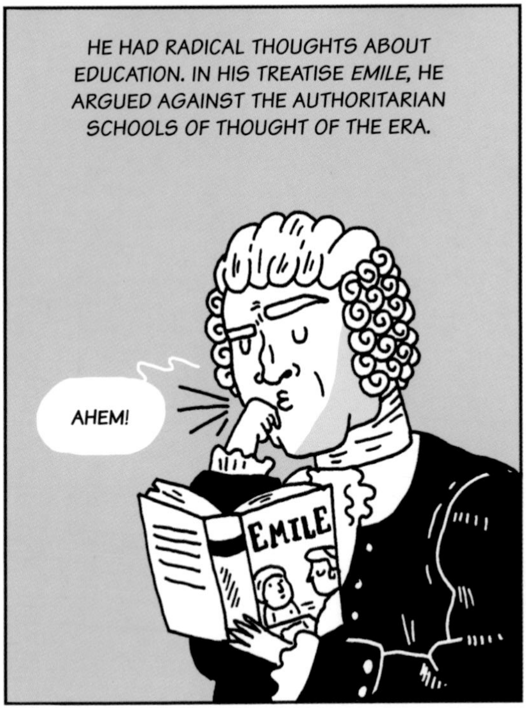
HE HAD RADICAL THOUGHTS ABOUT EDUCATION. IN HIS TREATISE *EMILE*, HE ARGUED AGAINST THE AUTHORITARIAN SCHOOLS OF THOUGHT OF THE ERA.
AHEM!
EMILE

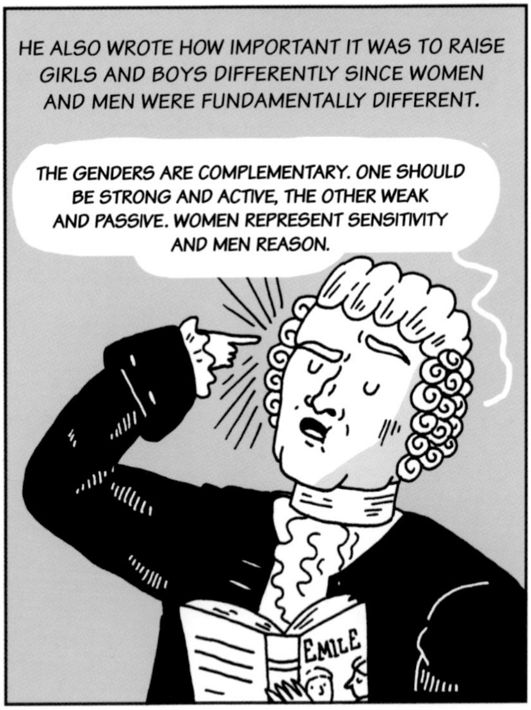
HE ALSO WROTE HOW IMPORTANT IT WAS TO RAISE GIRLS AND BOYS DIFFERENTLY SINCE WOMEN AND MEN WERE FUNDAMENTALLY DIFFERENT.
THE GENDERS ARE COMPLEMENTARY. ONE SHOULD BE STRONG AND ACTIVE, THE OTHER WEAK AND PASSIVE. WOMEN REPRESENT SENSITIVITY AND MEN REASON.
EMILE

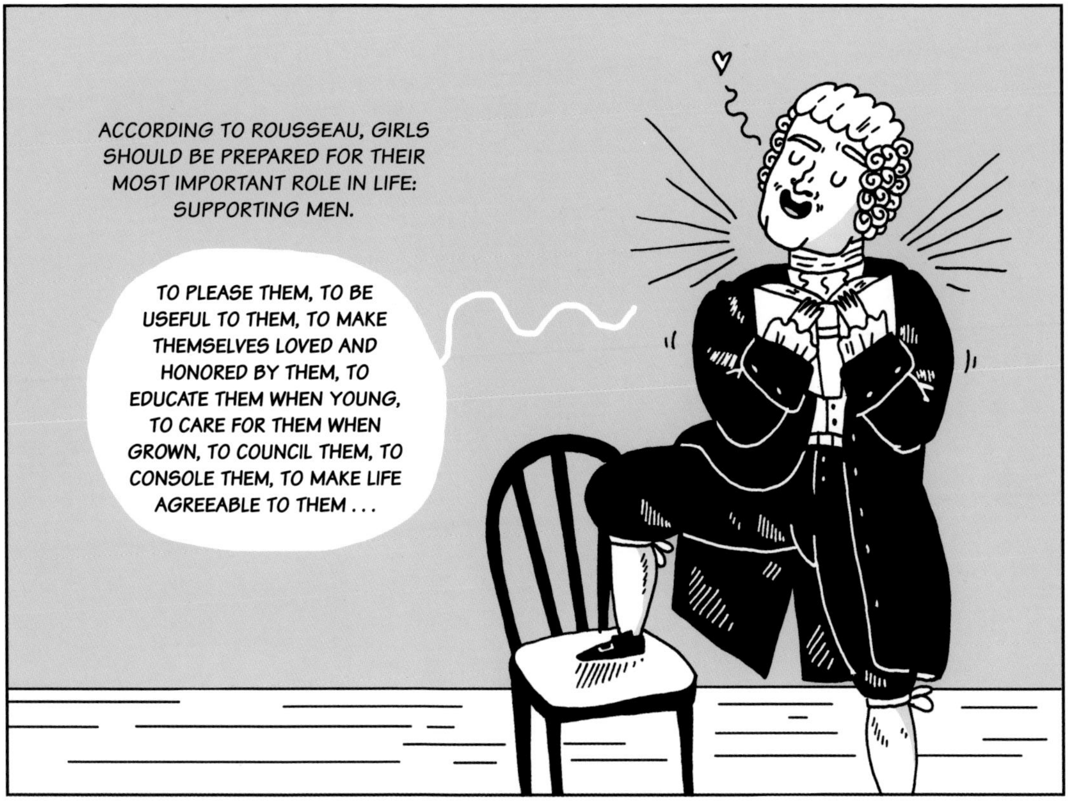
ACCORDING TO ROUSSEAU, GIRLS SHOULD BE PREPARED FOR THEIR MOST IMPORTANT ROLE IN LIFE: SUPPORTING MEN.
TO PLEASE THEM, TO BE USEFUL TO THEM, TO MAKE THEMSELVES LOVED AND HONORED BY THEM, TO EDUCATE THEM WHEN YOUNG, TO CARE FOR THEM WHEN GROWN, TO COUNCIL THEM, TO CONSOLE THEM, TO MAKE LIFE AGREEABLE TO THEM . . .

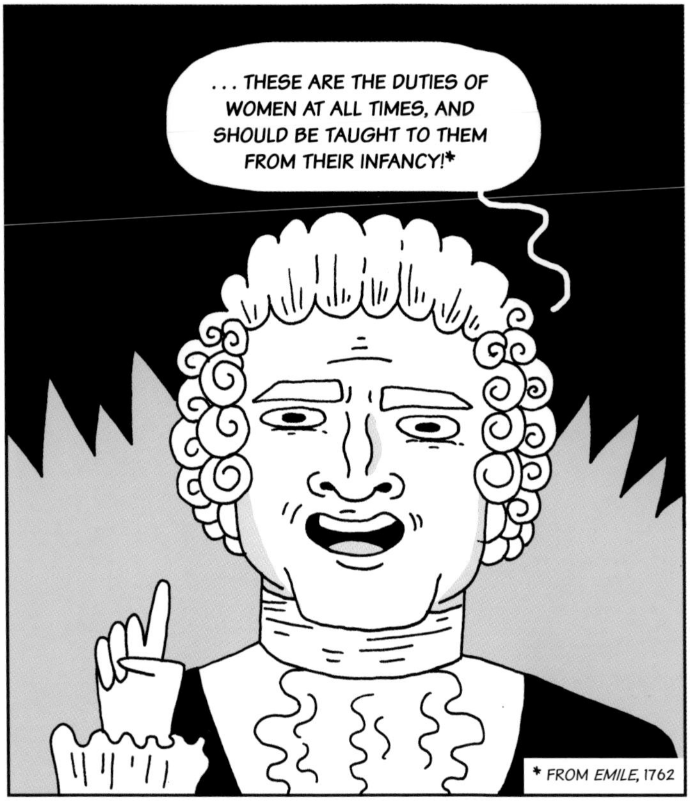
. . . THESE ARE THE DUTIES OF WOMEN AT ALL TIMES, AND SHOULD BE TAUGHT TO THEM FROM THEIR INFANCY!*
* FROM *EMILE*, 1762

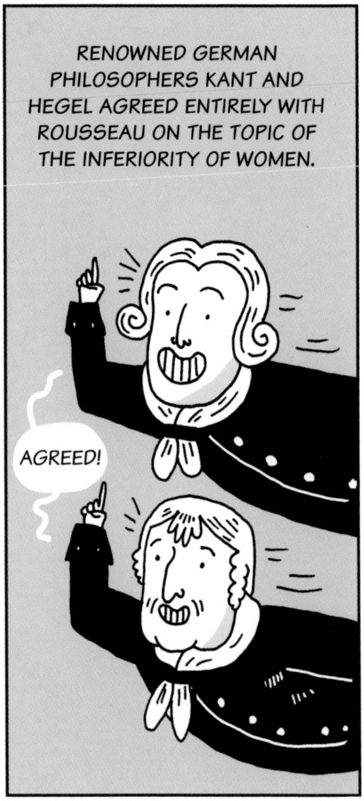
RENOWNED GERMAN PHILOSOPHERS KANT AND HEGEL AGREED ENTIRELY WITH ROUSSEAU ON THE TOPIC OF THE INFERIORITY OF WOMEN.
AGREED!

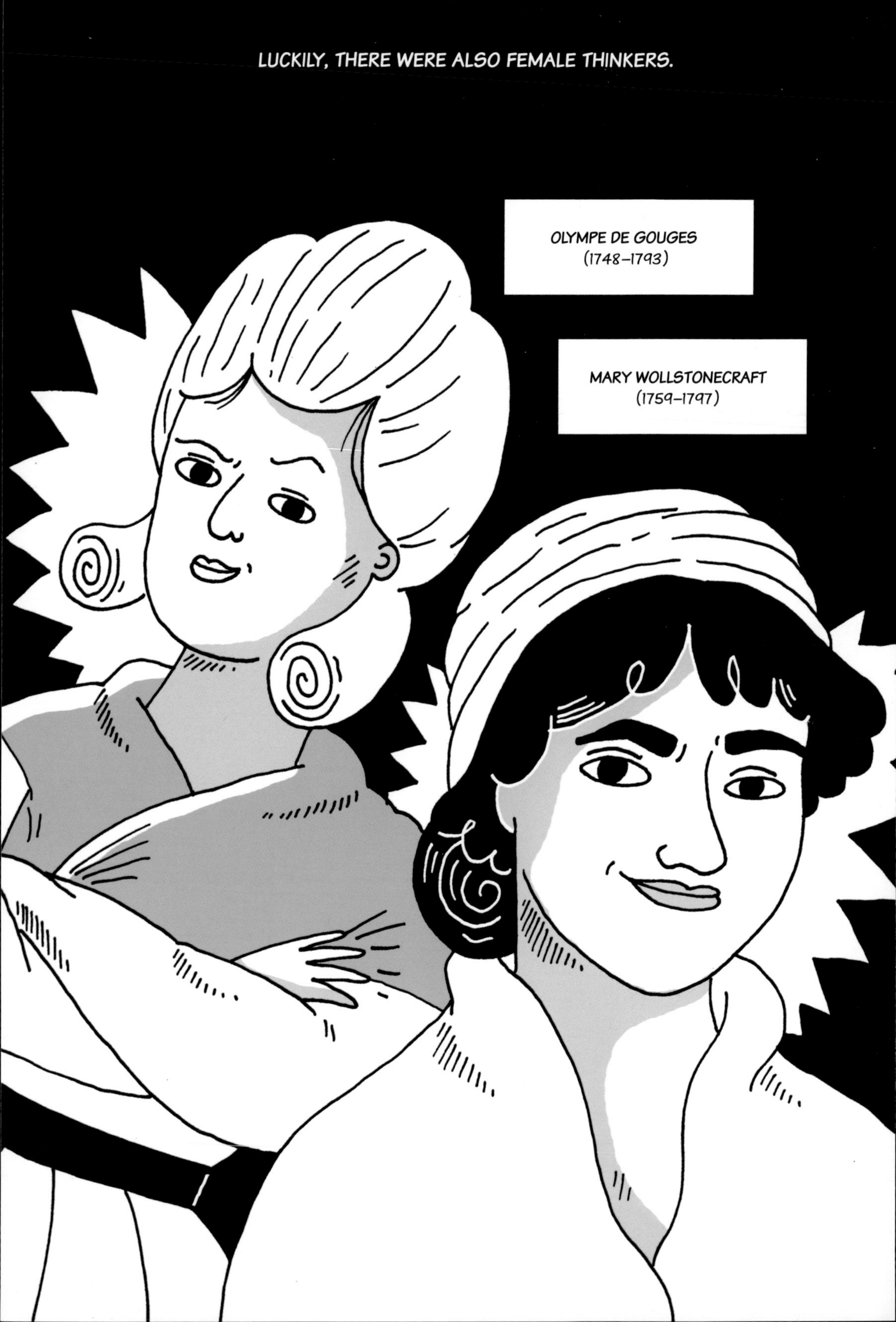
LUCKILY, THERE WERE ALSO FEMALE THINKERS.
OLYMPE DE GOUGES (1748–1793)
MARY WOLLSTONECRAFT (1759–1797)

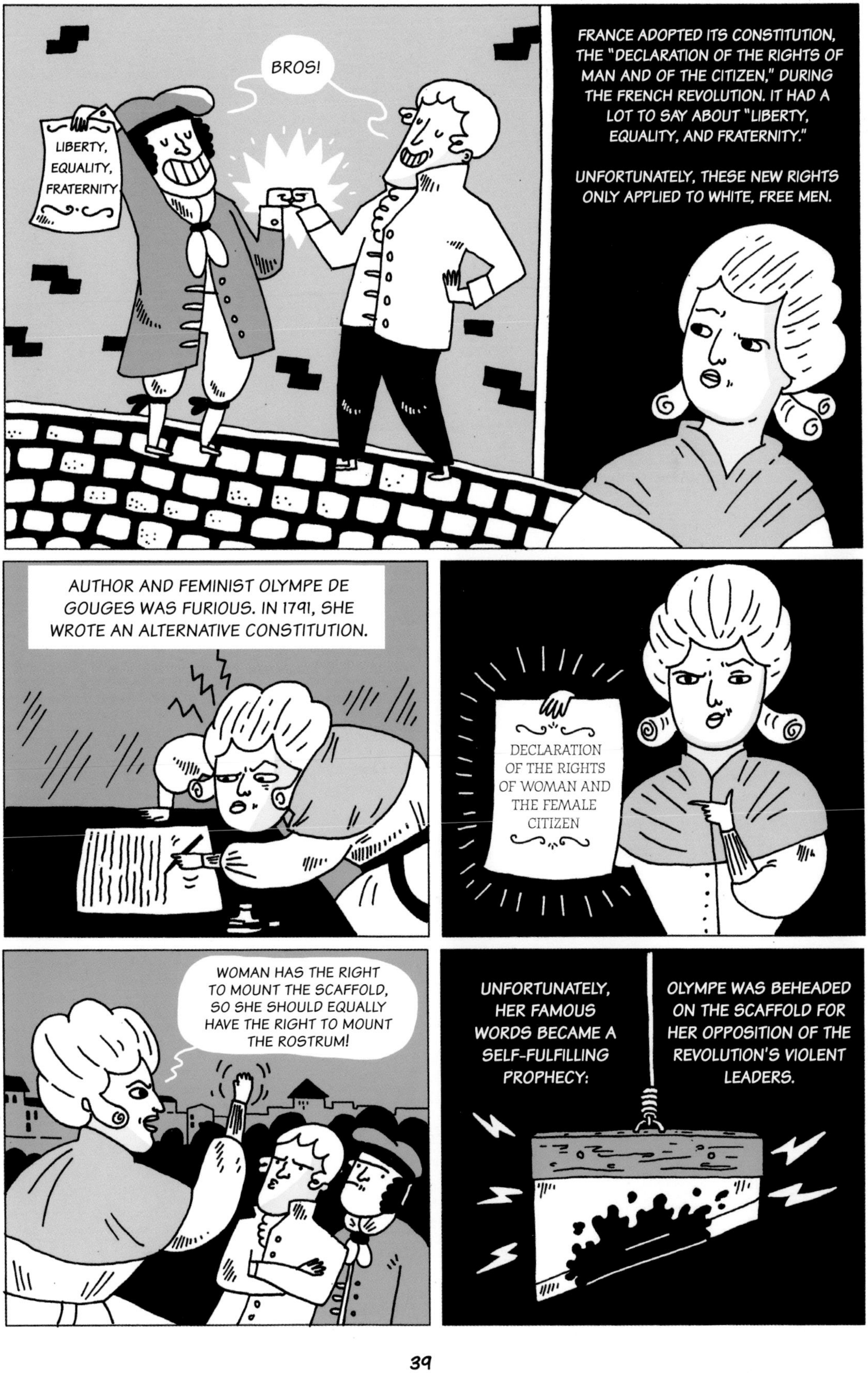
BROS!
LIBERTY, EQUALITY, FRATERNITY
FRANCE ADOPTED ITS CONSTITUTION, THE "DECLARATION OF THE RIGHTS OF MAN AND OF THE CITIZEN," DURING THE FRENCH REVOLUTION. IT HAD A LOT TO SAY ABOUT "LIBERTY, EQUALITY, AND FRATERNITY."
UNFORTUNATELY, THESE NEW RIGHTS ONLY APPLIED TO WHITE, FREE MEN.
AUTHOR AND FEMINIST OLYMPE DE GOUGES WAS FURIOUS. IN 1791, SHE WROTE AN ALTERNATIVE CONSTITUTION.
DECLARATION OF THE RIGHTS OF WOMAN AND THE FEMALE CITIZEN
WOMAN HAS THE RIGHT TO MOUNT THE SCAFFOLD, SO SHE SHOULD EQUALLY HAVE THE RIGHT TO MOUNT THE ROSTRUM!
UNFORTUNATELY, HER FAMOUS WORDS BECAME A SELF-FULFILLING PROPHECY:
OLYMPE WAS BEHEADED ON THE SCAFFOLD FOR HER OPPOSITION OF THE REVOLUTION'S VIOLENT LEADERS.

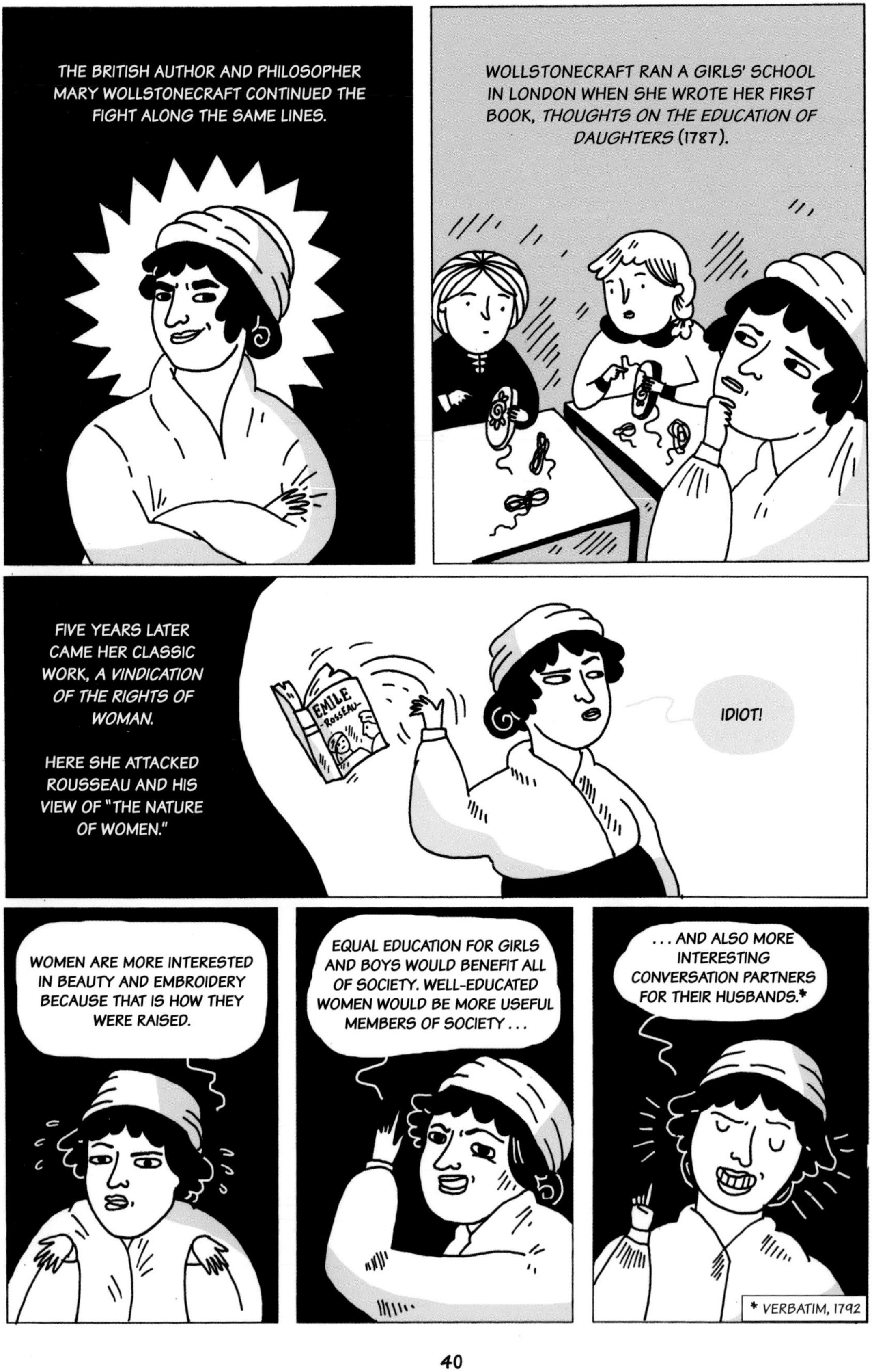
THE BRITISH AUTHOR AND PHILOSOPHER MARY WOLLSTONECRAFT CONTINUED THE FIGHT ALONG THE SAME LINES.
WOLLSTONECRAFT RAN A GIRLS' SCHOOL IN LONDON WHEN SHE WROTE HER FIRST BOOK, *THOUGHTS ON THE EDUCATION OF DAUGHTERS* (1787).
FIVE YEARS LATER CAME HER CLASSIC WORK, *A VINDICATION OF THE RIGHTS OF WOMAN.*
HERE SHE ATTACKED ROUSSEAU AND HIS VIEW OF "THE NATURE OF WOMEN."
EMILE
ROSSEAU
IDIOT!
WOMEN ARE MORE INTERESTED IN BEAUTY AND EMBROIDERY BECAUSE THAT IS HOW THEY WERE RAISED.
EQUAL EDUCATION FOR GIRLS AND BOYS WOULD BENEFIT ALL OF SOCIETY. WELL-EDUCATED WOMEN WOULD BE MORE USEFUL MEMBERS OF SOCIETY . . .
. . . AND ALSO MORE INTERESTING CONVERSATION PARTNERS FOR THEIR HUSBANDS.*
* VERBATIM, 1792

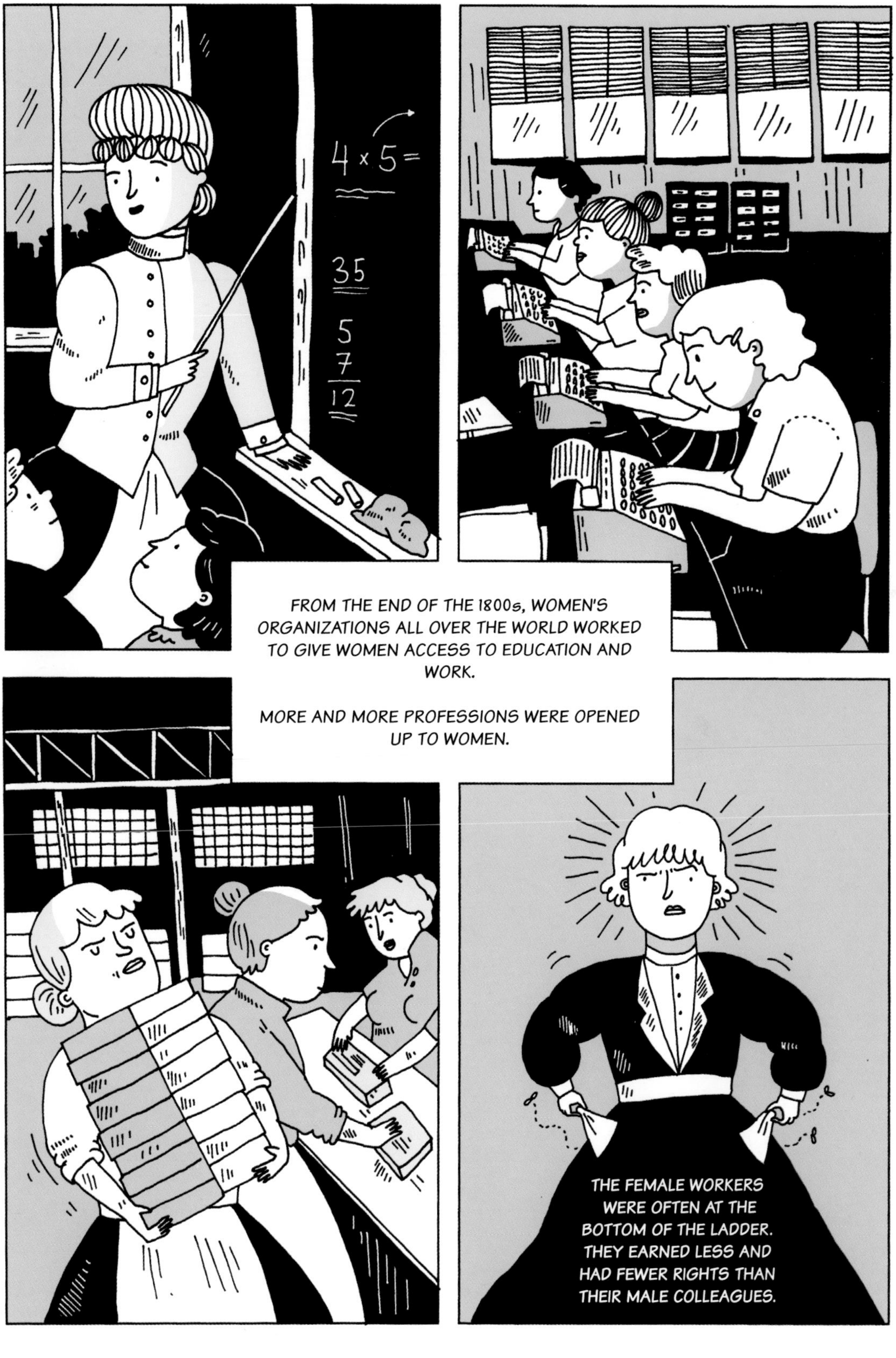
4 x 5 =
35
5
7
12
FROM THE END OF THE 1800s, WOMEN'S ORGANIZATIONS ALL OVER THE WORLD WORKED TO GIVE WOMEN ACCESS TO EDUCATION AND WORK.
MORE AND MORE PROFESSIONS WERE OPENED UP TO WOMEN.
THE FEMALE WORKERS WERE OFTEN AT THE BOTTOM OF THE LADDER. THEY EARNED LESS AND HAD FEWER RIGHTS THAN THEIR MALE COLLEAGUES.

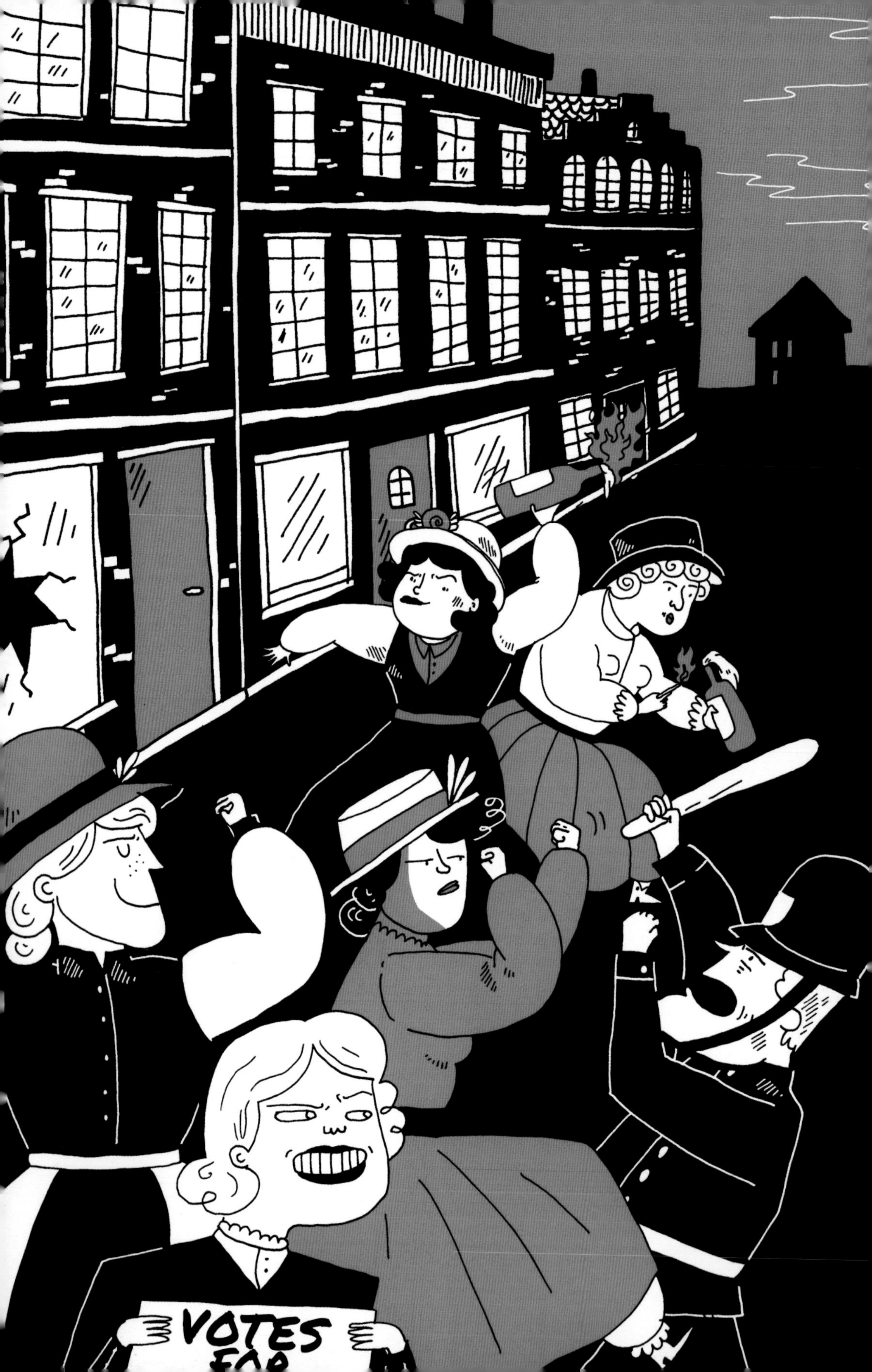
VOTES

SUFFERING SUFFRAGISTS

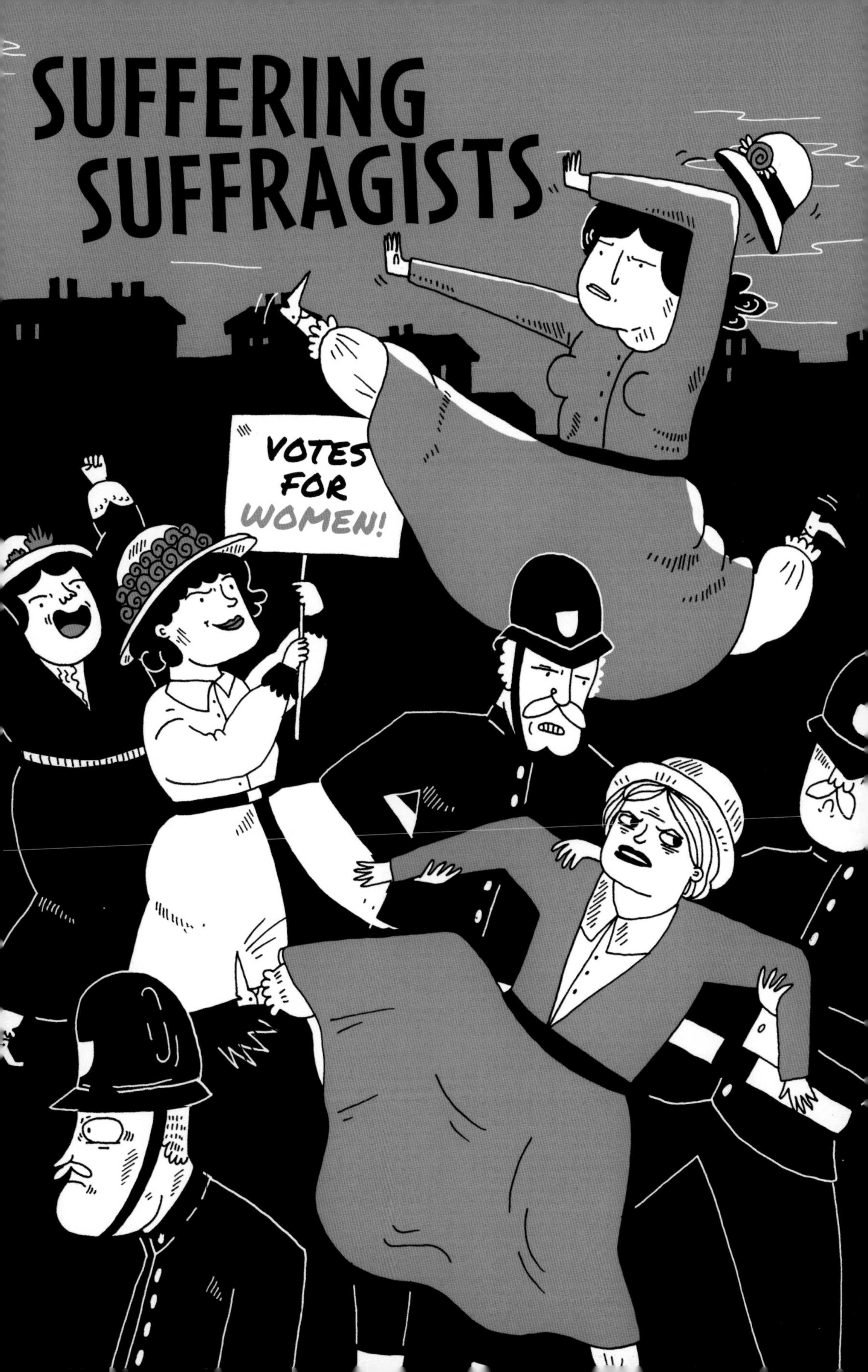
VOTES FOR WOMEN!

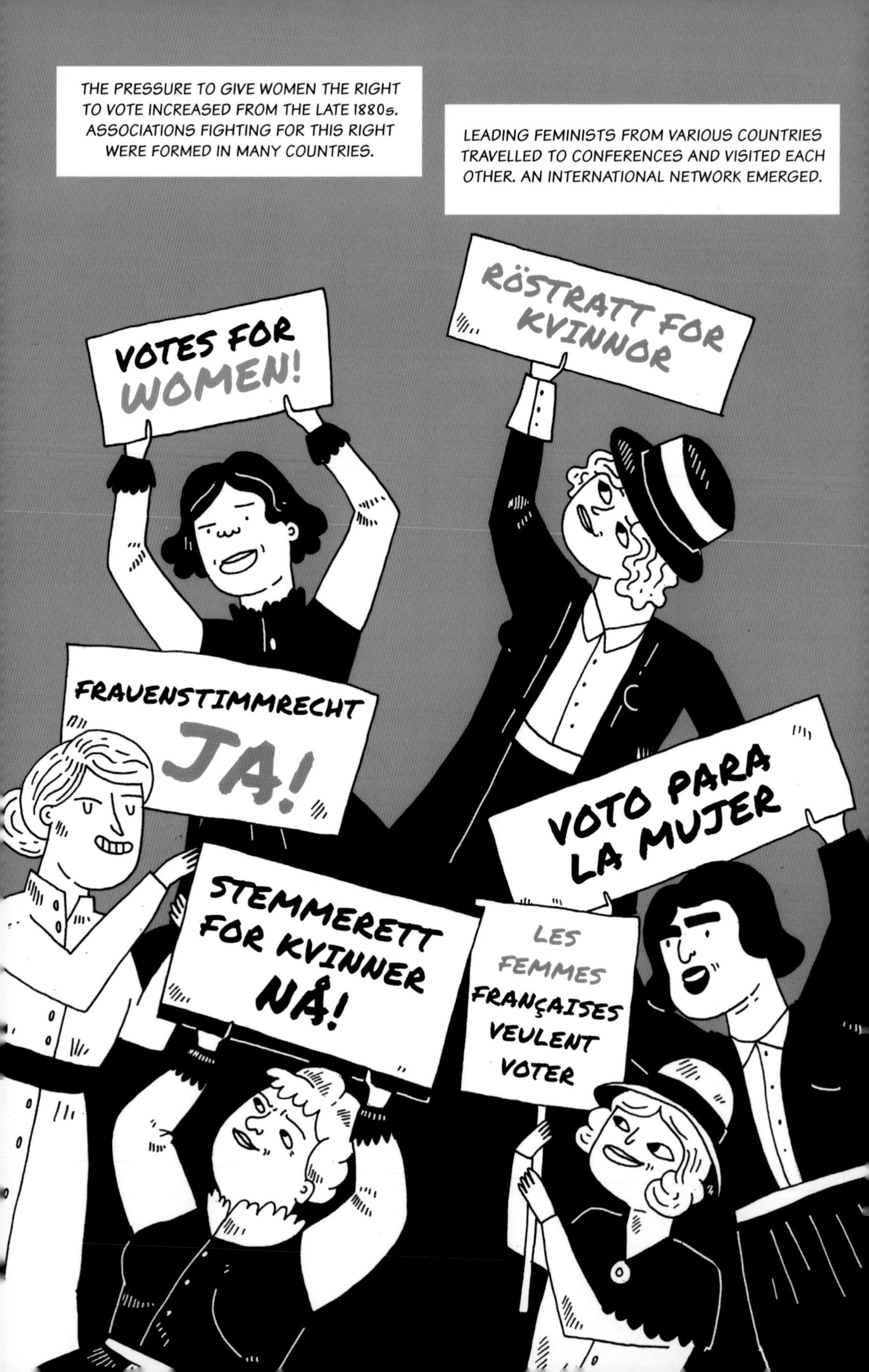
THE PRESSURE TO GIVE WOMEN THE RIGHT TO VOTE INCREASED FROM THE LATE 1880s. ASSOCIATIONS FIGHTING FOR THIS RIGHT WERE FORMED IN MANY COUNTRIES.
LEADING FEMINISTS FROM VARIOUS COUNTRIES TRAVELLED TO CONFERENCES AND VISITED EACH OTHER. AN INTERNATIONAL NETWORK EMERGED.
VOTES FOR WOMEN!
RÖSTRATT FOR KVINNOR
FRAUENSTIMMRECHT JA!
VOTO PARA LA MUJER
STEMMERETT FOR KVINNER NÅ!
LES FEMMES FRANÇAISES VEULENT VOTER

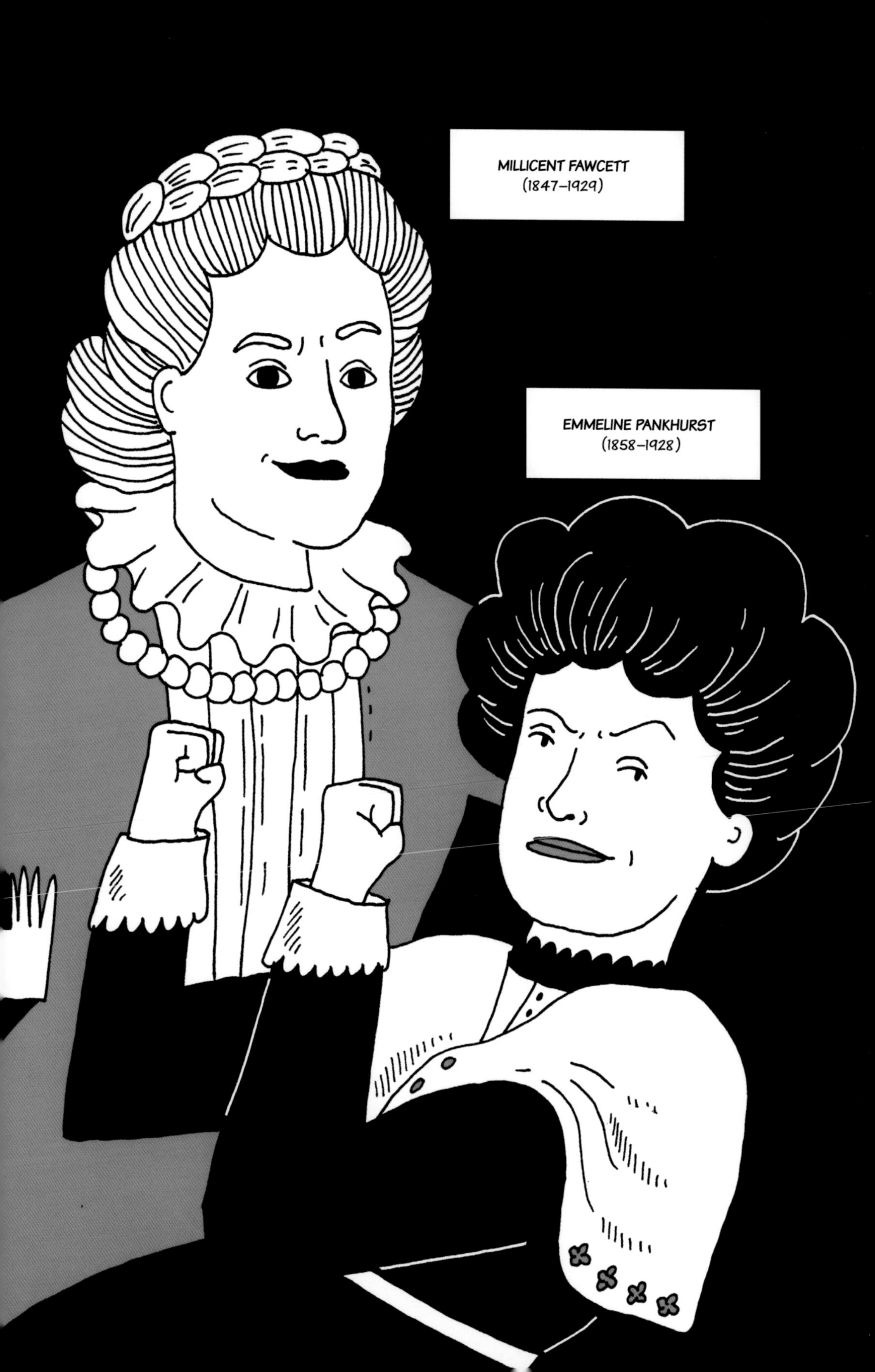

MILLICENT FAWCETT
(1847–1929)
EMMELINE PANKHURST
(1858–1928)

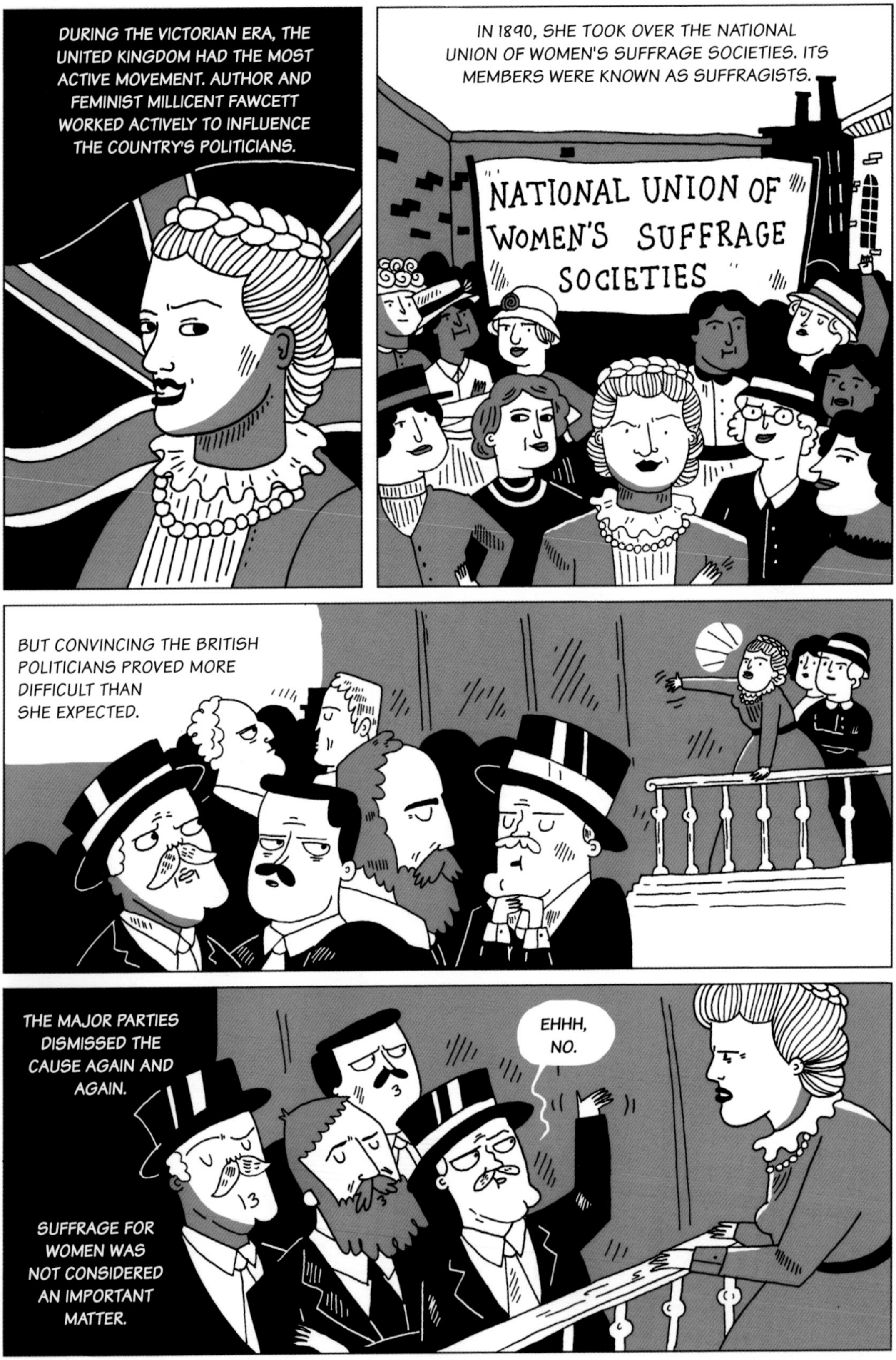

DURING THE VICTORIAN ERA, THE UNITED KINGDOM HAD THE MOST ACTIVE MOVEMENT. AUTHOR AND FEMINIST MILLICENT FAWCETT WORKED ACTIVELY TO INFLUENCE THE COUNTRY'S POLITICIANS.
IN 1890, SHE TOOK OVER THE NATIONAL UNION OF WOMEN'S SUFFRAGE SOCIETIES. ITS MEMBERS WERE KNOWN AS SUFFRAGISTS.
NATIONAL UNION OF WOMEN'S SUFFRAGE SOCIETIES
BUT CONVINCING THE BRITISH POLITICIANS PROVED MORE DIFFICULT THAN SHE EXPECTED.
THE MAJOR PARTIES DISMISSED THE CAUSE AGAIN AND AGAIN.
EHHH, NO.
SUFFRAGE FOR WOMEN WAS NOT CONSIDERED AN IMPORTANT MATTER.

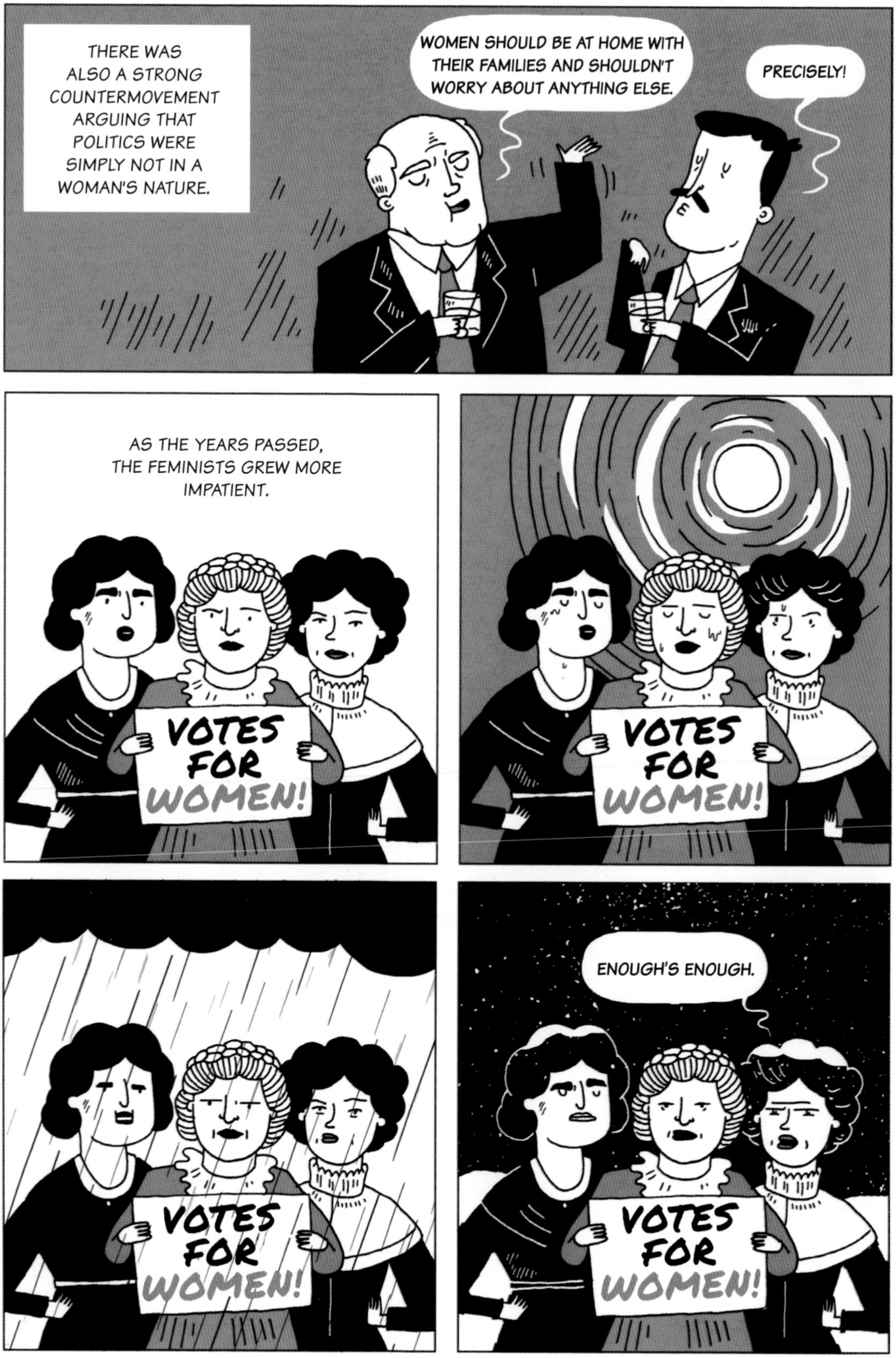
THERE WAS ALSO A STRONG COUNTERMOVEMENT ARGUING THAT POLITICS WERE SIMPLY NOT IN A WOMAN'S NATURE.
WOMEN SHOULD BE AT HOME WITH THEIR FAMILIES AND SHOULDN'T WORRY ABOUT ANYTHING ELSE.
PRECISELY!
AS THE YEARS PASSED, THE FEMINISTS GREW MORE IMPATIENT.
VOTES FOR WOMEN!
VOTES FOR WOMEN!
VOTES FOR WOMEN!
ENOUGH'S ENOUGH.
VOTES FOR WOMEN!

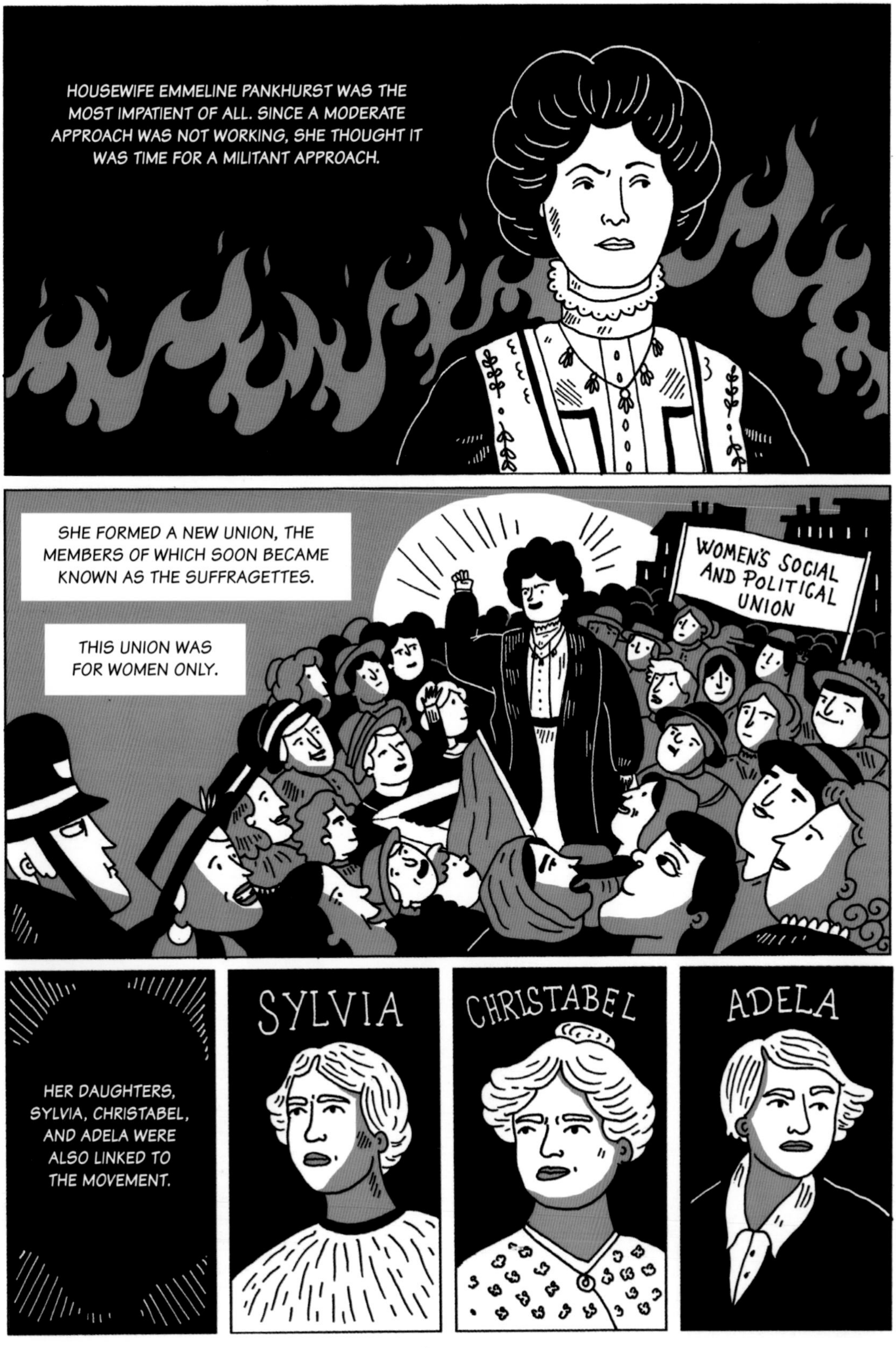
HOUSEWIFE EMMELINE PANKHURST WAS THE MOST IMPATIENT OF ALL. SINCE A MODERATE APPROACH WAS NOT WORKING, SHE THOUGHT IT WAS TIME FOR A MILITANT APPROACH.
SHE FORMED A NEW UNION, THE MEMBERS OF WHICH SOON BECAME KNOWN AS THE SUFFRAGETTES.
THIS UNION WAS FOR WOMEN ONLY.
WOMEN'S SOCIAL AND POLITICAL UNION
HER DAUGHTERS, SYLVIA, CHRISTABEL, AND ADELA WERE ALSO LINKED TO THE MOVEMENT.
SYLVIA
CHRISTABEL
ADELA

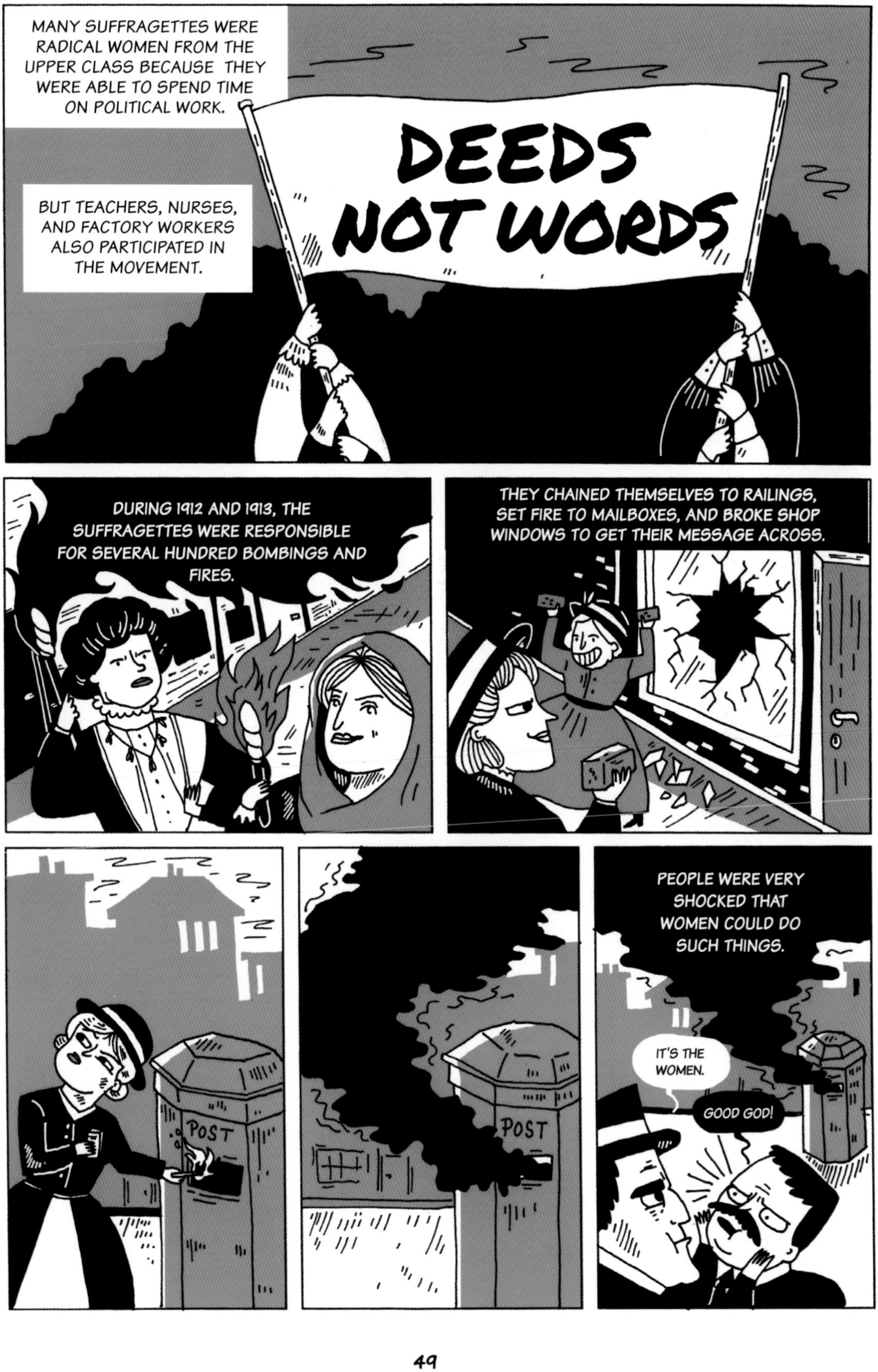
MANY SUFFRAGETTES WERE RADICAL WOMEN FROM THE UPPER CLASS BECAUSE THEY WERE ABLE TO SPEND TIME ON POLITICAL WORK.
DEEDS NOT WORDS
BUT TEACHERS, NURSES, AND FACTORY WORKERS ALSO PARTICIPATED IN THE MOVEMENT.
DURING 1912 AND 1913, THE SUFFRAGETTES WERE RESPONSIBLE FOR SEVERAL HUNDRED BOMBINGS AND FIRES.
THEY CHAINED THEMSELVES TO RAILINGS, SET FIRE TO MAILBOXES, AND BROKE SHOP WINDOWS TO GET THEIR MESSAGE ACROSS.
POST
POST
PEOPLE WERE VERY SHOCKED THAT WOMEN COULD DO SUCH THINGS.
IT'S THE WOMEN.
GOOD GOD!

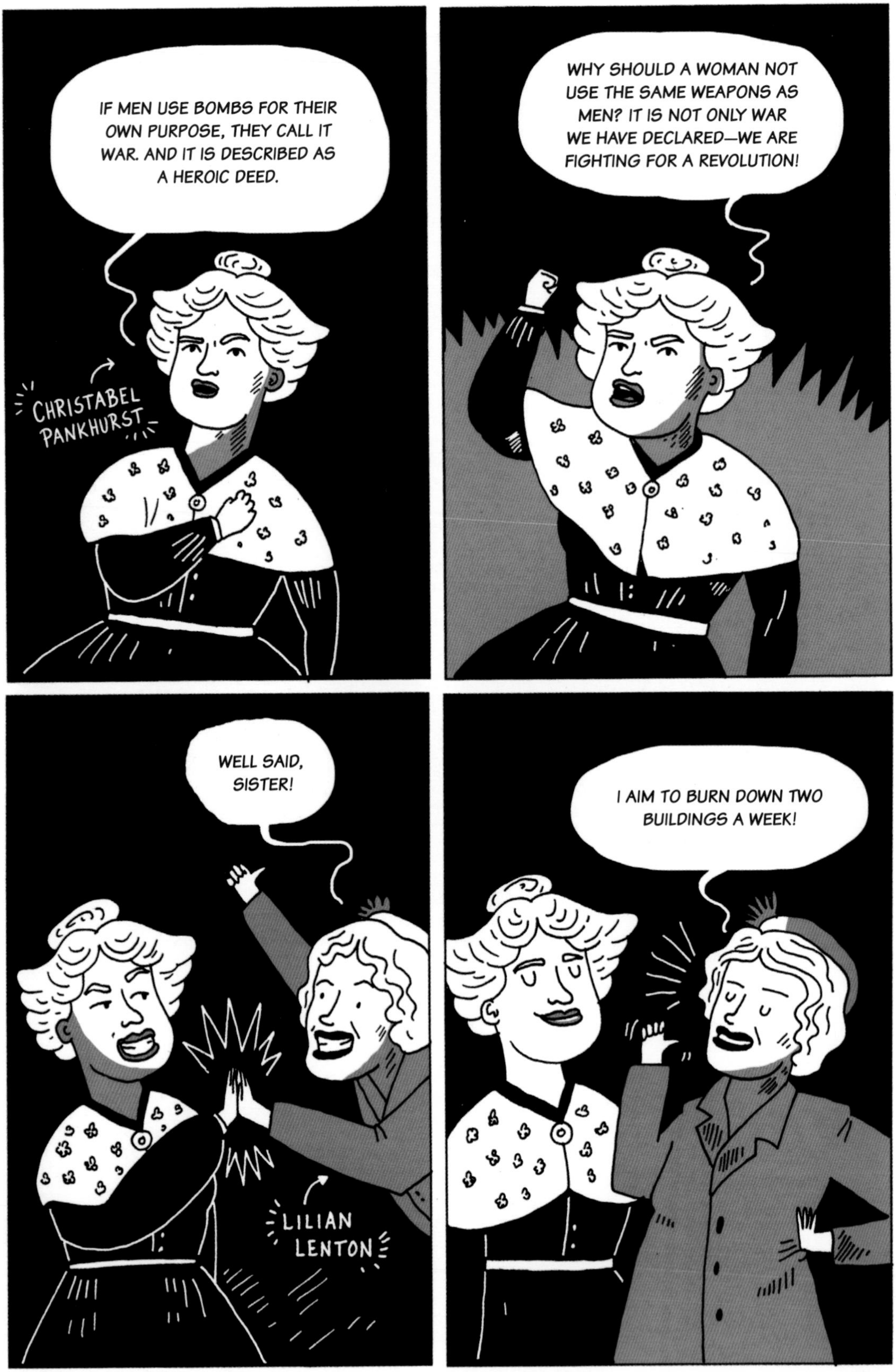
IF MEN USE BOMBS FOR THEIR OWN PURPOSE, THEY CALL IT WAR. AND IT IS DESCRIBED AS A HEROIC DEED.
CHRISTABEL PANKHURST
WHY SHOULD A WOMAN NOT USE THE SAME WEAPONS AS MEN? IT IS NOT ONLY WAR WE HAVE DECLARED—WE ARE FIGHTING FOR A REVOLUTION!
WELL SAID, SISTER!
LILIAN LENTON
I AIM TO BURN DOWN TWO BUILDINGS A WEEK!

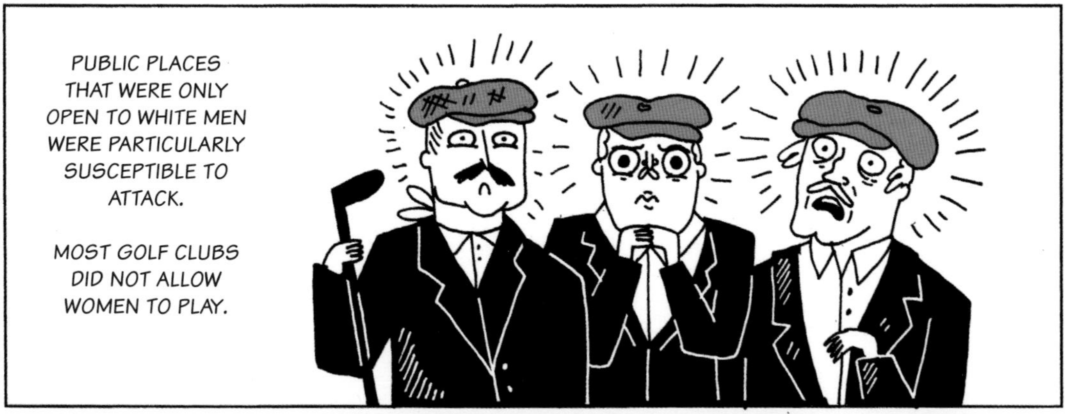
PUBLIC PLACES THAT WERE ONLY OPEN TO WHITE MEN WERE PARTICULARLY SUSCEPTIBLE TO ATTACK.
MOST GOLF CLUBS DID NOT ALLOW WOMEN TO PLAY.

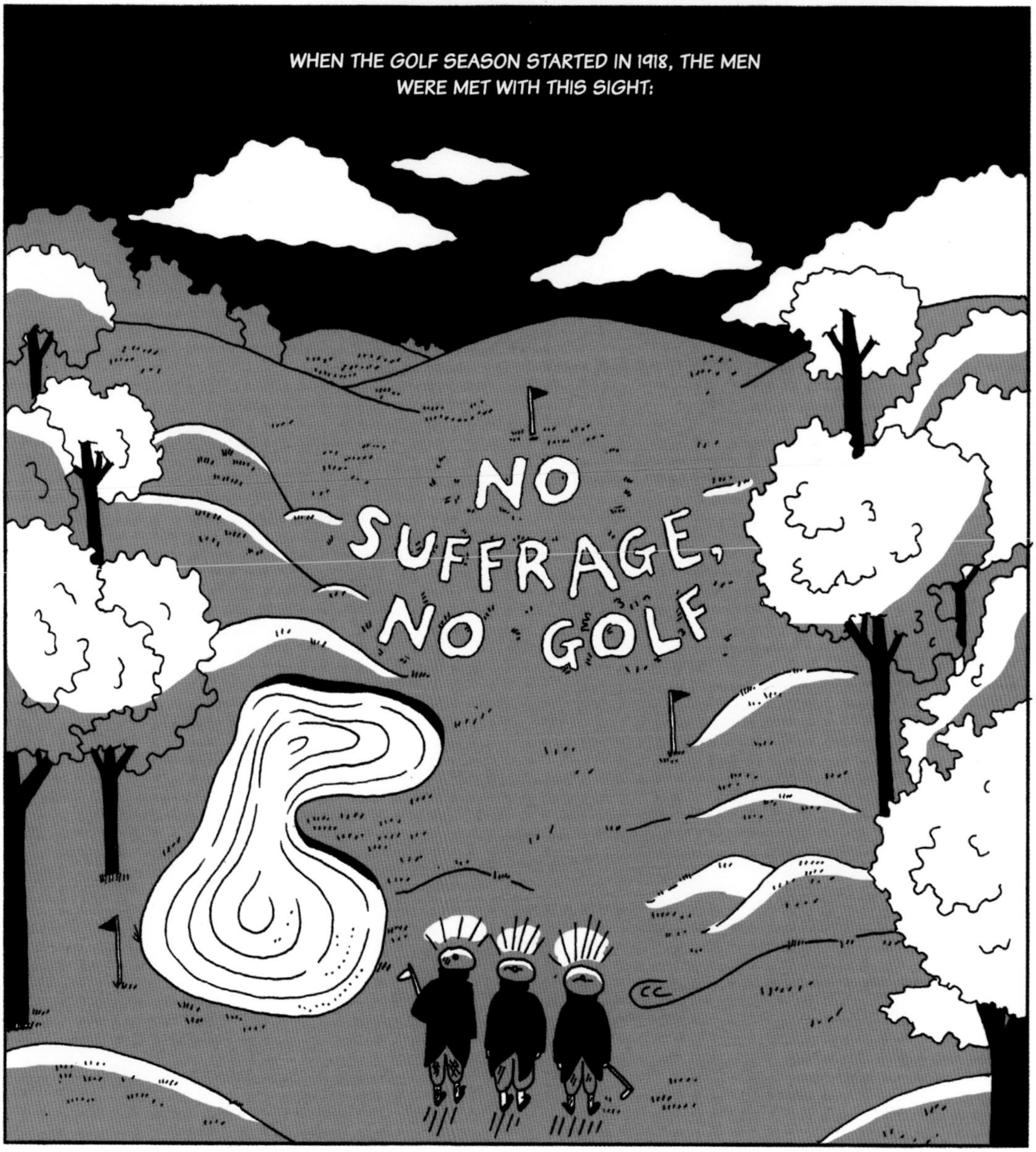
WHEN THE GOLF SEASON STARTED IN 1918, THE MEN WERE MET WITH THIS SIGHT:
NO SUFFRAGE, NO GOLF

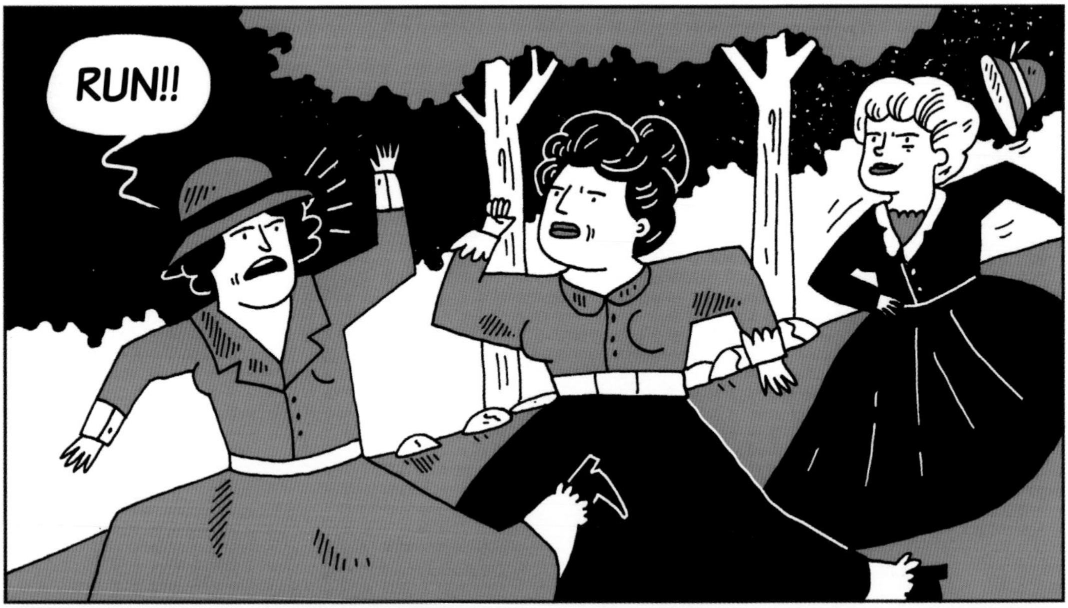
RUN!!

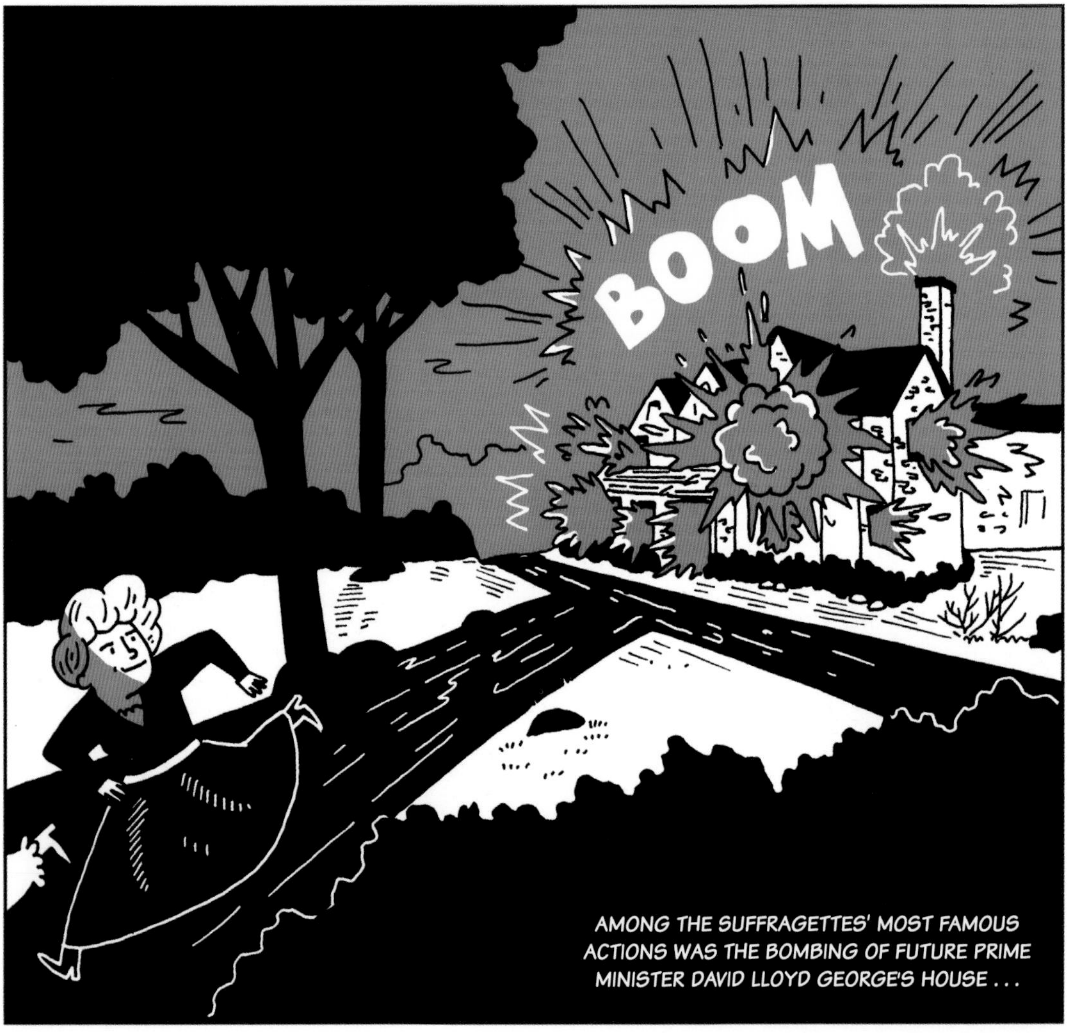
BOOM
AMONG THE SUFFRAGETTES' MOST FAMOUS ACTIONS WAS THE BOMBING OF FUTURE PRIME MINISTER DAVID LLOYD GEORGE'S HOUSE . . .

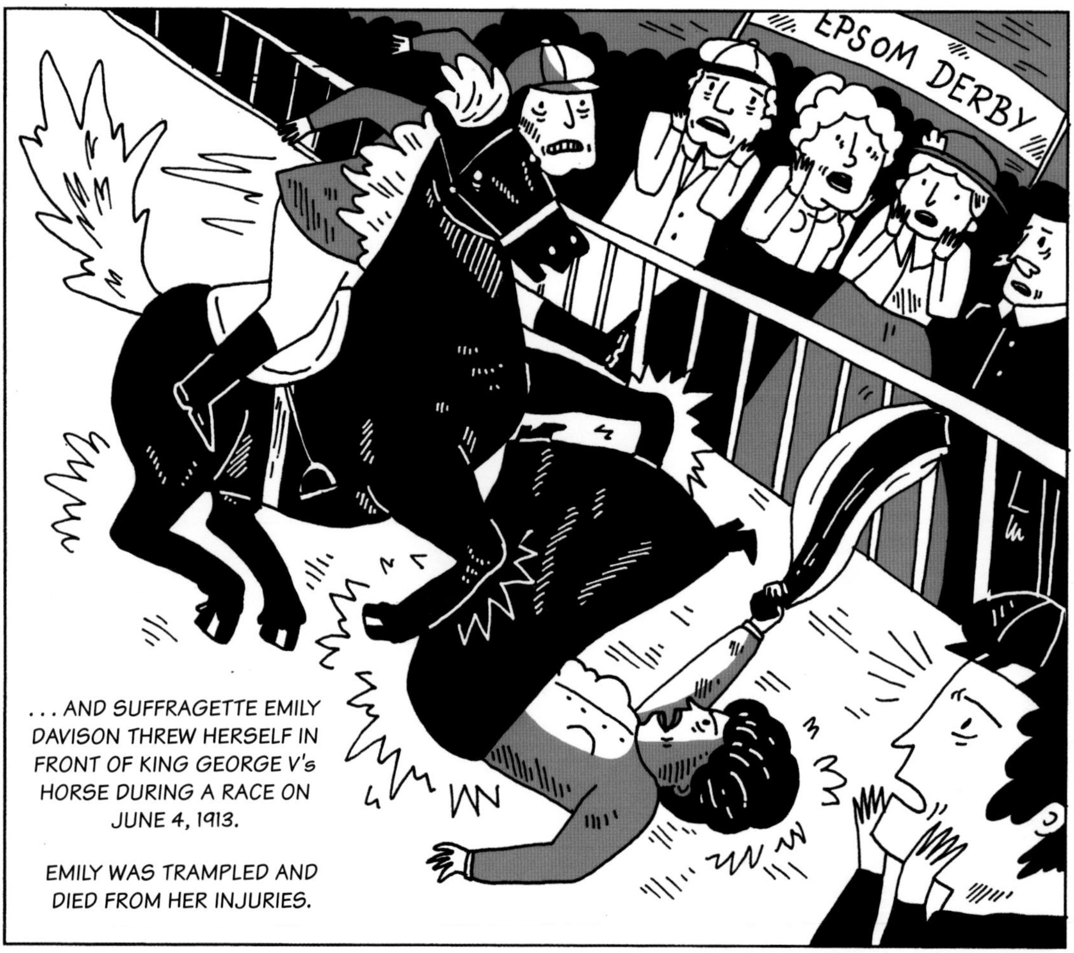
EPSOM DERBY
. . . AND SUFFRAGETTE EMILY DAVISON THREW HERSELF IN FRONT OF KING GEORGE V's HORSE DURING A RACE ON JUNE 4, 1913.
EMILY WAS TRAMPLED AND DIED FROM HER INJURIES.

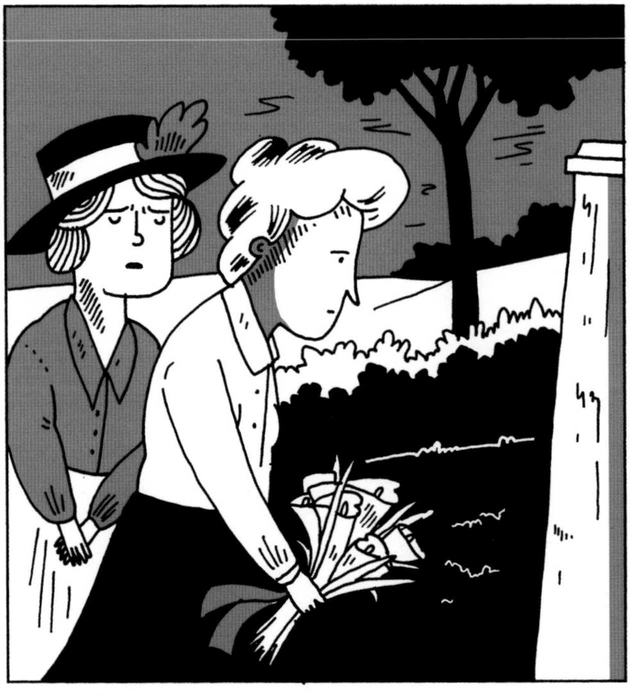

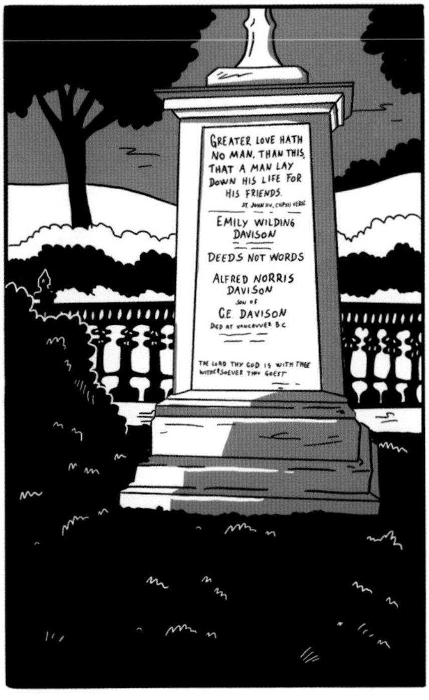
GREATER LOVE HATH NO MAN, THAN THIS, THAT A MAN LAY DOWN HIS LIFE FOR HIS FRIENDS.
EMILY WILDING DAVISON
DEEDS NOT WORDS
ALFRED NORRIS DAVISON
SON OF
G.E. DAVISON
DIED AT VANCOUVER B.C.
THE LORD THY GOD IS WITH THEE WITHERSOEVER THOU GOEST

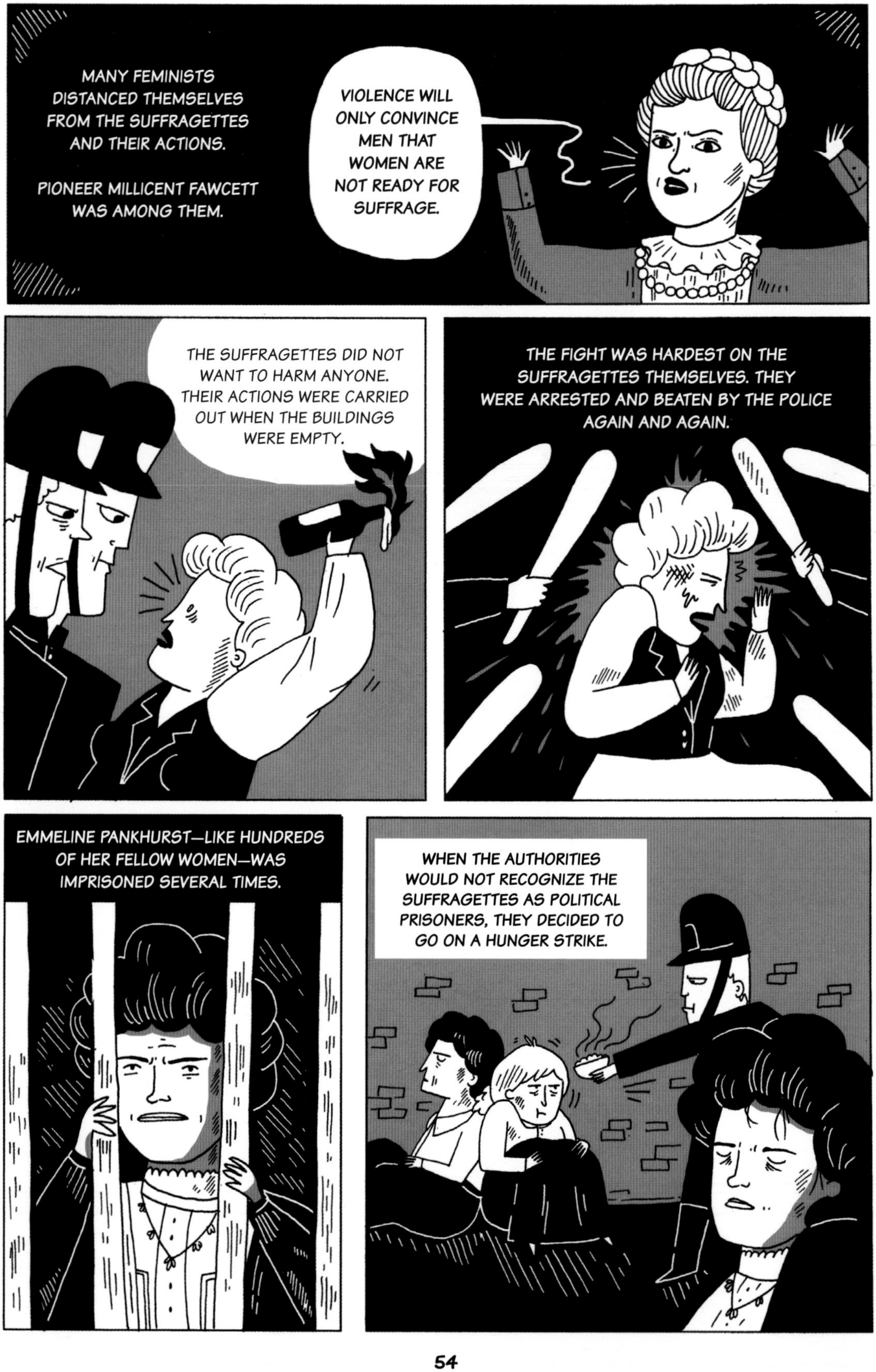
MANY FEMINISTS DISTANCED THEMSELVES FROM THE SUFFRAGETTES AND THEIR ACTIONS.
PIONEER MILLICENT FAWCETT WAS AMONG THEM.
VIOLENCE WILL ONLY CONVINCE MEN THAT WOMEN ARE NOT READY FOR SUFFRAGE.
THE SUFFRAGETTES DID NOT WANT TO HARM ANYONE. THEIR ACTIONS WERE CARRIED OUT WHEN THE BUILDINGS WERE EMPTY.
THE FIGHT WAS HARDEST ON THE SUFFRAGETTES THEMSELVES. THEY WERE ARRESTED AND BEATEN BY THE POLICE AGAIN AND AGAIN.
EMMELINE PANKHURST—LIKE HUNDREDS OF HER FELLOW WOMEN—WAS IMPRISONED SEVERAL TIMES.
WHEN THE AUTHORITIES WOULD NOT RECOGNIZE THE SUFFRAGETTES AS POLITICAL PRISONERS, THEY DECIDED TO GO ON A HUNGER STRIKE.

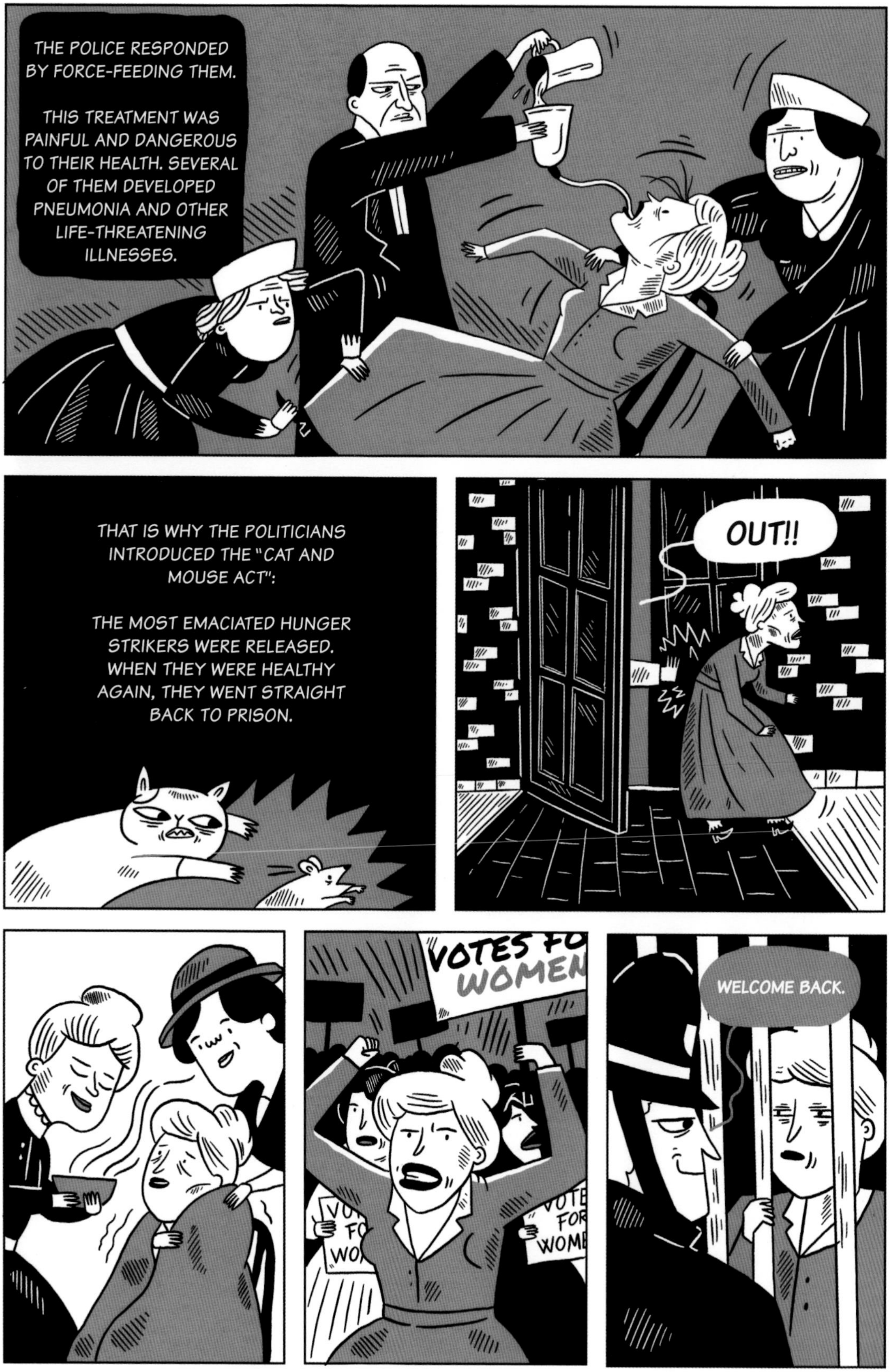
THE POLICE RESPONDED BY FORCE-FEEDING THEM.
THIS TREATMENT WAS PAINFUL AND DANGEROUS TO THEIR HEALTH. SEVERAL OF THEM DEVELOPED PNEUMONIA AND OTHER LIFE-THREATENING ILLNESSES.
THAT IS WHY THE POLITICIANS INTRODUCED THE "CAT AND MOUSE ACT":
THE MOST EMACIATED HUNGER STRIKERS WERE RELEASED. WHEN THEY WERE HEALTHY AGAIN, THEY WENT STRAIGHT BACK TO PRISON.
OUT!!
WELCOME BACK.

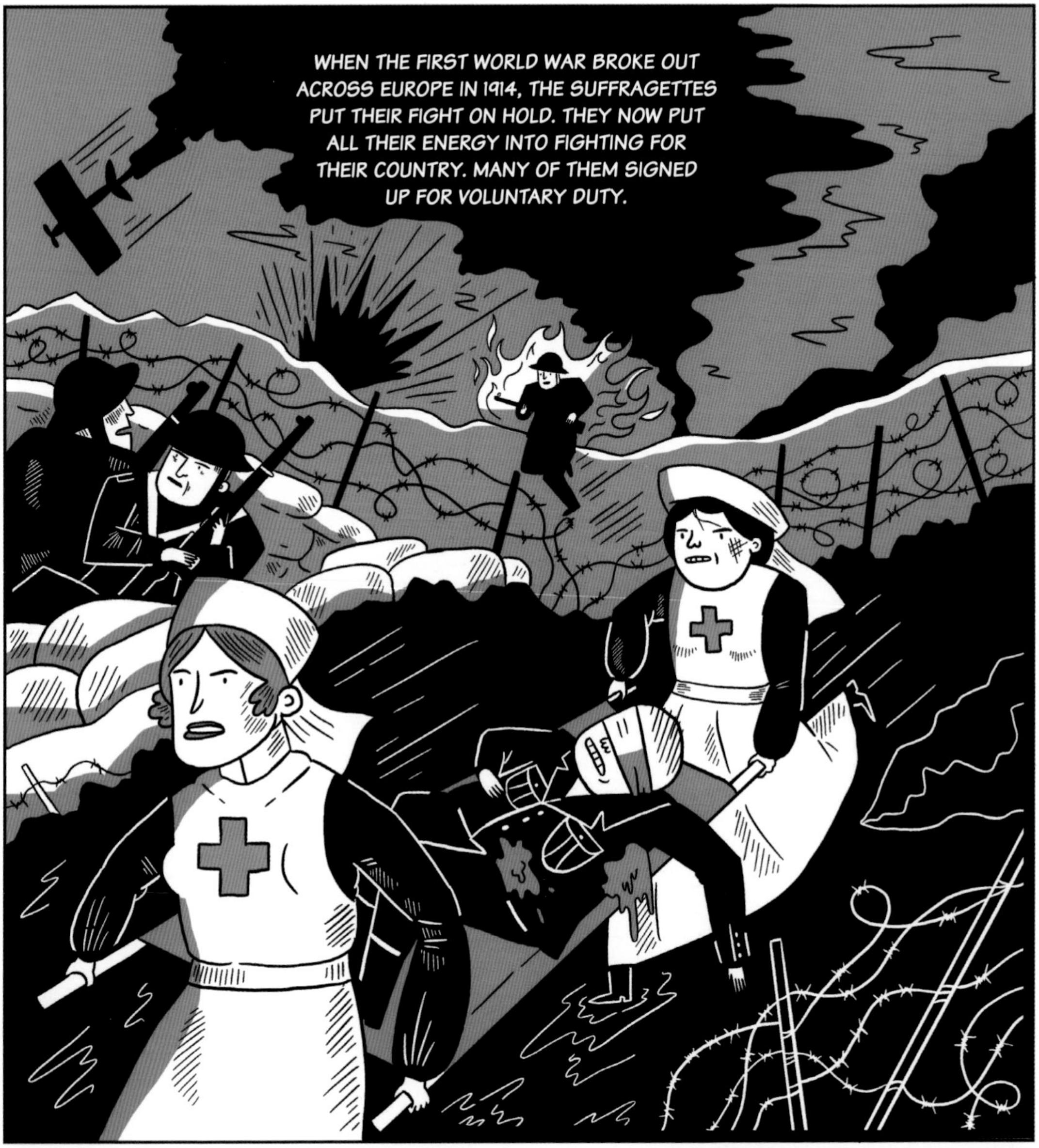
WHEN THE FIRST WORLD WAR BROKE OUT ACROSS EUROPE IN 1914, THE SUFFRAGETTES PUT THEIR FIGHT ON HOLD. THEY NOW PUT ALL THEIR ENERGY INTO FIGHTING FOR THEIR COUNTRY. MANY OF THEM SIGNED UP FOR VOLUNTARY DUTY.

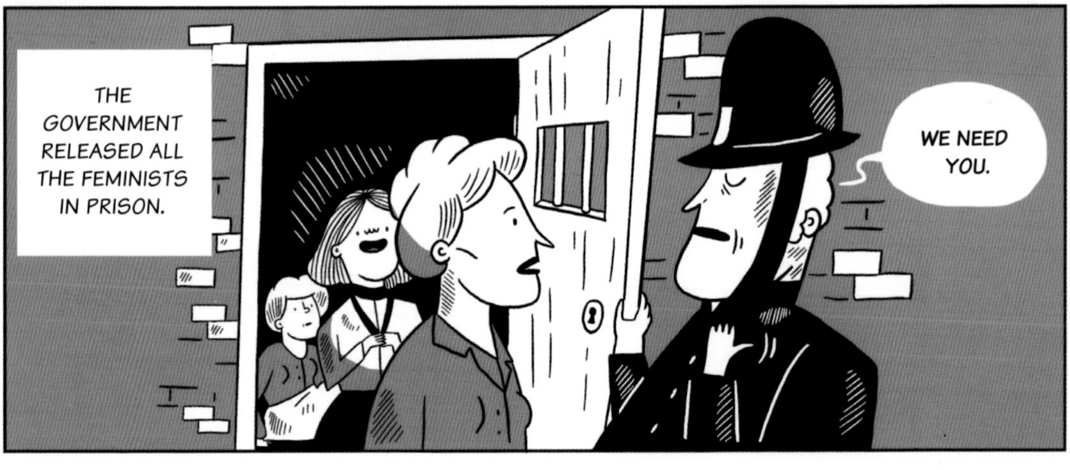
THE GOVERNMENT RELEASED ALL THE FEMINISTS IN PRISON.
WE NEED YOU.

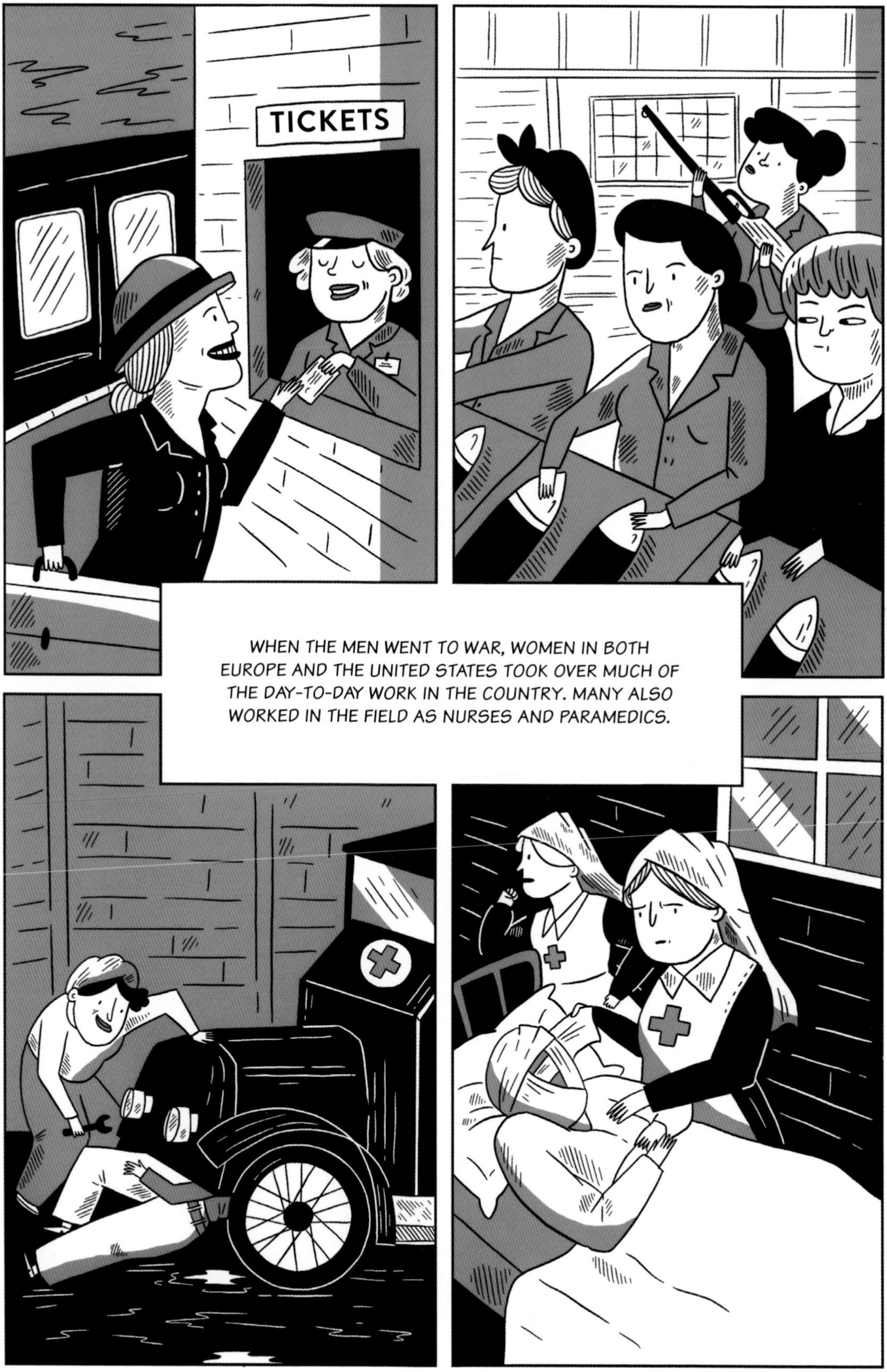
TICKETS
WHEN THE MEN WENT TO WAR, WOMEN IN BOTH EUROPE AND THE UNITED STATES TOOK OVER MUCH OF THE DAY-TO-DAY WORK IN THE COUNTRY. MANY ALSO WORKED IN THE FIELD AS NURSES AND PARAMEDICS.

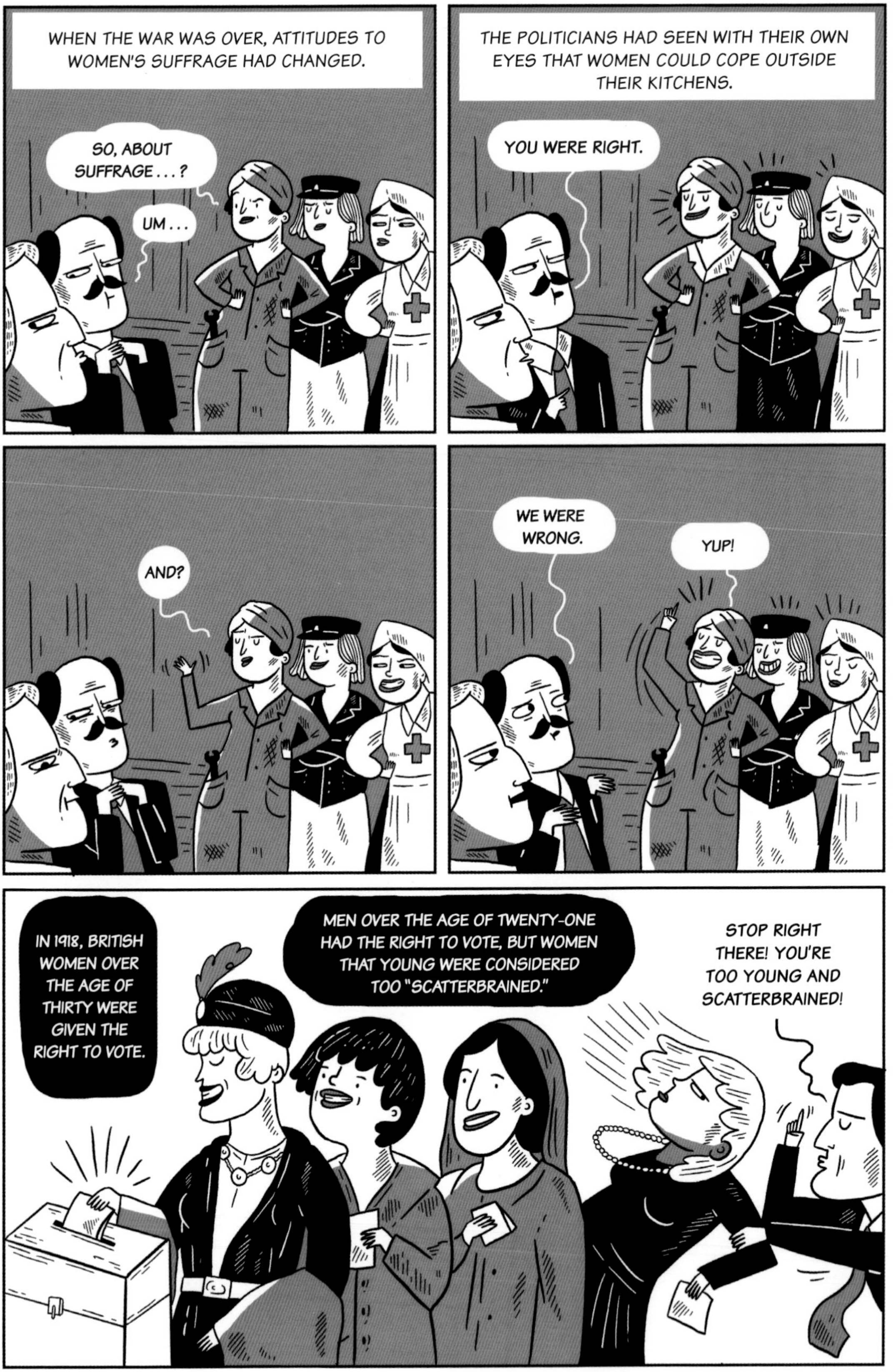
WHEN THE WAR WAS OVER, ATTITUDES TO WOMEN'S SUFFRAGE HAD CHANGED.
SO, ABOUT SUFFRAGE . . . ?
UM . . .
THE POLITICIANS HAD SEEN WITH THEIR OWN EYES THAT WOMEN COULD COPE OUTSIDE THEIR KITCHENS.
YOU WERE RIGHT.
AND?
WE WERE WRONG.
YUP!
IN 1918, BRITISH WOMEN OVER THE AGE OF THIRTY WERE GIVEN THE RIGHT TO VOTE.
MEN OVER THE AGE OF TWENTY-ONE HAD THE RIGHT TO VOTE, BUT WOMEN THAT YOUNG WERE CONSIDERED TOO "SCATTERBRAINED."
STOP RIGHT THERE! YOU'RE TOO YOUNG AND SCATTERBRAINED!

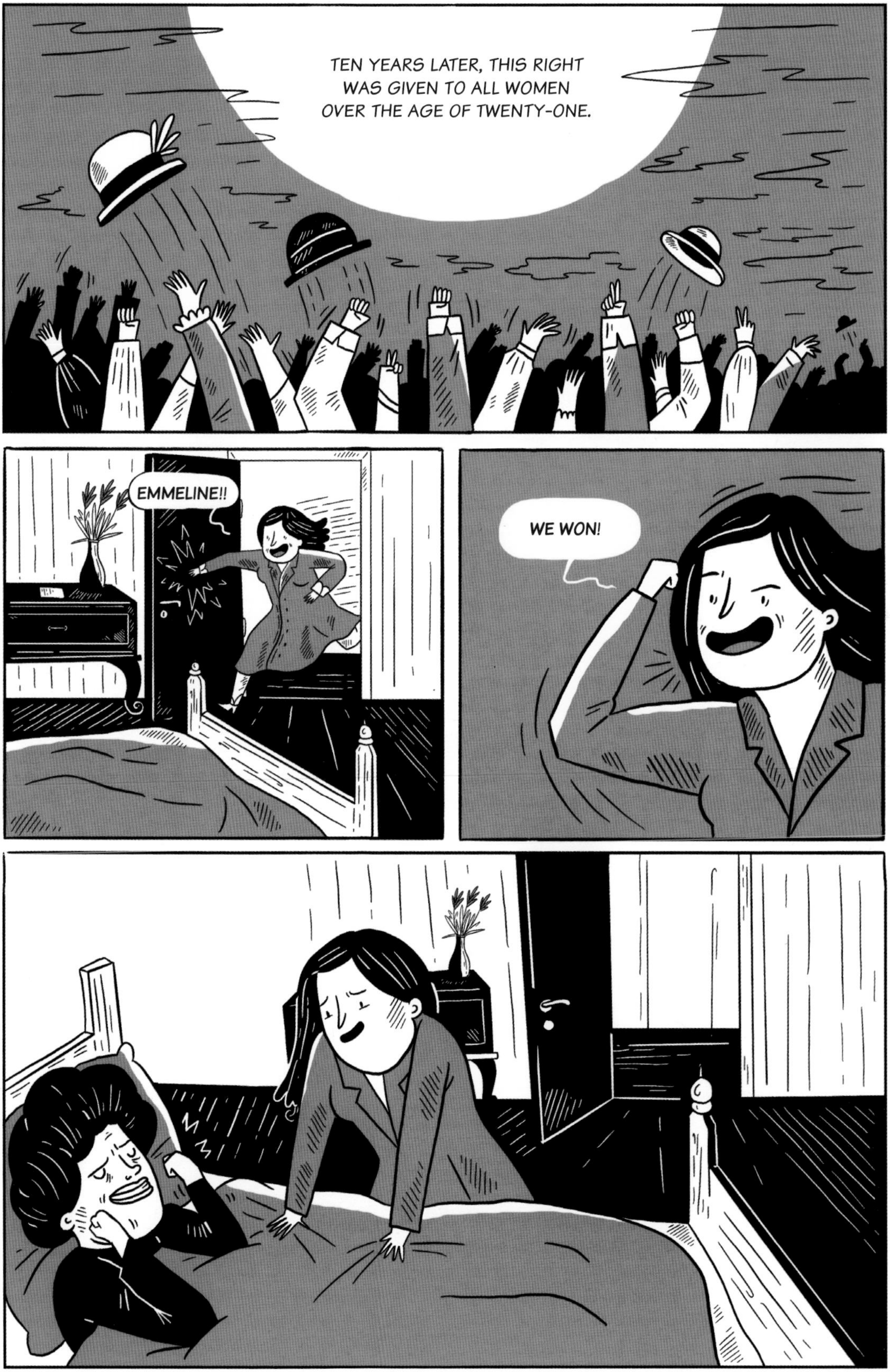
TEN YEARS LATER, THIS RIGHT WAS GIVEN TO ALL WOMEN OVER THE AGE OF TWENTY-ONE.
EMMELINE!!
WE WON!

THE FIRST COUNTRY IN THE WORLD TO GIVE WOMEN THE RIGHT TO VOTE WITH NO RESTRICTIONS WAS NEW ZEALAND. FINLAND WAS THE FIRST COUNTRY IN EUROPE.

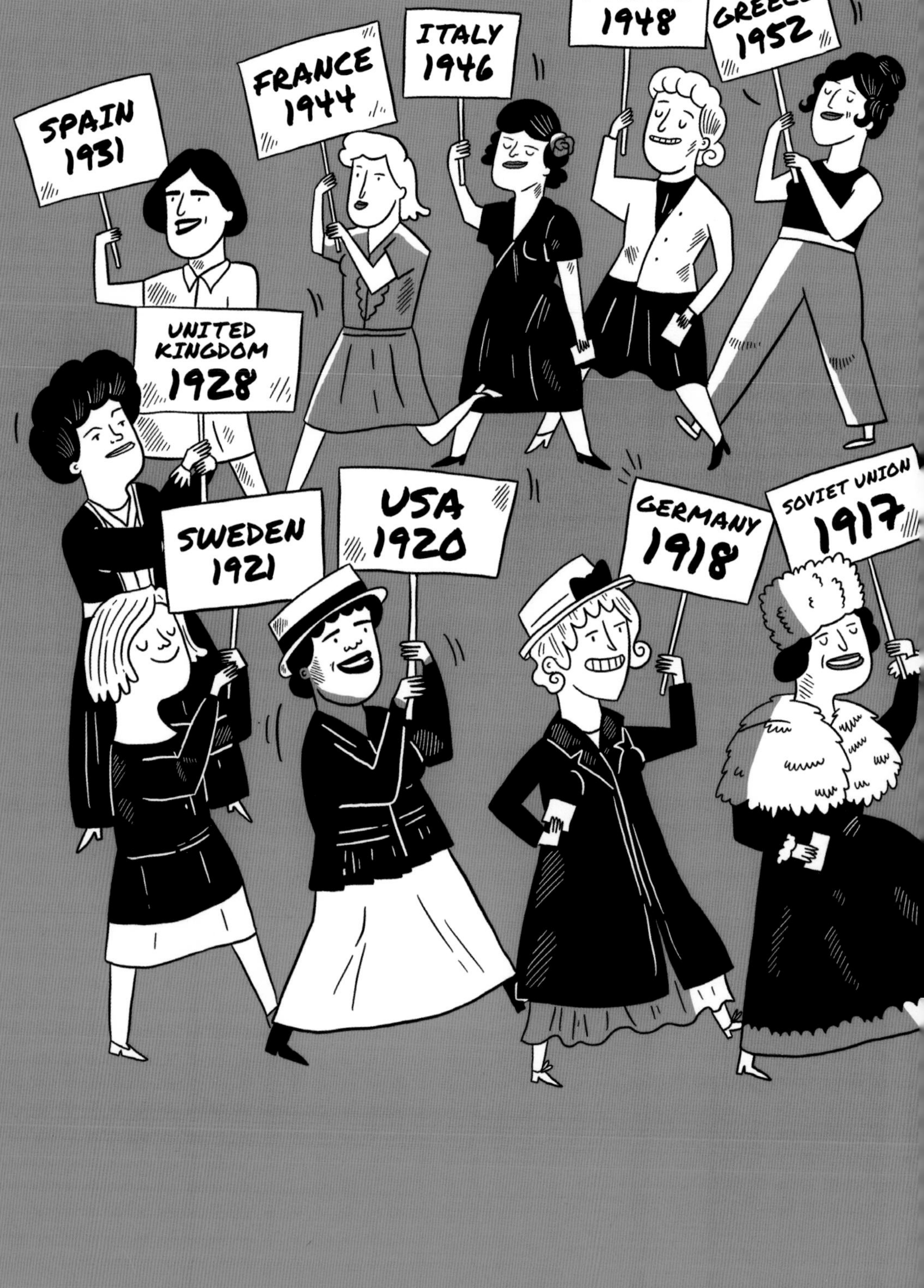
SPAIN 1931
FRANCE 1944
ITALY 1946
ISRAEL 1948
GREECE 1952
UNITED KINGDOM 1928
SWEDEN 1921
USA 1920
GERMANY 1918
SOVIET UNION 1917

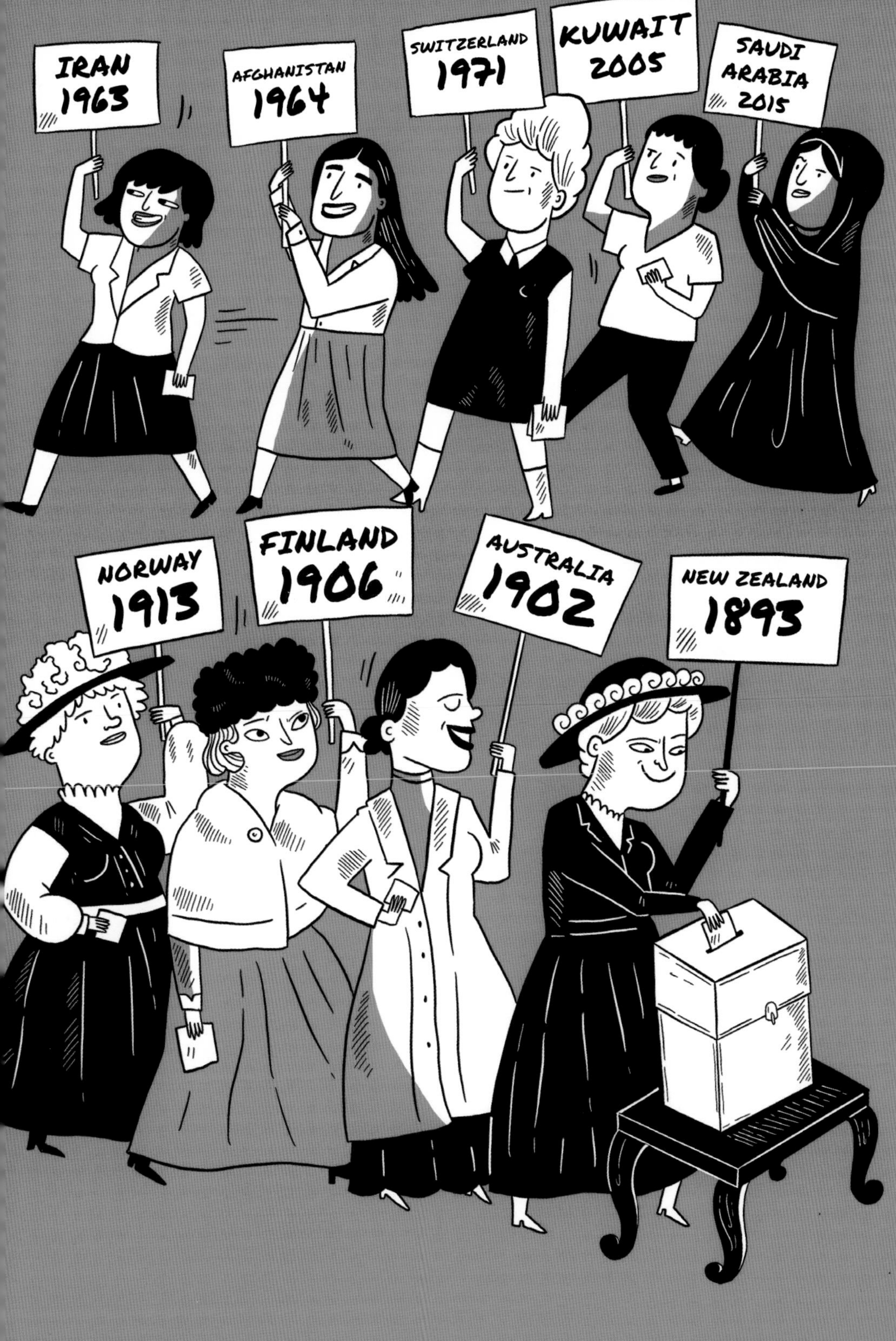
IRAN 1963
AFGHANISTAN 1964
SWITZERLAND 1971
KUWAIT 2005
SAUDI ARABIA 2015
NORWAY 1913
FINLAND 1906
AUSTRALIA 1902
NEW ZEALAND 1893

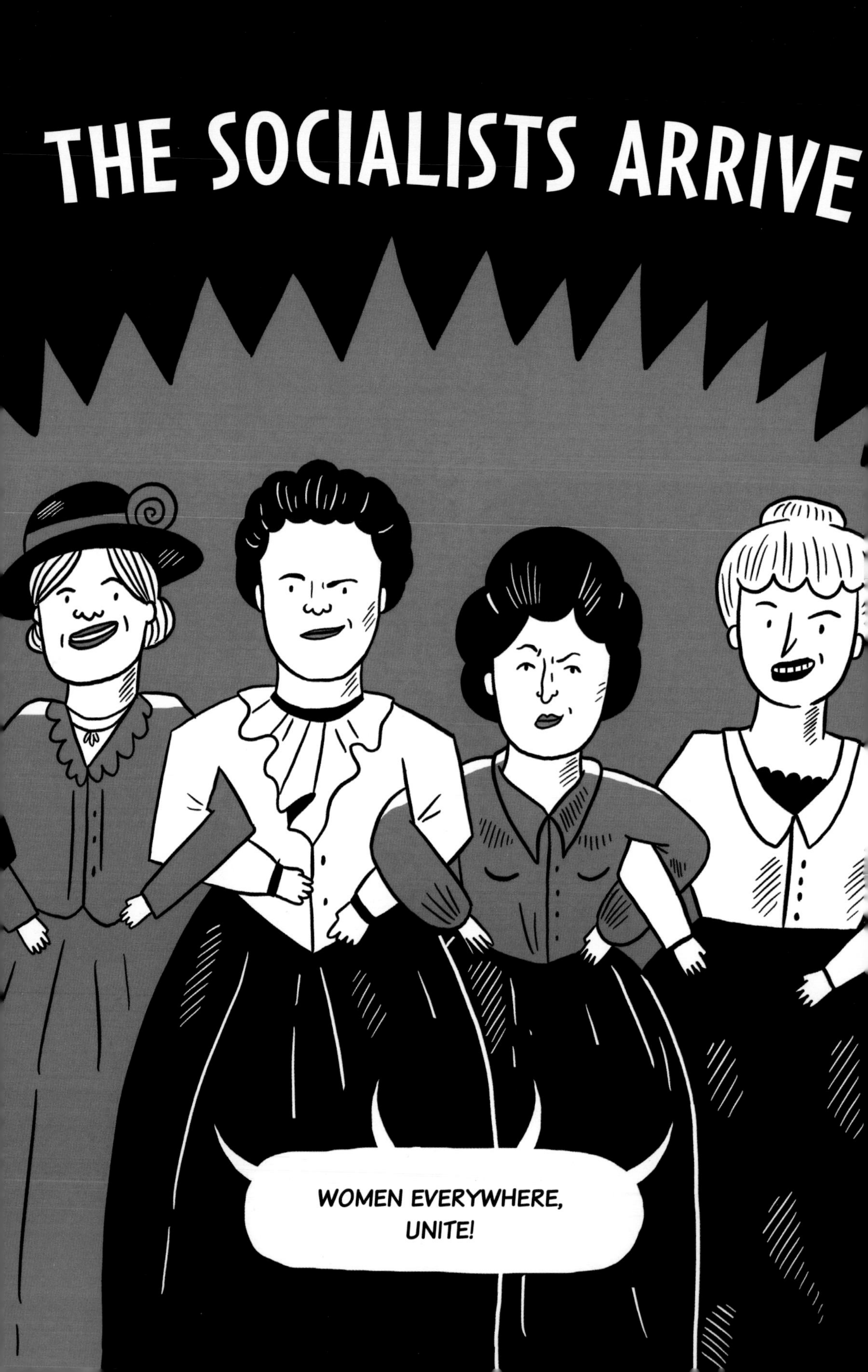
THE SOCIALISTS ARRIVE
WOMEN EVERYWHERE, UNITE!

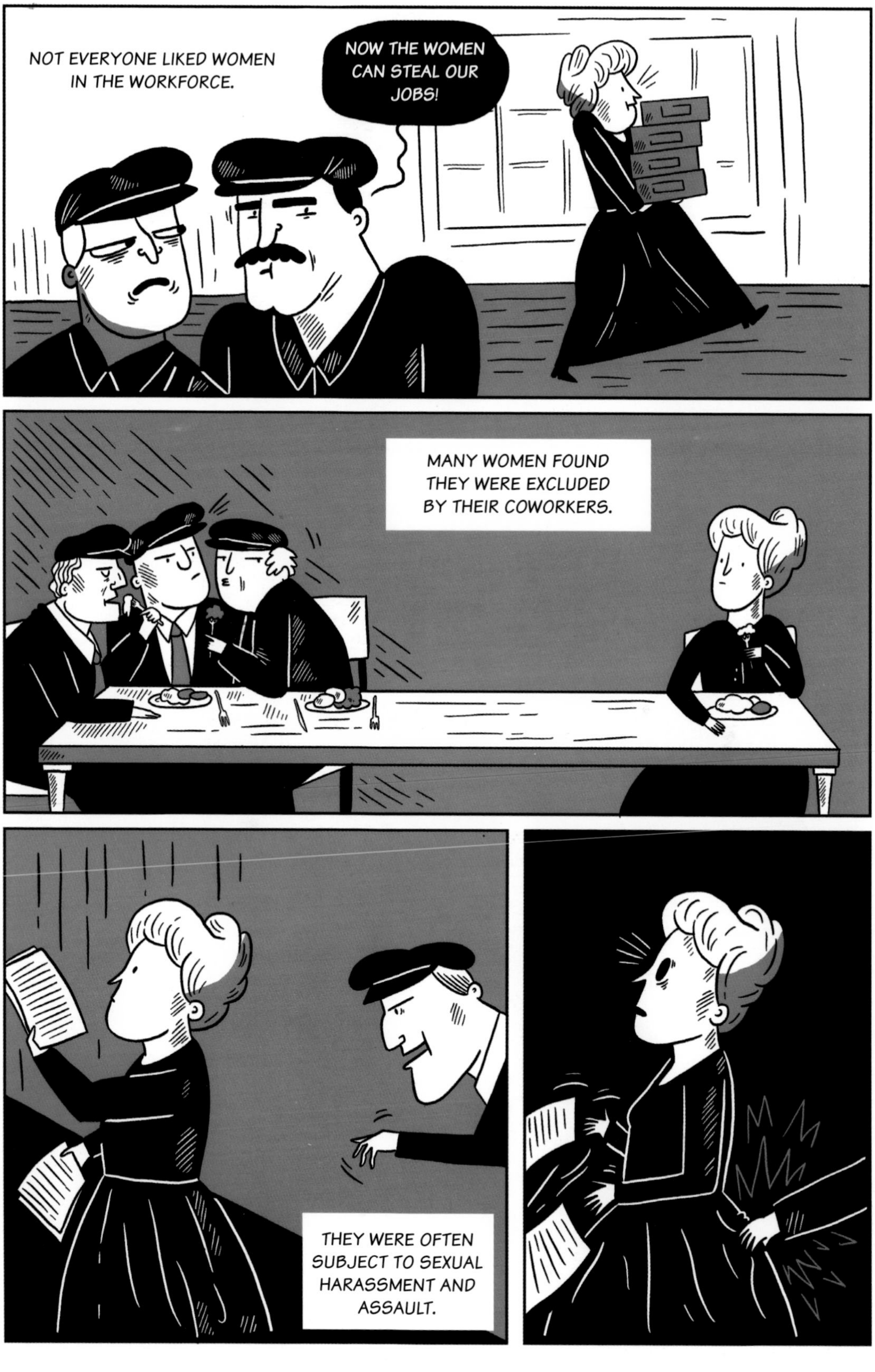
NOT EVERYONE LIKED WOMEN IN THE WORKFORCE.
NOW THE WOMEN CAN STEAL OUR JOBS!
MANY WOMEN FOUND THEY WERE EXCLUDED BY THEIR COWORKERS.
THEY WERE OFTEN SUBJECT TO SEXUAL HARASSMENT AND ASSAULT.

THE FEMALE WORKERS WERE TREATED WORSE THAN THE MEN.

THEY WERE PAID LESS THAN MEN . . .

. . . AND THEY WERE OFTEN FIRED FIRST.

YOUR HUSBAND CAN LOOK AFTER YOU!

UNTIL NOW, THE WOMEN'S MOVEMENT IN EUROPE AND AMERICA HAD BEEN DOMINATED BY MIDDLE-CLASS WOMEN.

AT THE BEGINNING OF THE 1900s, WORKING-CLASS WOMEN ALSO STARTED TO MOBILIZE.

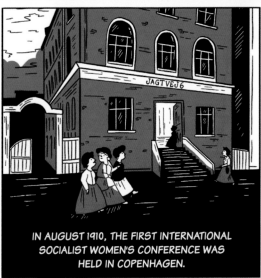

IN AUGUST 1910, THE FIRST INTERNATIONAL SOCIALIST WOMEN'S CONFERENCE WAS HELD IN COPENHAGEN.

THE SOCIALISTS CONSIDERED THE WOMEN'S MOVEMENT PART OF THE CLASS STRUGGLE.

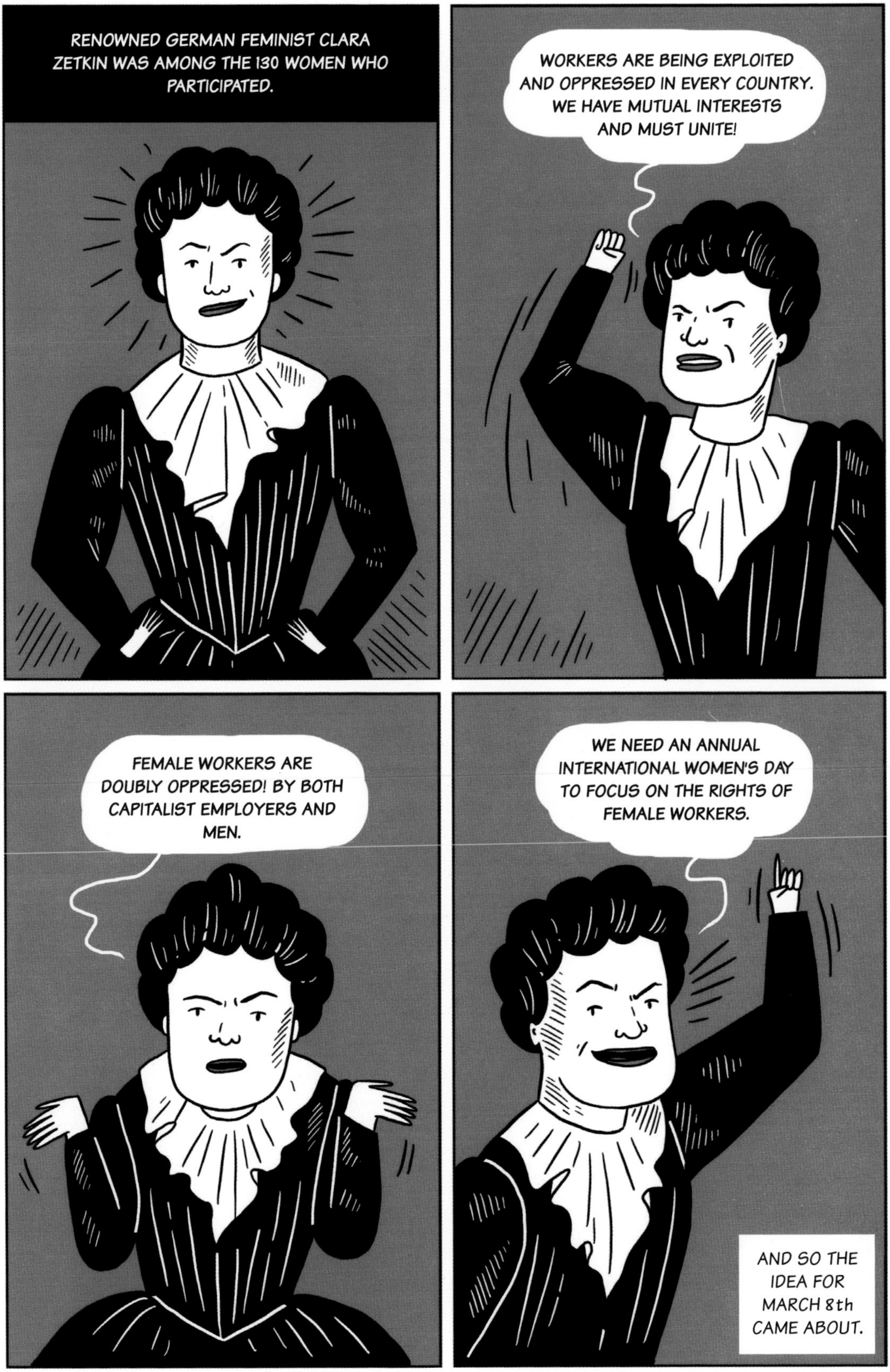
RENOWNED GERMAN FEMINIST CLARA ZETKIN WAS AMONG THE 130 WOMEN WHO PARTICIPATED.
WORKERS ARE BEING EXPLOITED AND OPPRESSED IN EVERY COUNTRY. WE HAVE MUTUAL INTERESTS AND MUST UNITE!
FEMALE WORKERS ARE DOUBLY OPPRESSED! BY BOTH CAPITALIST EMPLOYERS AND MEN.
WE NEED AN ANNUAL INTERNATIONAL WOMEN'S DAY TO FOCUS ON THE RIGHTS OF FEMALE WORKERS.
AND SO THE IDEA FOR MARCH 8th CAME ABOUT.

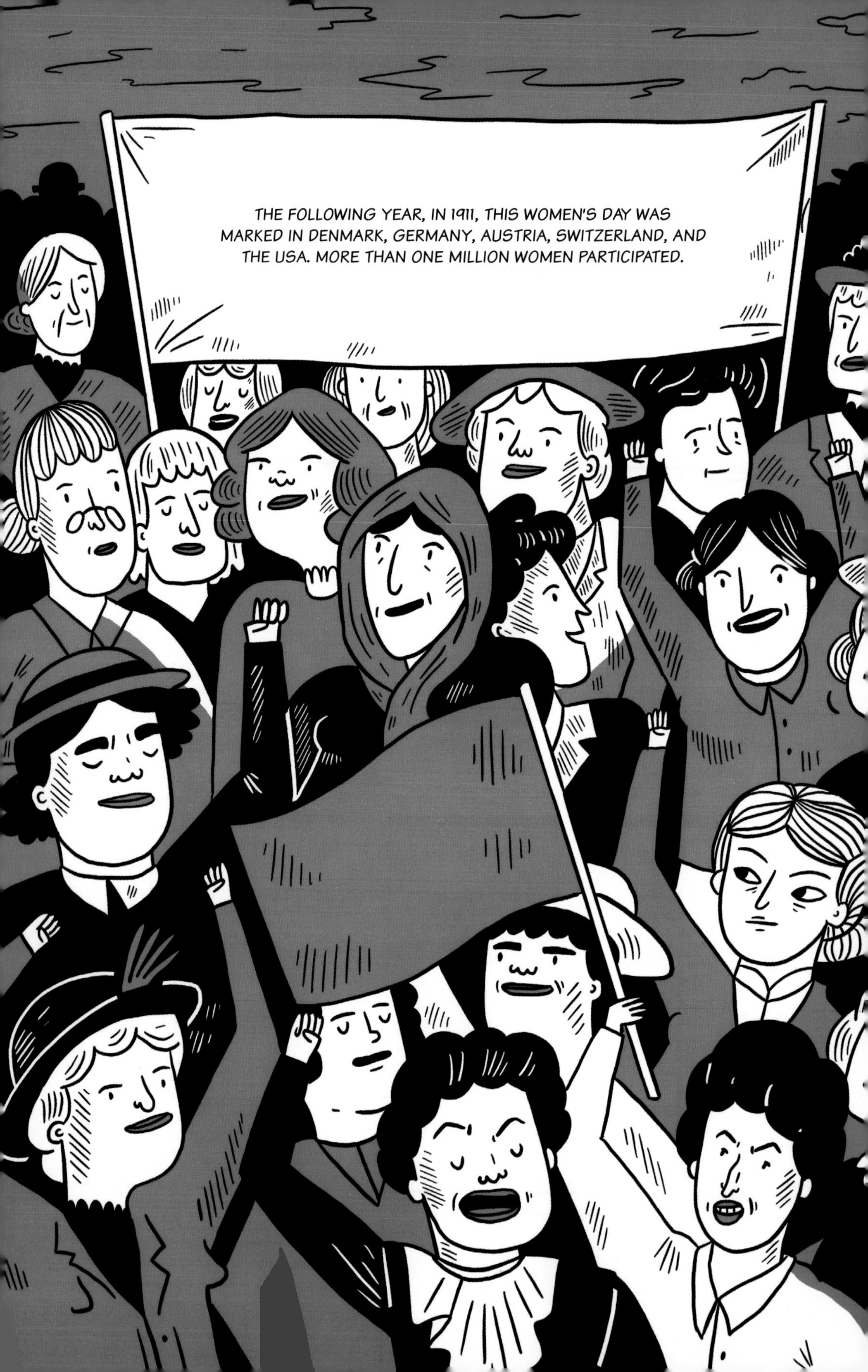
THE FOLLOWING YEAR, IN 1911, THIS WOMEN'S DAY WAS MARKED IN DENMARK, GERMANY, AUSTRIA, SWITZERLAND, AND THE USA. MORE THAN ONE MILLION WOMEN PARTICIPATED.

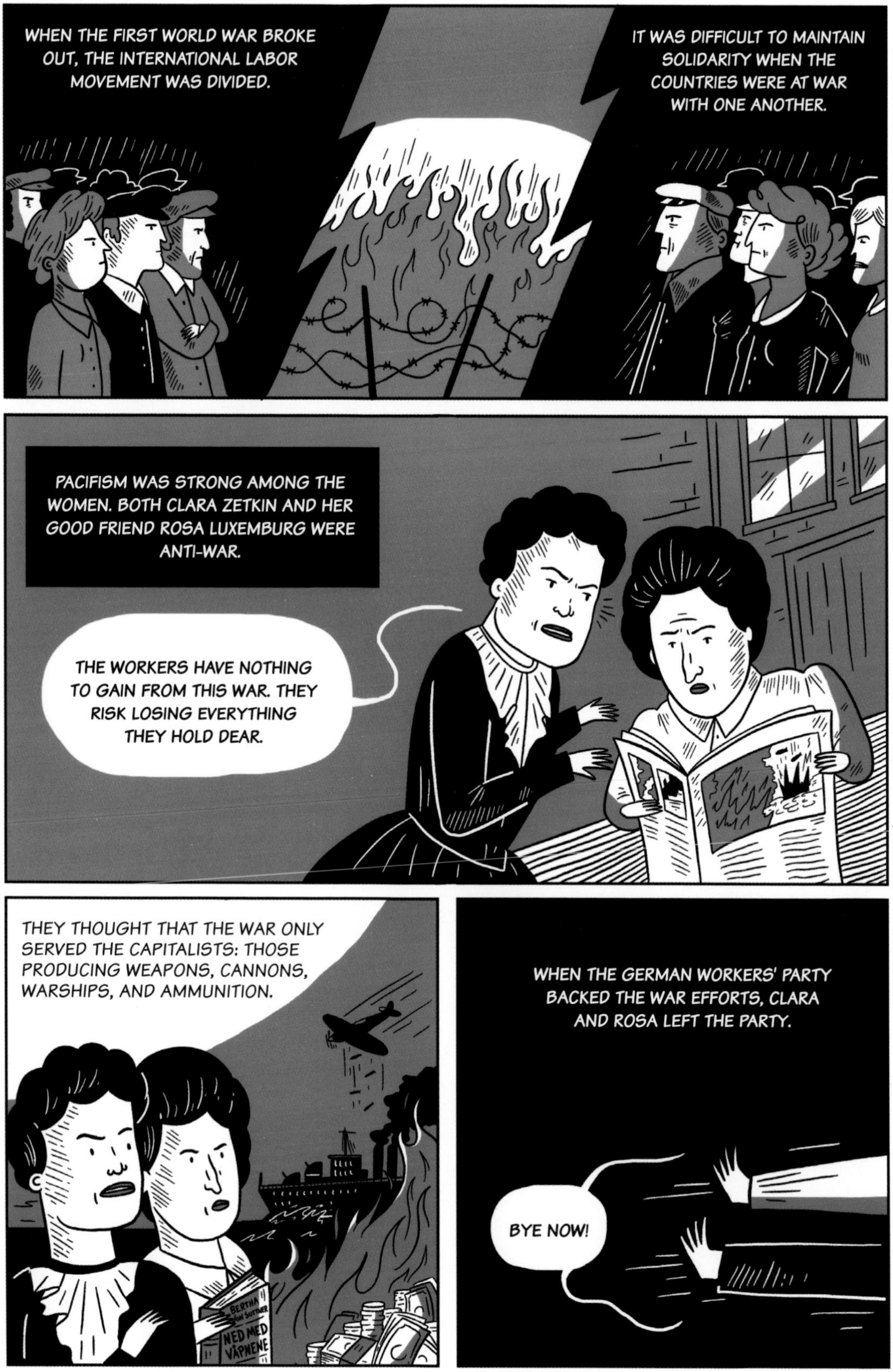
WHEN THE FIRST WORLD WAR BROKE OUT, THE INTERNATIONAL LABOR MOVEMENT WAS DIVIDED.
IT WAS DIFFICULT TO MAINTAIN SOLIDARITY WHEN THE COUNTRIES WERE AT WAR WITH ONE ANOTHER.
PACIFISM WAS STRONG AMONG THE WOMEN. BOTH CLARA ZETKIN AND HER GOOD FRIEND ROSA LUXEMBURG WERE ANTI-WAR.
THE WORKERS HAVE NOTHING TO GAIN FROM THIS WAR. THEY RISK LOSING EVERYTHING THEY HOLD DEAR.
THEY THOUGHT THAT THE WAR ONLY SERVED THE CAPITALISTS: THOSE PRODUCING WEAPONS, CANNONS, WARSHIPS, AND AMMUNITION.
BERTHA von SUTTNER
NED MED VÅPNENE
WHEN THE GERMAN WORKERS' PARTY BACKED THE WAR EFFORTS, CLARA AND ROSA LEFT THE PARTY.
BYE NOW!

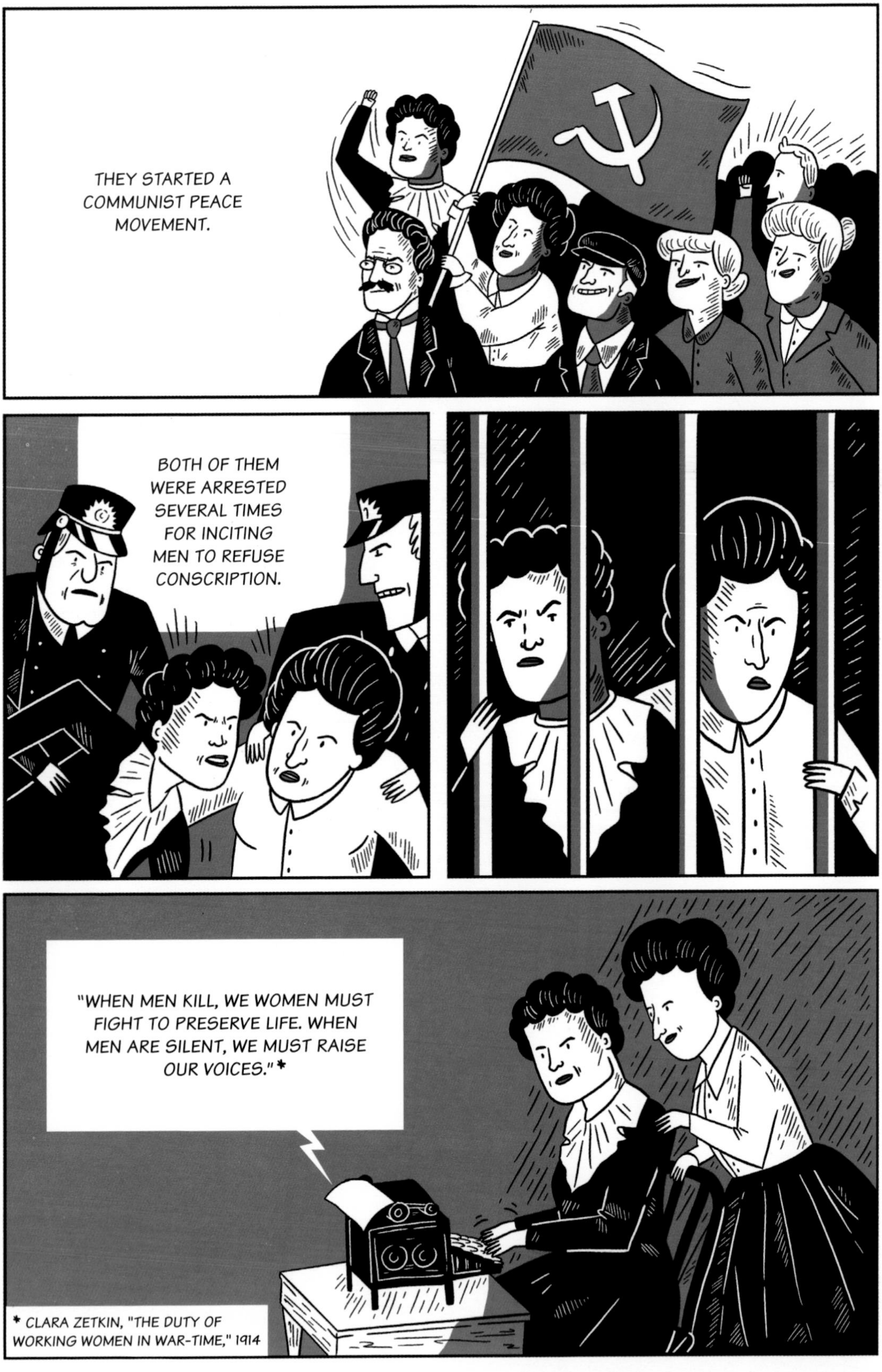
THEY STARTED A COMMUNIST PEACE MOVEMENT.
BOTH OF THEM WERE ARRESTED SEVERAL TIMES FOR INCITING MEN TO REFUSE CONSCRIPTION.
"WHEN MEN KILL, WE WOMEN MUST FIGHT TO PRESERVE LIFE. WHEN MEN ARE SILENT, WE MUST RAISE OUR VOICES."*
* CLARA ZETKIN, "THE DUTY OF WORKING WOMEN IN WAR-TIME," 1914

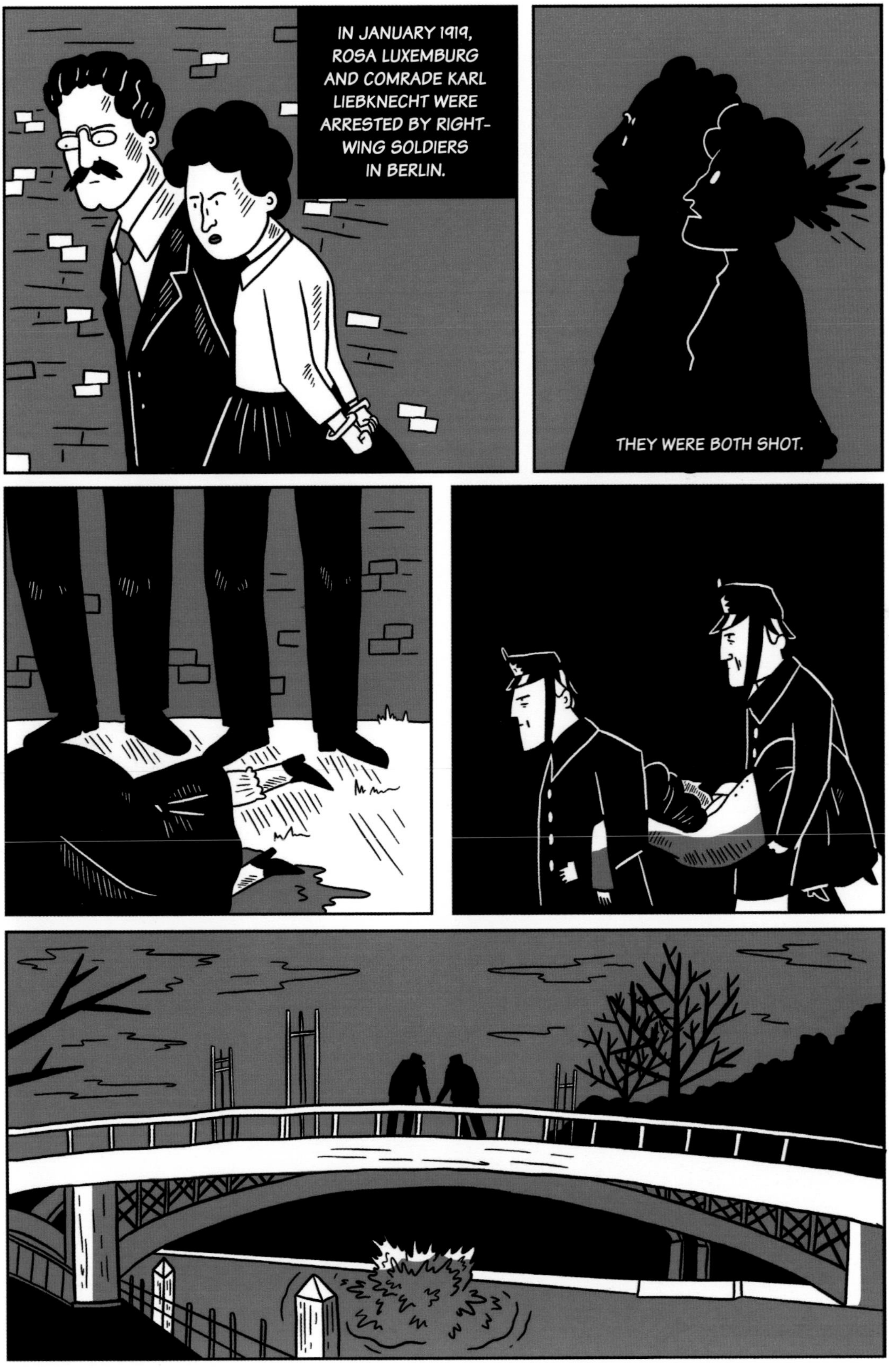
IN JANUARY 1919, ROSA LUXEMBURG AND COMRADE KARL LIEBKNECHT WERE ARRESTED BY RIGHT-WING SOLDIERS IN BERLIN.
THEY WERE BOTH SHOT.

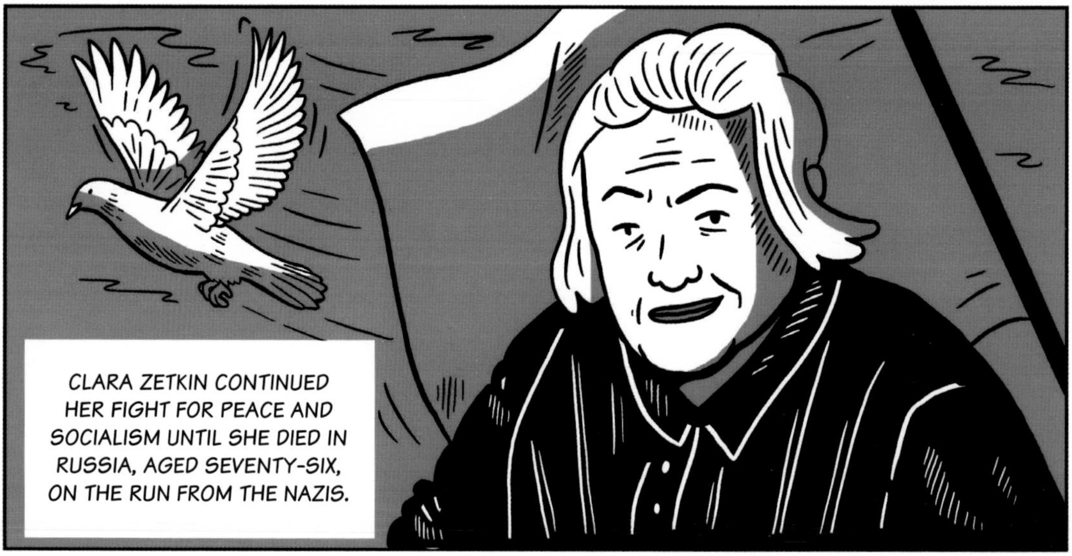
CLARA ZETKIN CONTINUED HER FIGHT FOR PEACE AND SOCIALISM UNTIL SHE DIED IN RUSSIA, AGED SEVENTY-SIX, ON THE RUN FROM THE NAZIS.

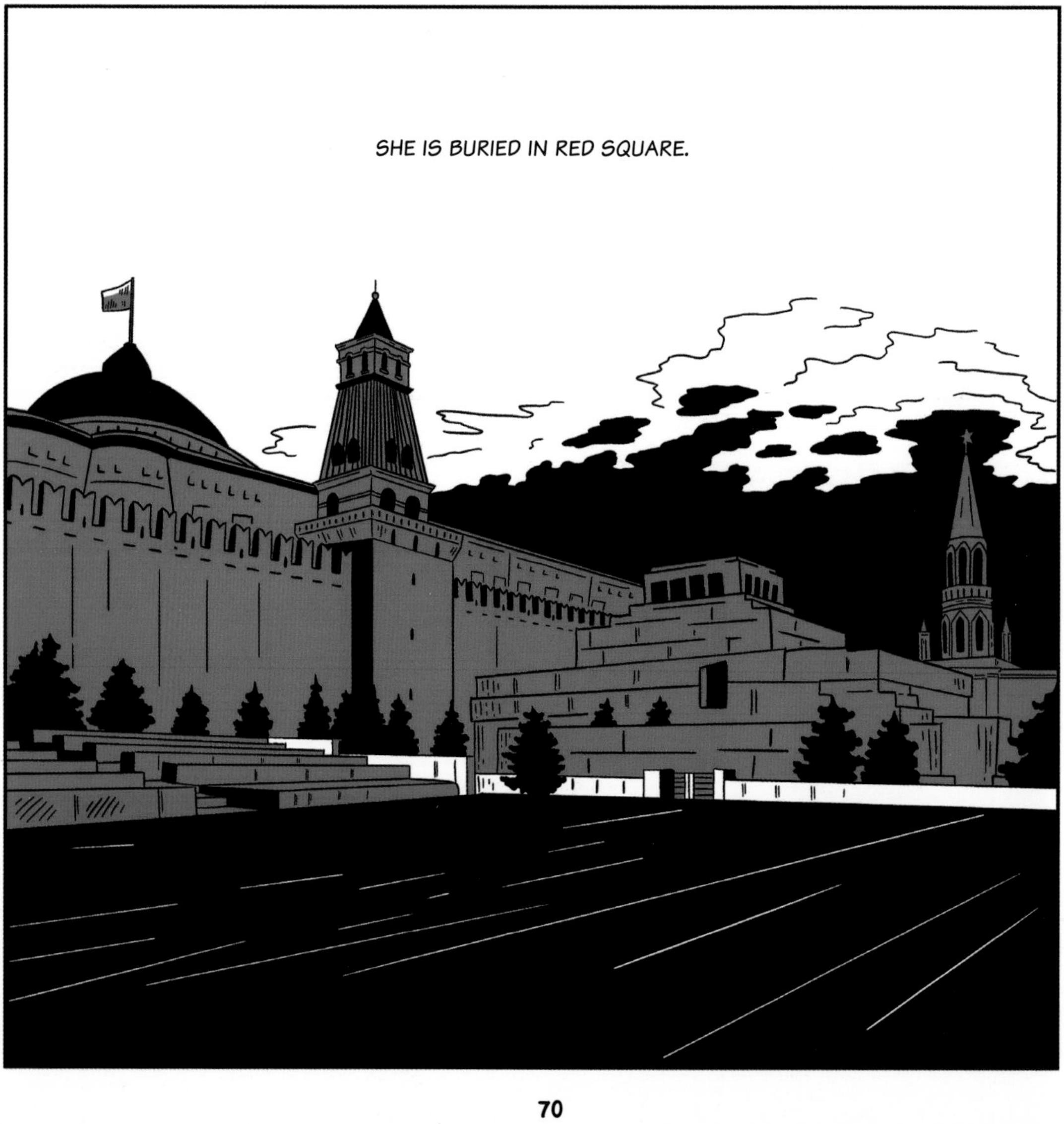
SHE IS BURIED IN RED SQUARE.

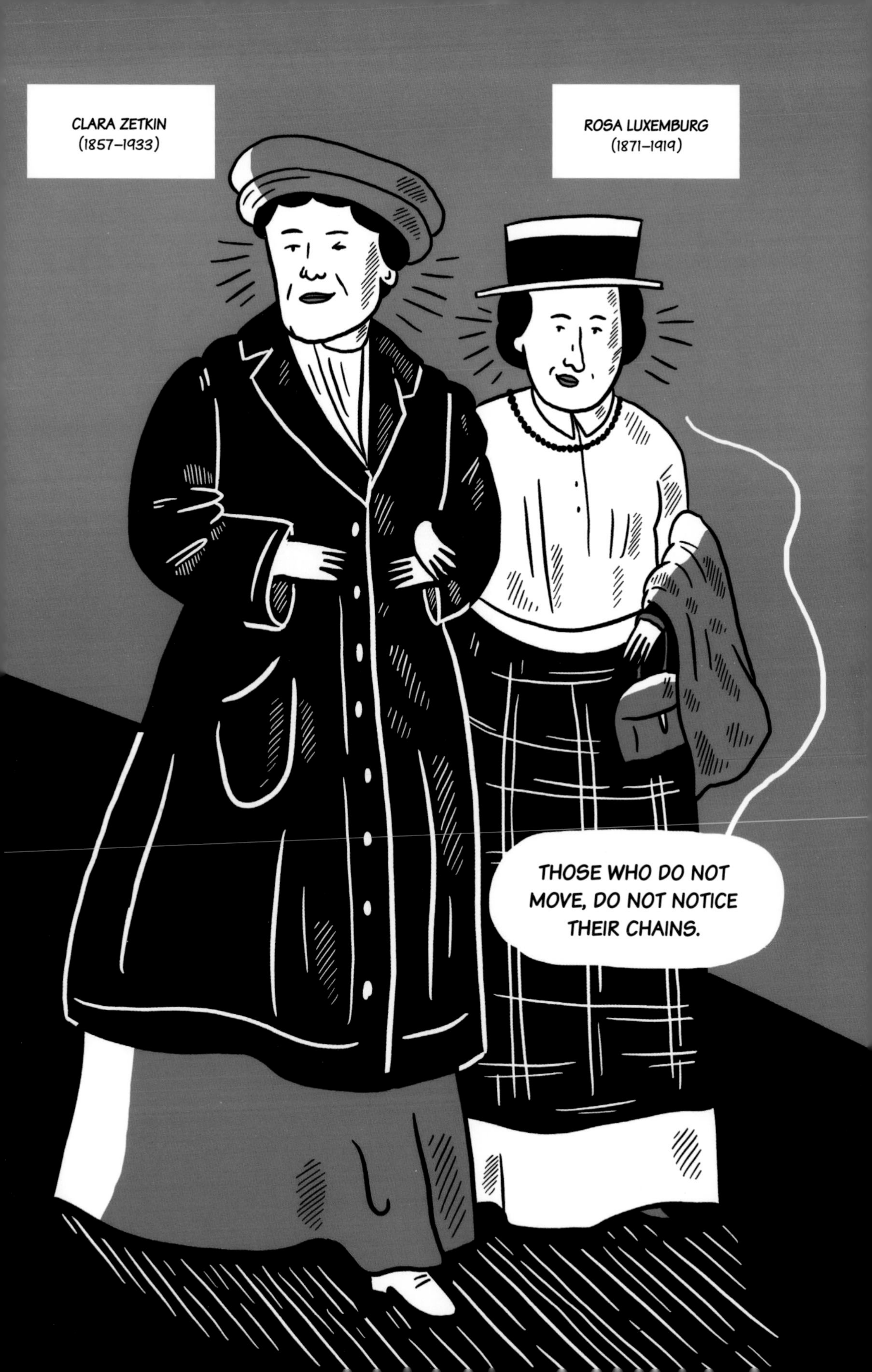
CLARA ZETKIN
(1857–1933)
ROSA LUXEMBURG
(1871–1919)
THOSE WHO DO NOT MOVE, DO NOT NOTICE THEIR CHAINS.

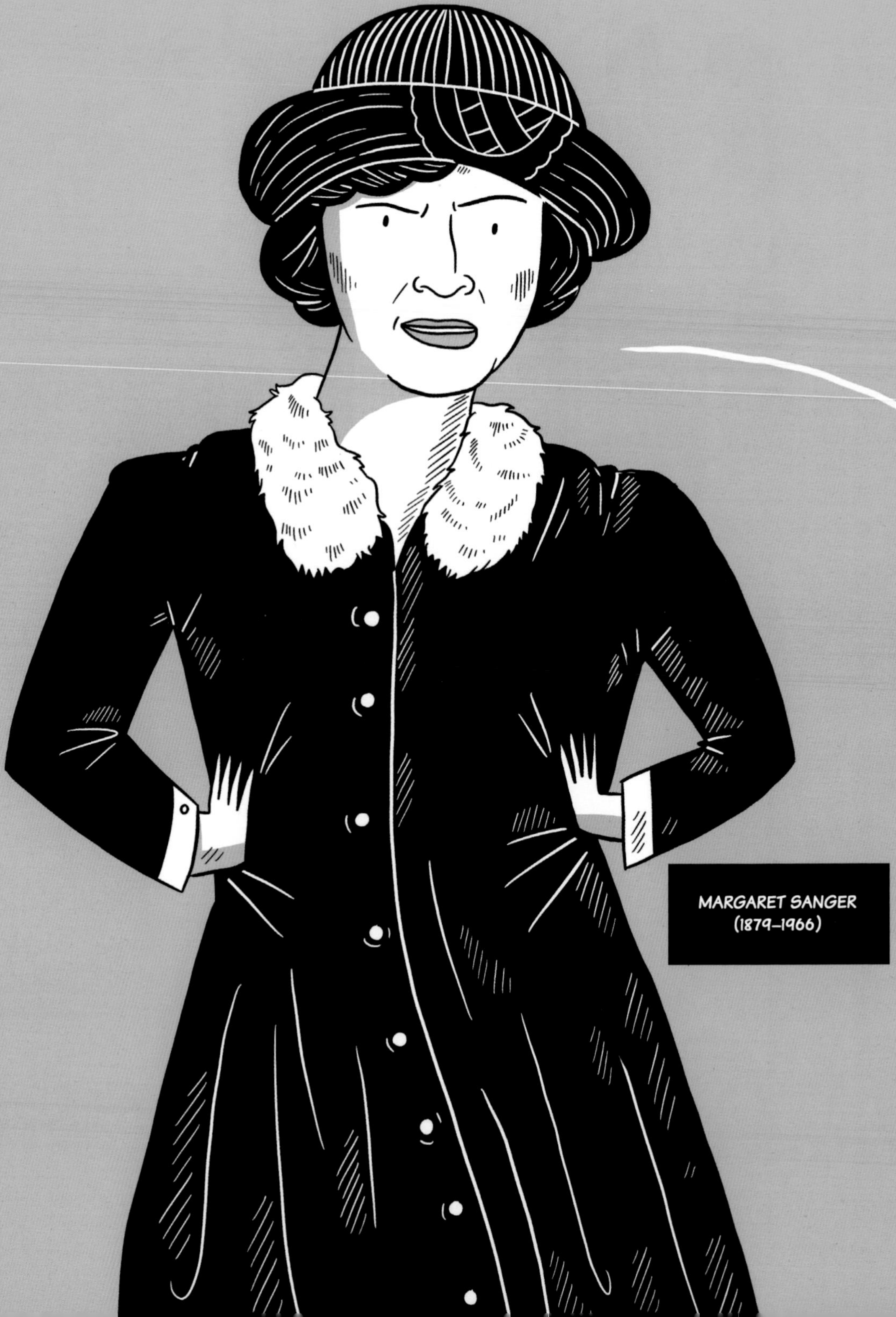
MARGARET SANGER
(1879–1966)

THE STRUGGLE FOR FEMALE BODILY INTEGRITY

NO WOMAN CAN CALL HERSELF FREE WHO DOES NOT OWN AND CONTROL HER BODY.

IN THE PAST, FAMILIES OFTEN HAD MANY CHILDREN, PARTICULARLY POOR FAMILIES.

CONTRACEPTION OPTIONS WERE UNRELIABLE AND THERE WAS NOWHERE TO GET A LEGAL ABORTION.

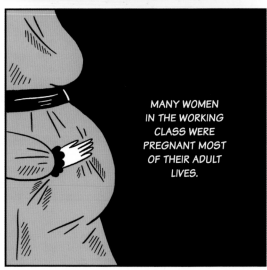

MANY WOMEN IN THE WORKING CLASS WERE PREGNANT MOST OF THEIR ADULT LIVES.

MANY WOMEN WERE HARMED—OR KILLED— DURING CHILDBIRTH AND ILLEGAL ABORTIONS.

THIS WORRIED AMERICAN NURSE MARGARET SANGER, WHO LIVED IN NEW YORK IN THE EARLY 1900s.

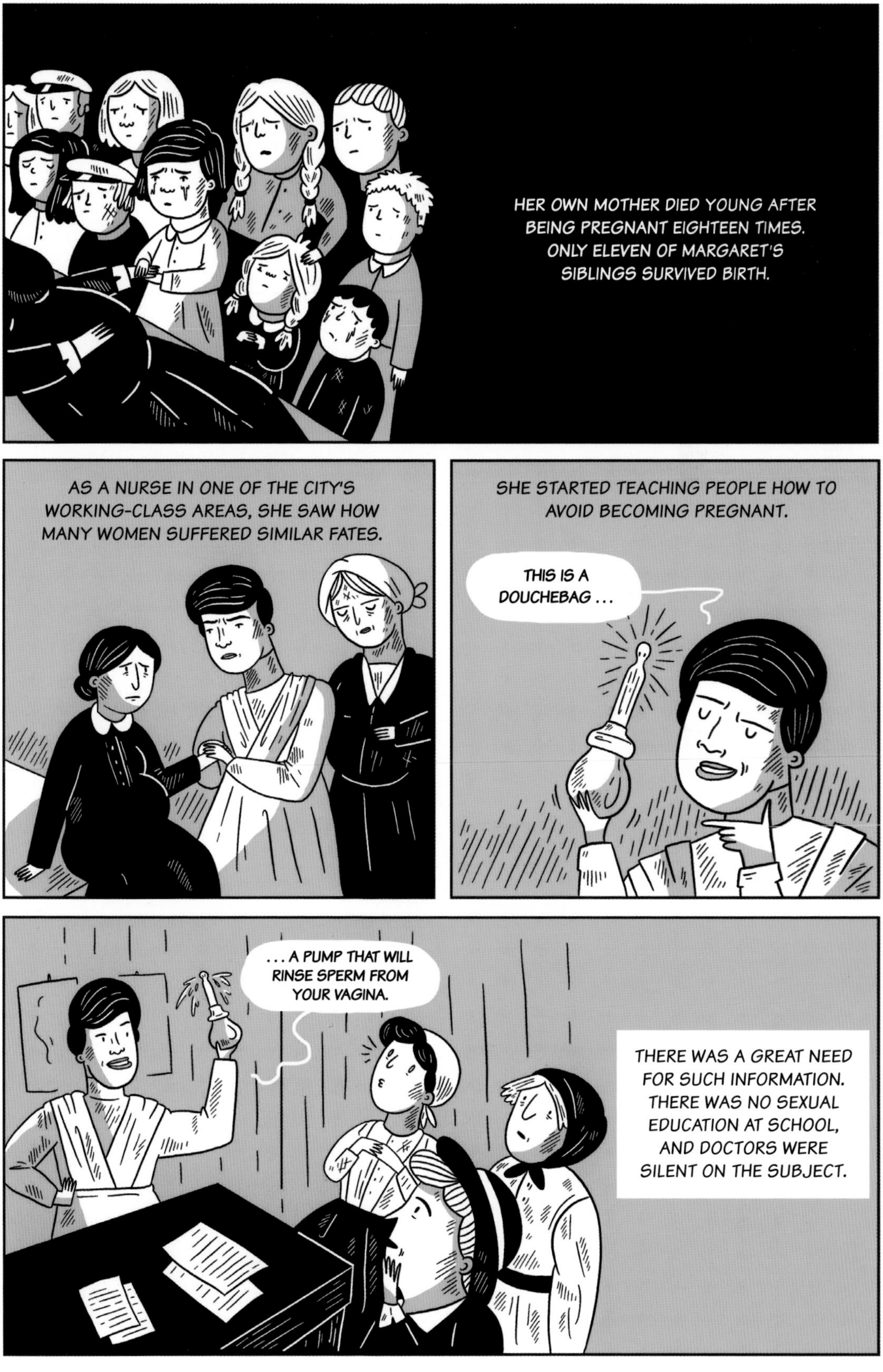
HER OWN MOTHER DIED YOUNG AFTER BEING PREGNANT EIGHTEEN TIMES. ONLY ELEVEN OF MARGARET'S SIBLINGS SURVIVED BIRTH.
AS A NURSE IN ONE OF THE CITY'S WORKING-CLASS AREAS, SHE SAW HOW MANY WOMEN SUFFERED SIMILAR FATES.
SHE STARTED TEACHING PEOPLE HOW TO AVOID BECOMING PREGNANT.
THIS IS A DOUCHEBAG . . .
. . . A PUMP THAT WILL RINSE SPERM FROM YOUR VAGINA.
THERE WAS A GREAT NEED FOR SUCH INFORMATION. THERE WAS NO SEXUAL EDUCATION AT SCHOOL, AND DOCTORS WERE SILENT ON THE SUBJECT.

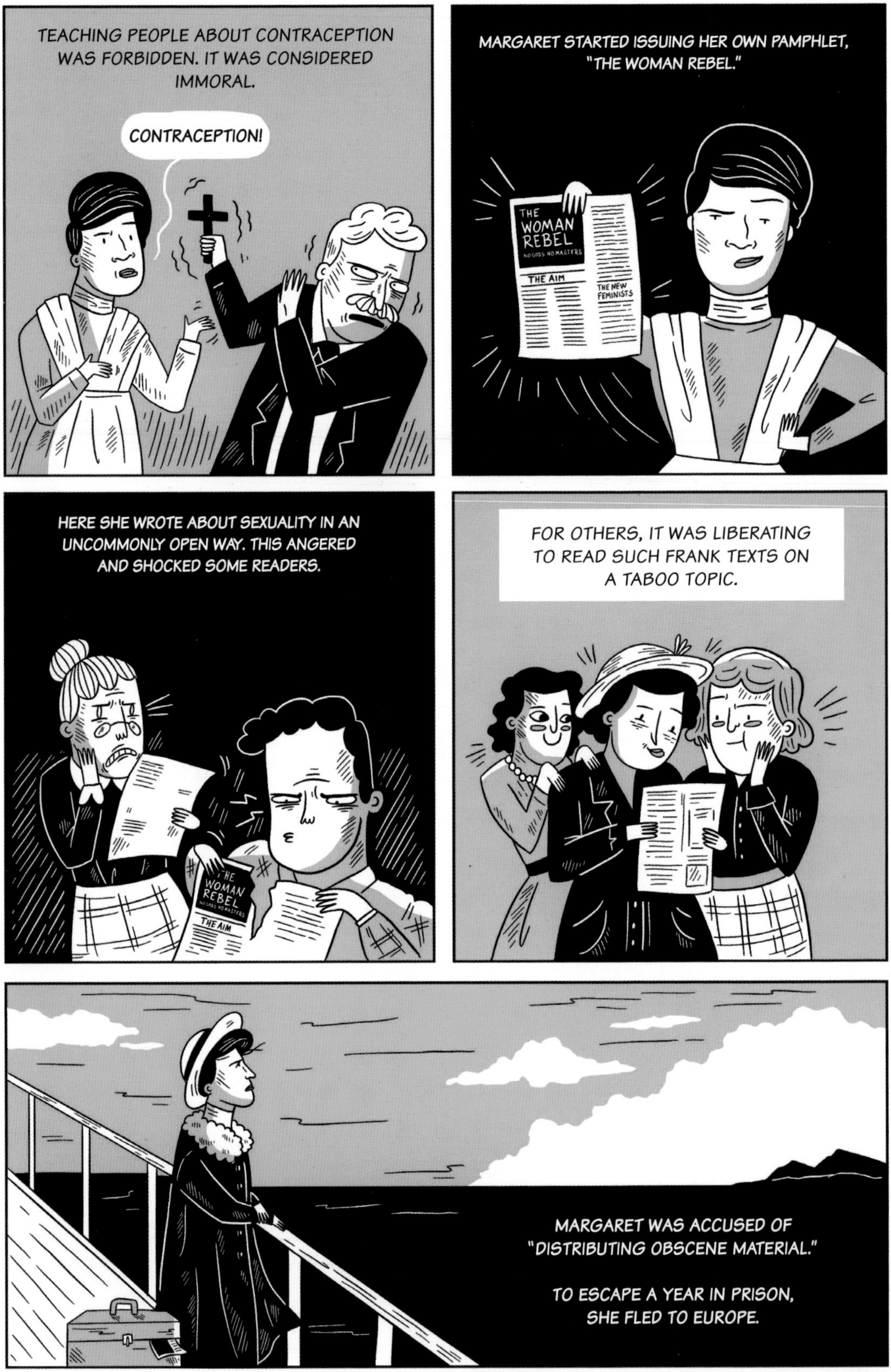
TEACHING PEOPLE ABOUT CONTRACEPTION WAS FORBIDDEN. IT WAS CONSIDERED IMMORAL.
CONTRACEPTION!
MARGARET STARTED ISSUING HER OWN PAMPHLET, "THE WOMAN REBEL."
THE WOMAN REBEL
NO GODS NO MASTERS
THE AIM
THE NEW FEMINISTS
HERE SHE WROTE ABOUT SEXUALITY IN AN UNCOMMONLY OPEN WAY. THIS ANGERED AND SHOCKED SOME READERS.
THE WOMAN REBEL
THE AIM
FOR OTHERS, IT WAS LIBERATING TO READ SUCH FRANK TEXTS ON A TABOO TOPIC.
MARGARET WAS ACCUSED OF "DISTRIBUTING OBSCENE MATERIAL."
TO ESCAPE A YEAR IN PRISON, SHE FLED TO EUROPE.

SOME EUROPEAN COUNTRIES HAD A MORE LIBERAL OPINION OF CONTRACEPTION. WHEN MARGARET VISITED A DUTCH WOMEN'S CLINIC IN 1915, SHE LEARNED ABOUT DIAPHRAGMS.

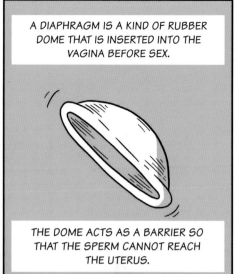

A DIAPHRAGM IS A KIND OF RUBBER DOME THAT IS INSERTED INTO THE VAGINA BEFORE SEX.

THE DOME ACTS AS A BARRIER SO THAT THE SPERM CANNOT REACH THE UTERUS.

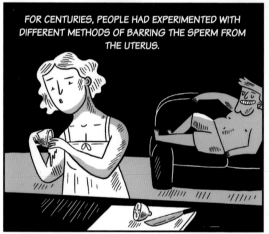

FOR CENTURIES, PEOPLE HAD EXPERIMENTED WITH DIFFERENT METHODS OF BARRING THE SPERM FROM THE UTERUS.

IT WAS ONLY WHEN MODERN RUBBER TECHNOLOGY BECAME AVAILABLE IN THE LATE 1800s THAT DIAPHRAGMS STARTED BEING PRODUCED.

MARGARET DECIDED TO IMPORT THEM ILLEGALLY TO THE USA.

BACK HOME, SHE OPENED THE USA'S FIRST WOMEN'S CLINIC TOGETHER WITH HER LITTLE SISTER, ETHEL.

46 AMBOY STREET

THE CLINIC WAS ONLY OPEN FOR TEN DAYS BEFORE THE SISTERS WERE ARRESTED.

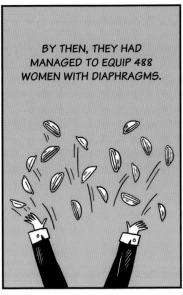

BY THEN, THEY HAD MANAGED TO EQUIP 488 WOMEN WITH DIAPHRAGMS.

AFTER A SECOND ARREST, MARGARET AND ETHEL WERE SENTENCED TO THIRTY DAYS IN PRISON.

THEIR ARRESTS DID NOT GO UNNOTICED. MORE AND MORE PEOPLE SIDED WITH THEM.

THE AUTHORITIES FINALLY RELENTED. DOCTORS WERE ALLOWED TO GIVE ADVICE ON CONTRACEPTION—AND IN SOME CASES, TO DISTRIBUTE IT.

MARGARET CONTINUED TO SPREAD HER MESSAGE INTERNATIONALLY. SHE LED CAMPAIGNS FOR FAMILY PLANNING IN INDIA AND JAPAN, AMONG OTHER PLACES.

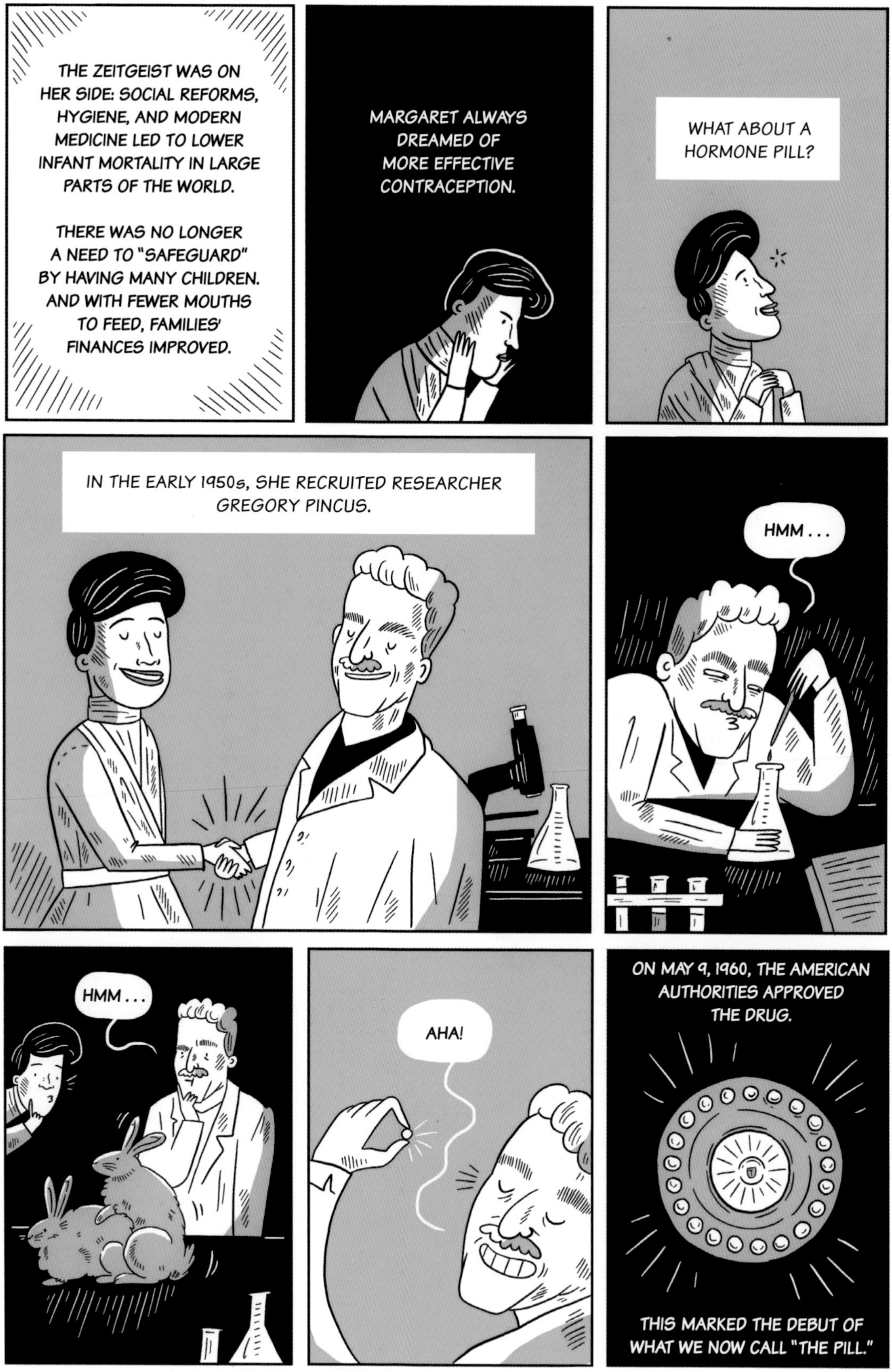
THE ZEITGEIST WAS ON HER SIDE: SOCIAL REFORMS, HYGIENE, AND MODERN MEDICINE LED TO LOWER INFANT MORTALITY IN LARGE PARTS OF THE WORLD.
THERE WAS NO LONGER A NEED TO "SAFEGUARD" BY HAVING MANY CHILDREN. AND WITH FEWER MOUTHS TO FEED, FAMILIES' FINANCES IMPROVED.
MARGARET ALWAYS DREAMED OF MORE EFFECTIVE CONTRACEPTION.
WHAT ABOUT A HORMONE PILL?
IN THE EARLY 1950s, SHE RECRUITED RESEARCHER GREGORY PINCUS.
HMM . . .
HMM . . .
AHA!
ON MAY 9, 1960, THE AMERICAN AUTHORITIES APPROVED THE DRUG.
THIS MARKED THE DEBUT OF WHAT WE NOW CALL "THE PILL."

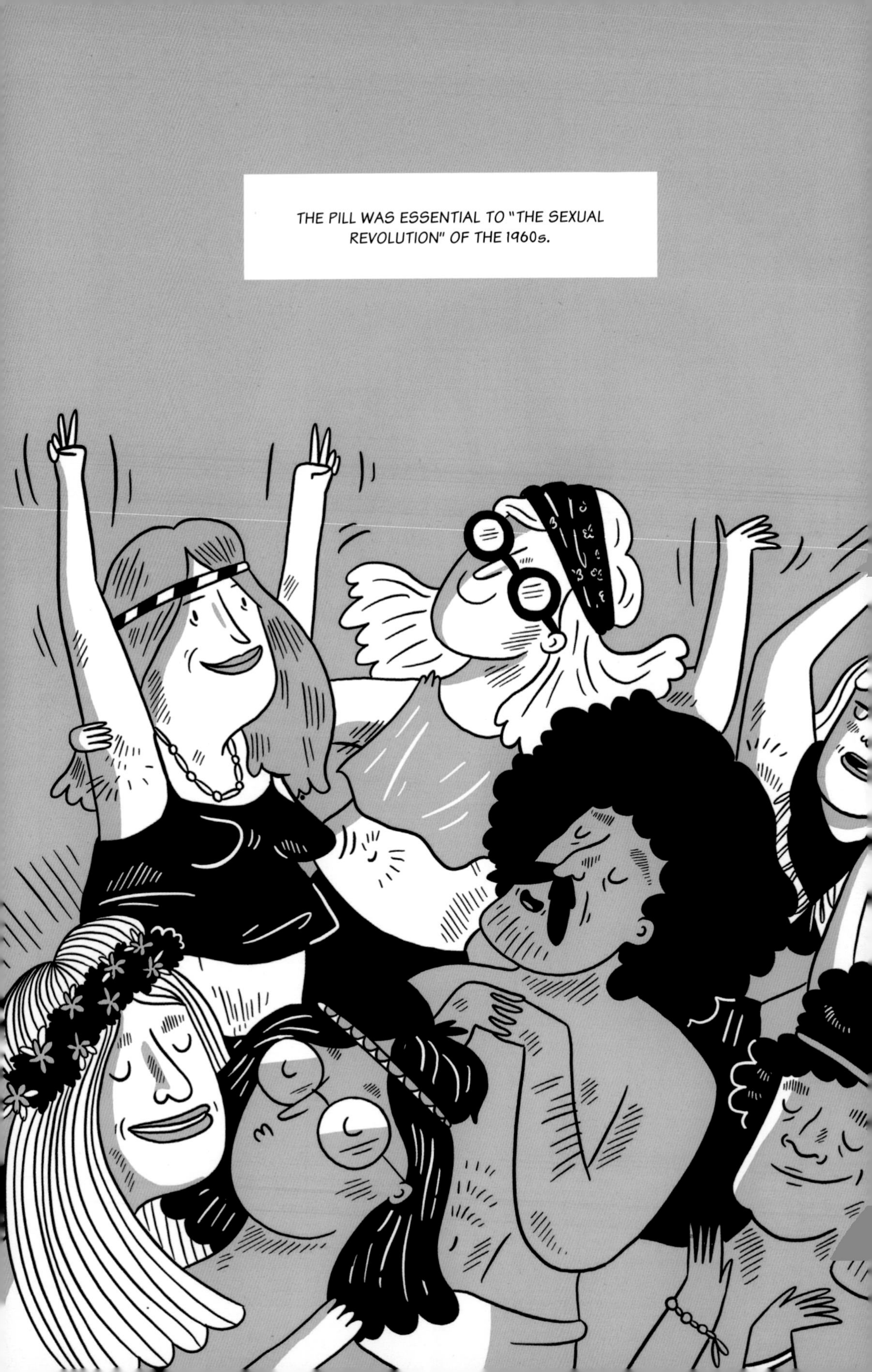
THE PILL WAS ESSENTIAL TO "THE SEXUAL REVOLUTION" OF THE 1960s.

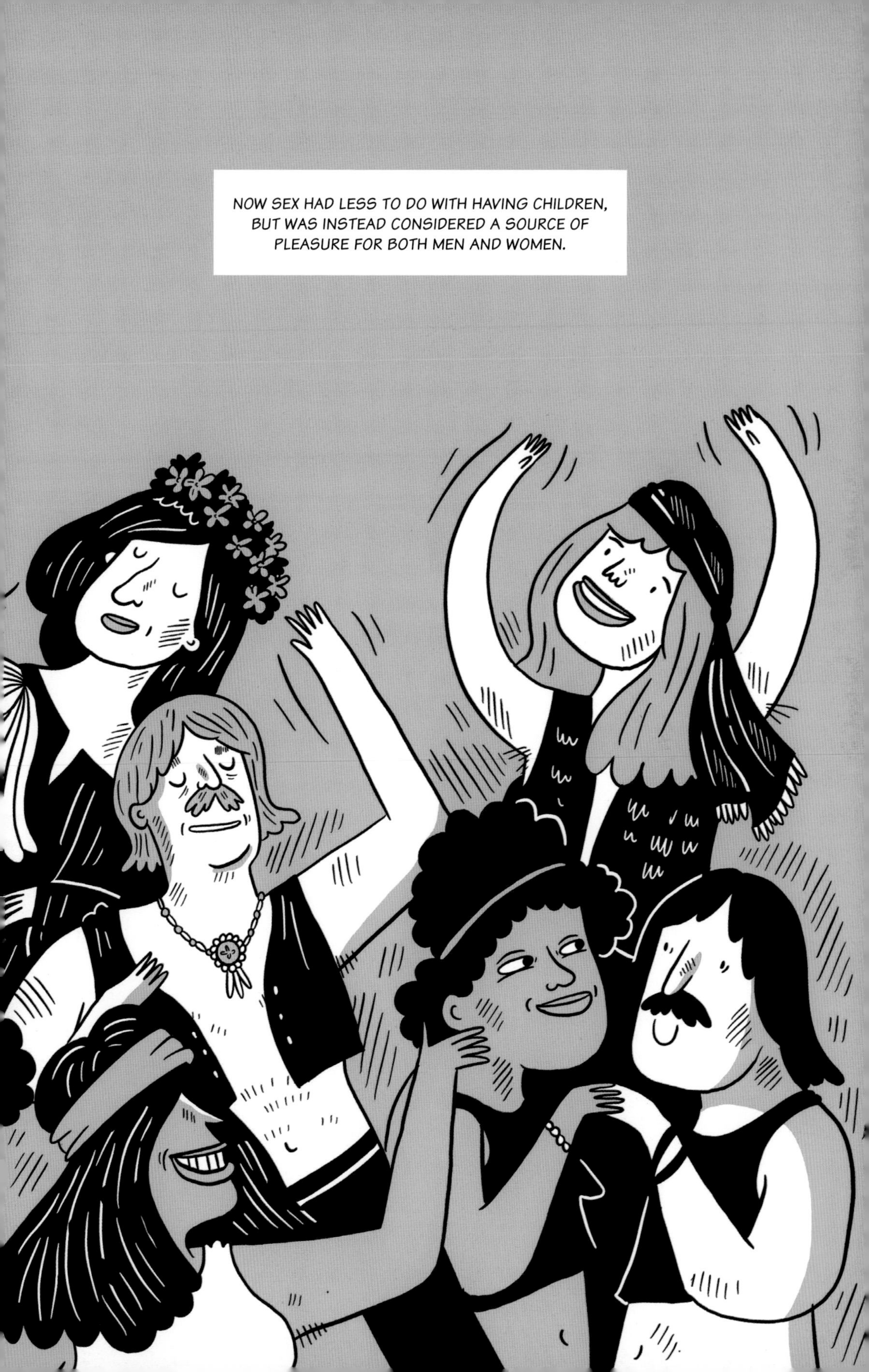
NOW SEX HAD LESS TO DO WITH HAVING CHILDREN, BUT WAS INSTEAD CONSIDERED A SOURCE OF PLEASURE FOR BOTH MEN AND WOMEN.

NO MORE
KNITTING NEEDLES,
"WISE WOMEN,"
OR PAINFUL MEMORIES!

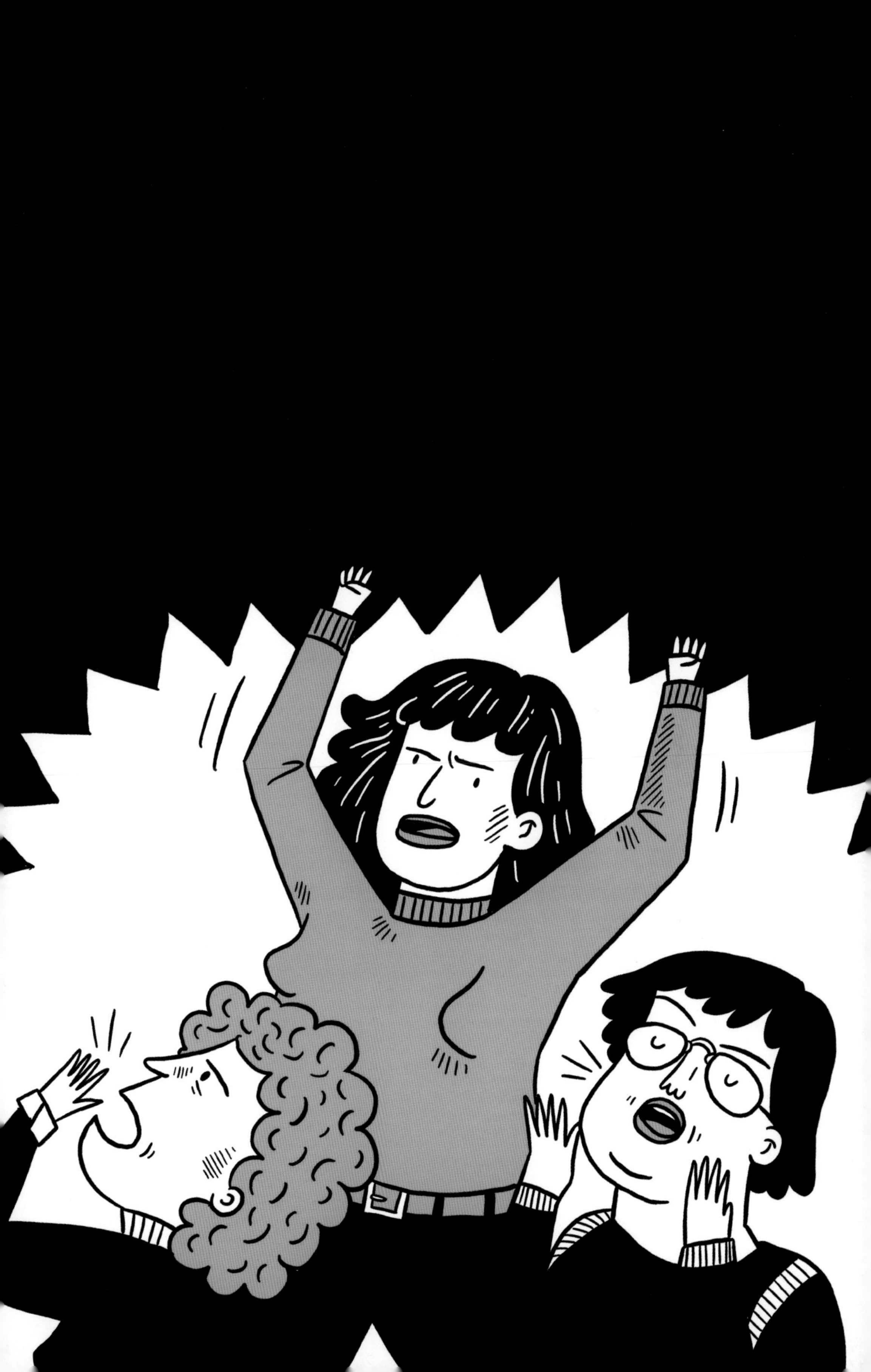

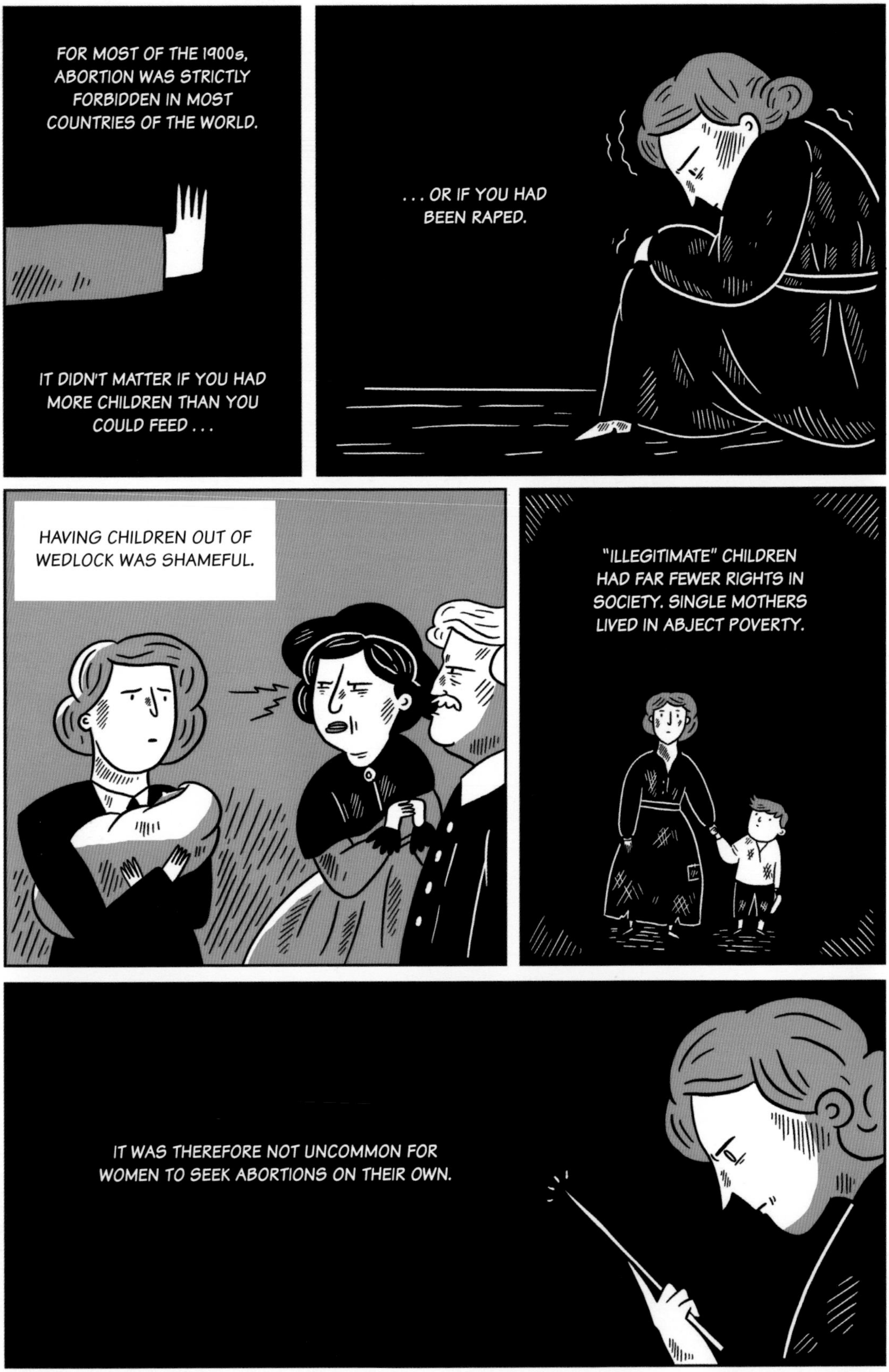
FOR MOST OF THE 1900s, ABORTION WAS STRICTLY FORBIDDEN IN MOST COUNTRIES OF THE WORLD.
IT DIDN'T MATTER IF YOU HAD MORE CHILDREN THAN YOU COULD FEED . . .
. . . OR IF YOU HAD BEEN RAPED.
HAVING CHILDREN OUT OF WEDLOCK WAS SHAMEFUL.
"ILLEGITIMATE" CHILDREN HAD FAR FEWER RIGHTS IN SOCIETY. SINGLE MOTHERS LIVED IN ABJECT POVERTY.
IT WAS THEREFORE NOT UNCOMMON FOR WOMEN TO SEEK ABORTIONS ON THEIR OWN.

SOME VISITED ILLEGAL CLINICS . . .

. . . OR "WISE WOMEN."

OTHERS MADE DESPERATE ATTEMPTS
USING KNITTING NEEDLES . . .

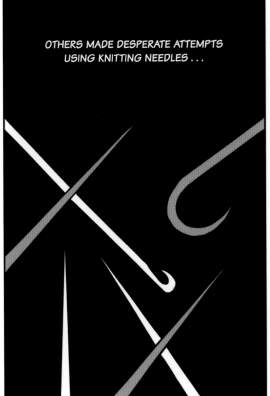

. . . OR BY "FALLING."

IN SOME EUROPEAN COUNTRIES, ABORTION WAS PERMITTED IN RARE EXCEPTIONS. YOU WOULD BE BROUGHT BEFORE A COMMITTEE TO EXPLAIN WHY YOU WANTED AN ABORTION.

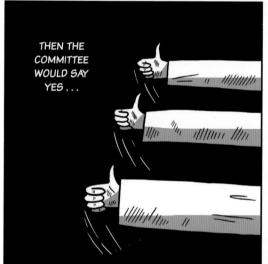

THEN THE COMMITTEE WOULD SAY YES . . .

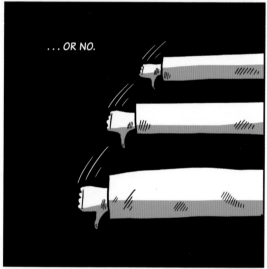

. . . OR NO.

IN 1973, A NEW LAW GAVE WOMEN IN THE USA THE RIGHT TO CHOOSE WHETHER THEY WANTED AN ABORTION. IT WAS CALLED *ROE V. WADE*.

THE CASE BEGAN WHEN TWENTY-ONE-YEAR-OLD NORMA MCCORVEY IN DALLAS, TEXAS, FELL PREGNANT WITH HER THIRD CHILD.

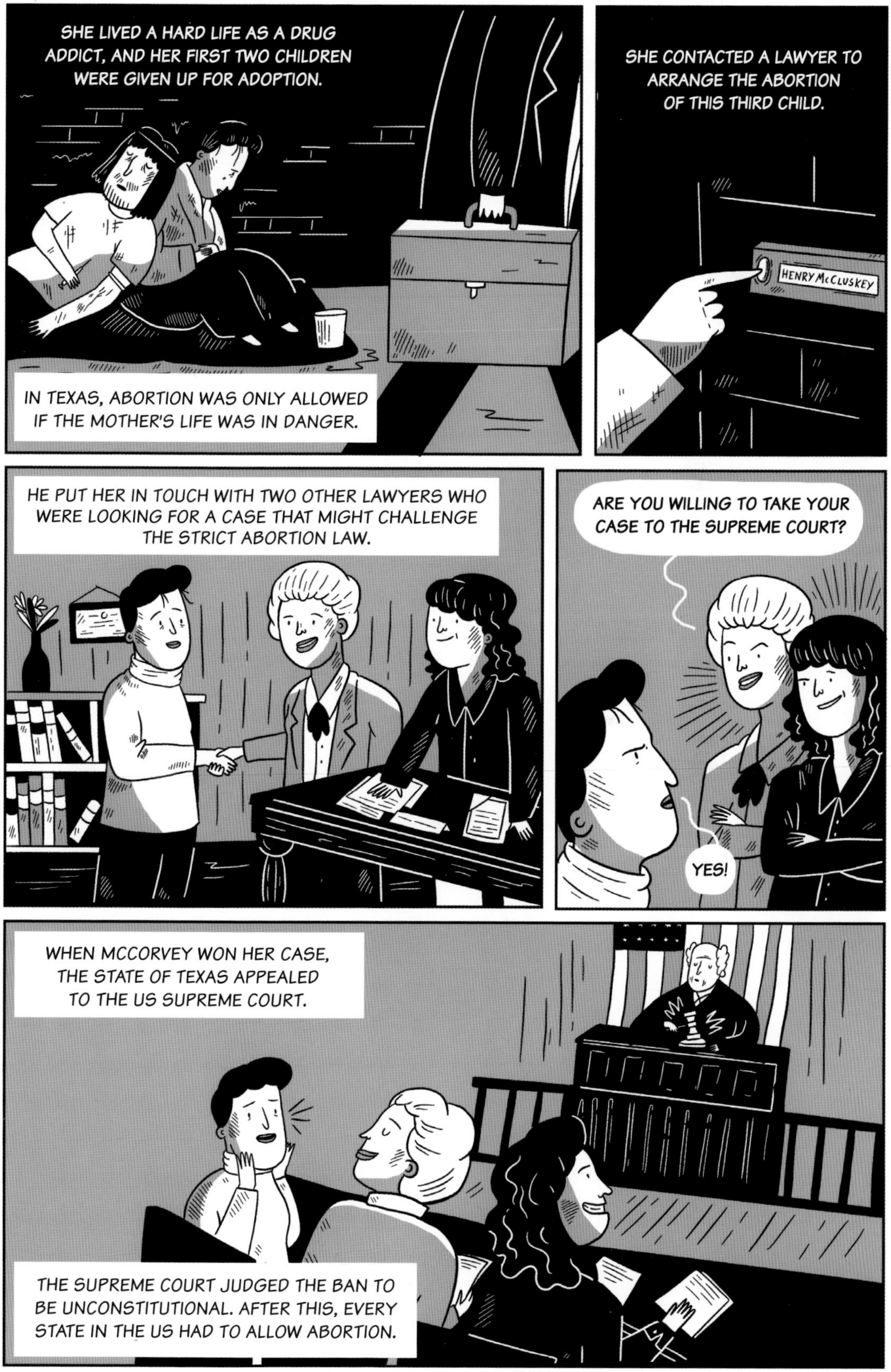
SHE LIVED A HARD LIFE AS A DRUG ADDICT, AND HER FIRST TWO CHILDREN WERE GIVEN UP FOR ADOPTION.
IN TEXAS, ABORTION WAS ONLY ALLOWED IF THE MOTHER'S LIFE WAS IN DANGER.
SHE CONTACTED A LAWYER TO ARRANGE THE ABORTION OF THIS THIRD CHILD.
HENRY McCLUSKEY
HE PUT HER IN TOUCH WITH TWO OTHER LAWYERS WHO WERE LOOKING FOR A CASE THAT MIGHT CHALLENGE THE STRICT ABORTION LAW.
ARE YOU WILLING TO TAKE YOUR CASE TO THE SUPREME COURT?
YES!
WHEN MCCORVEY WON HER CASE, THE STATE OF TEXAS APPEALED TO THE US SUPREME COURT.
THE SUPREME COURT JUDGED THE BAN TO BE UNCONSTITUTIONAL. AFTER THIS, EVERY STATE IN THE US HAD TO ALLOW ABORTION.

THIS JUDGMENT IN 1973 GARNERED A LOT OF ATTENTION WORLDWIDE. IN THE YEARS THAT FOLLOWED, PEOPLE FOUGHT FOR THIS RIGHT IN A NUMBER OF OTHER WESTERN COUNTRIES.

BUT THE DEBATE CONTINUES. THE AMERICAN PEOPLE ARE DIVIDED, AND MANY ARE OPPOSING THE LAW IN ANY WAY POSSIBLE.

PRO-CHOICE

PRO-LIFE

IN 1976, AN ABORTION CLINIC IN OREGON WAS TORCHED BY AN ARSONIST, JOSEPH STOCKETT.

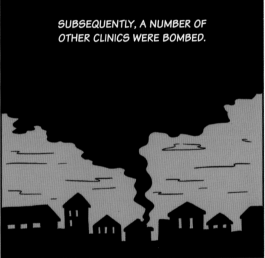

SUBSEQUENTLY, A NUMBER OF OTHER CLINICS WERE BOMBED.

SINCE 1990, AT LEAST ELEVEN DOCTORS AND CLINIC STAFF MEMBERS HAVE BEEN MURDERED ACROSS THE NATION. ATTEMPTS HAD BEEN MADE TO KILL MANY OTHERS.

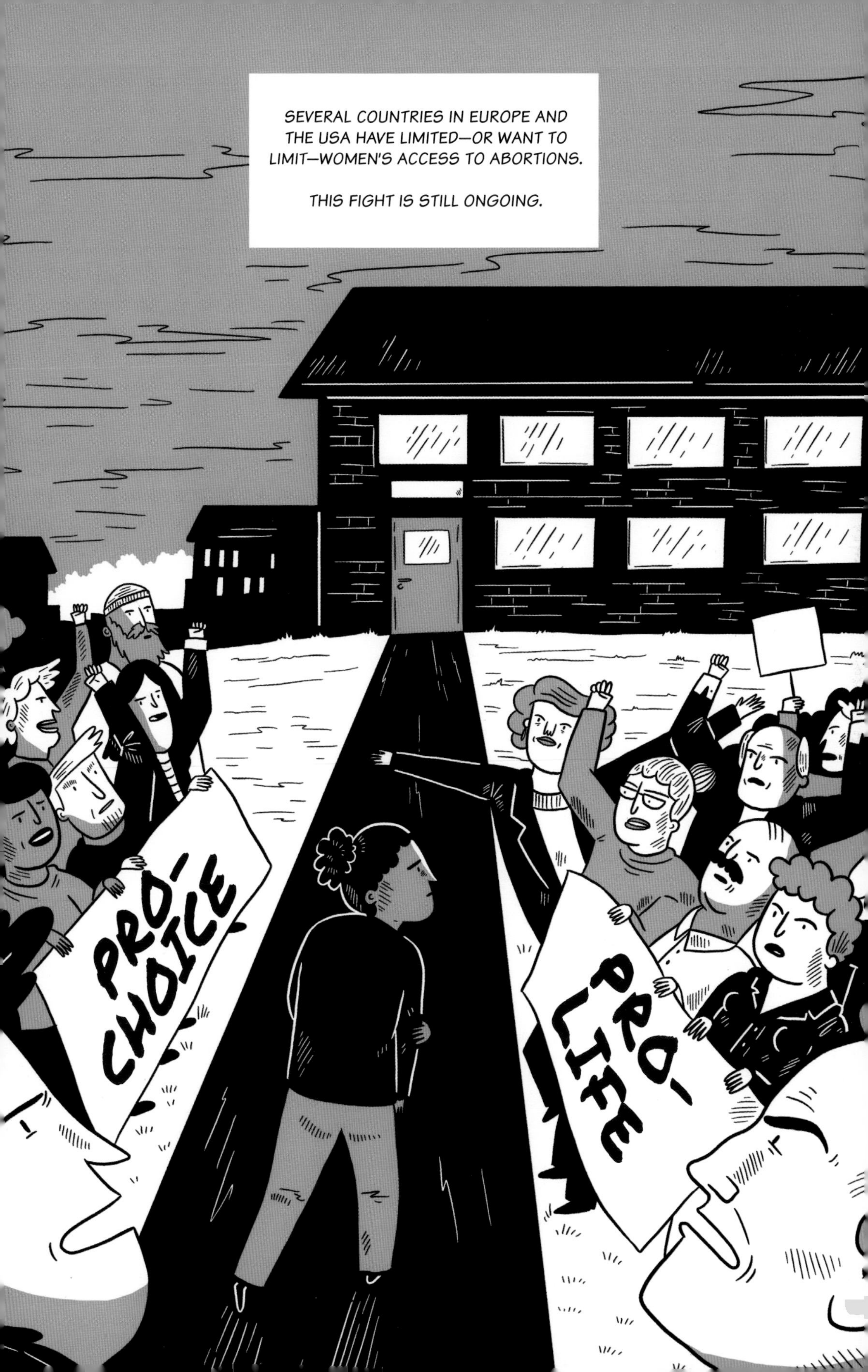
SEVERAL COUNTRIES IN EUROPE AND THE USA HAVE LIMITED—OR WANT TO LIMIT—WOMEN'S ACCESS TO ABORTIONS.
THIS FIGHT IS STILL ONGOING.
PRO-CHOICE
PRO-LIFE

WE TRADITIONALLY TALK ABOUT WAVES IN THE HISTORY OF AMERICAN AND EUROPEAN FEMINISM. THE FIRST WAVE WAS THE ACTIVISM FOR WOMEN'S RIGHTS TO VOTE IN THE LATE 19th CENTURY.

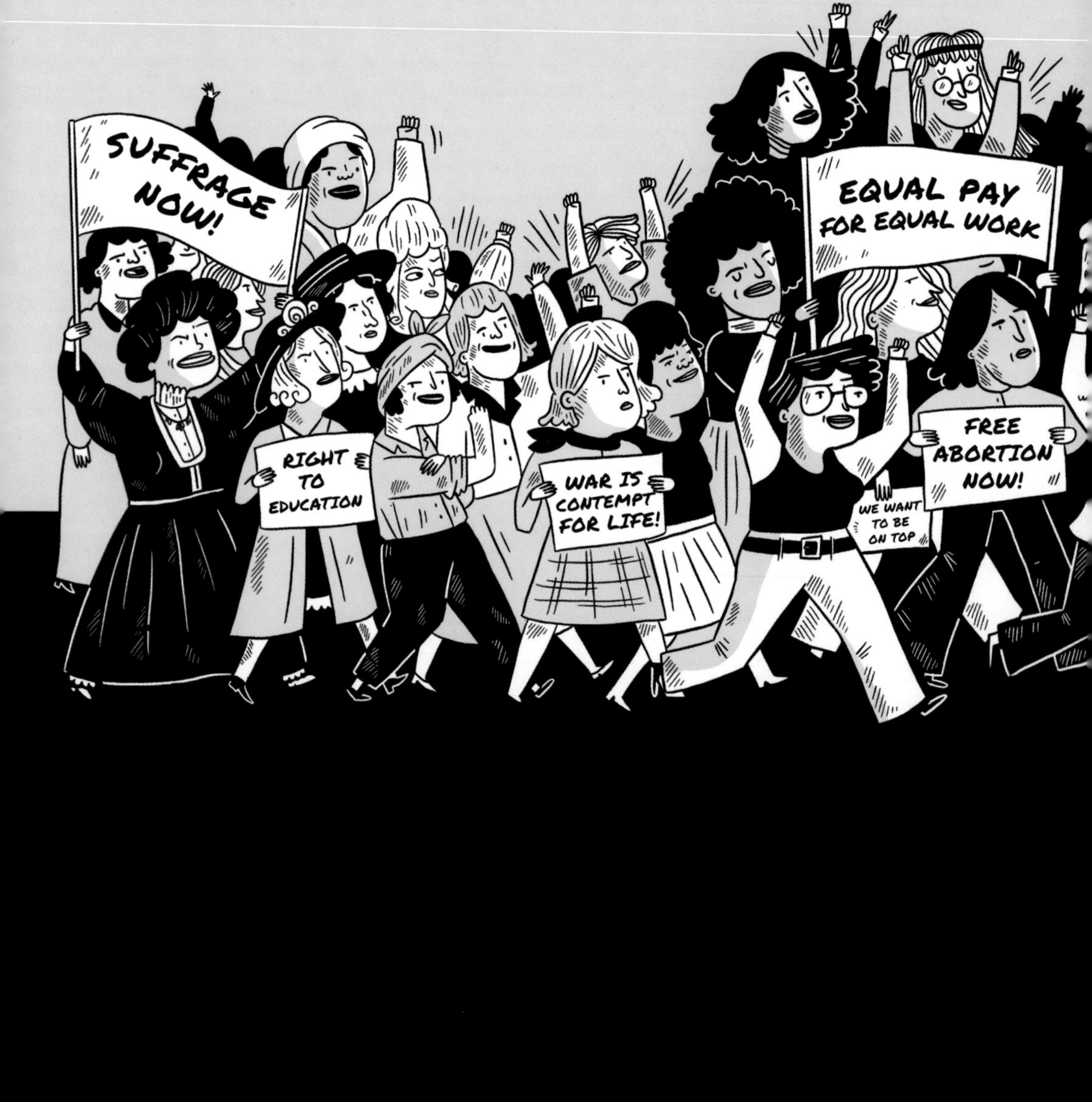
SUFFRAGE NOW!
RIGHT TO EDUCATION
WAR IS CONTEMPT FOR LIFE!
EQUAL PAY FOR EQUAL WORK
WE WANT TO BE ON TOP
FREE ABORTION NOW!

THE AMERICAN WOMEN'S MOVEMENT IN THE 1970s IS CONSIDERED THE SECOND WAVE. THE THIRD WAVE CAME DURING THE 1990s, WITH AN INCREASED FOCUS ON DIVERSITY AND INDIVIDUAL FREEDOM.

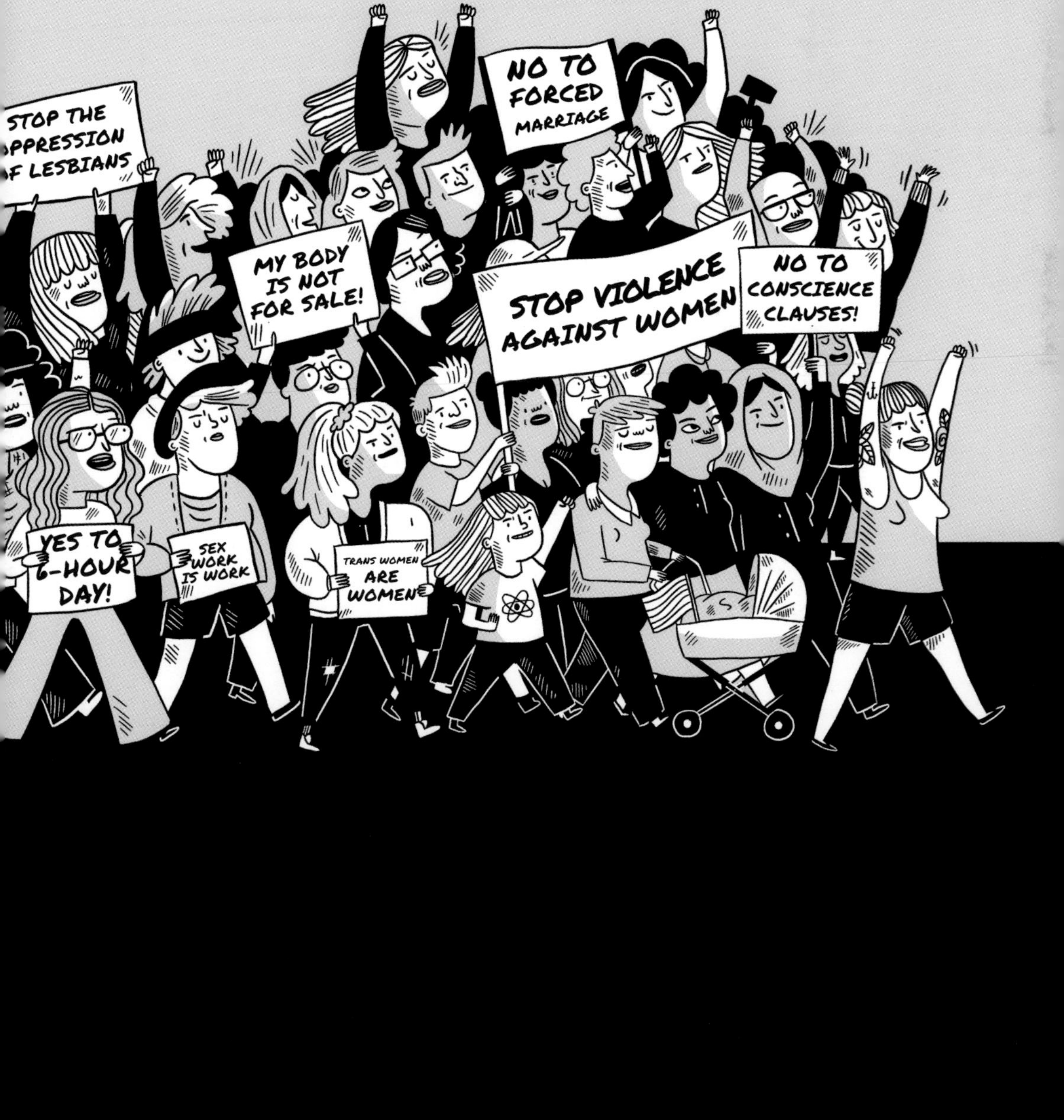

NO TO FORCED MARRIAGE
STOP THE PPRESSION F LESBIANS
MY BODY IS NOT FOR SALE!
STOP VIOLENCE AGAINST WOMEN
NO TO CONSCIENCE CLAUSES!
YES TO 6-HOUR DAY!
SEX WORK IS WORK
TRANS WOMEN ARE WOMEN

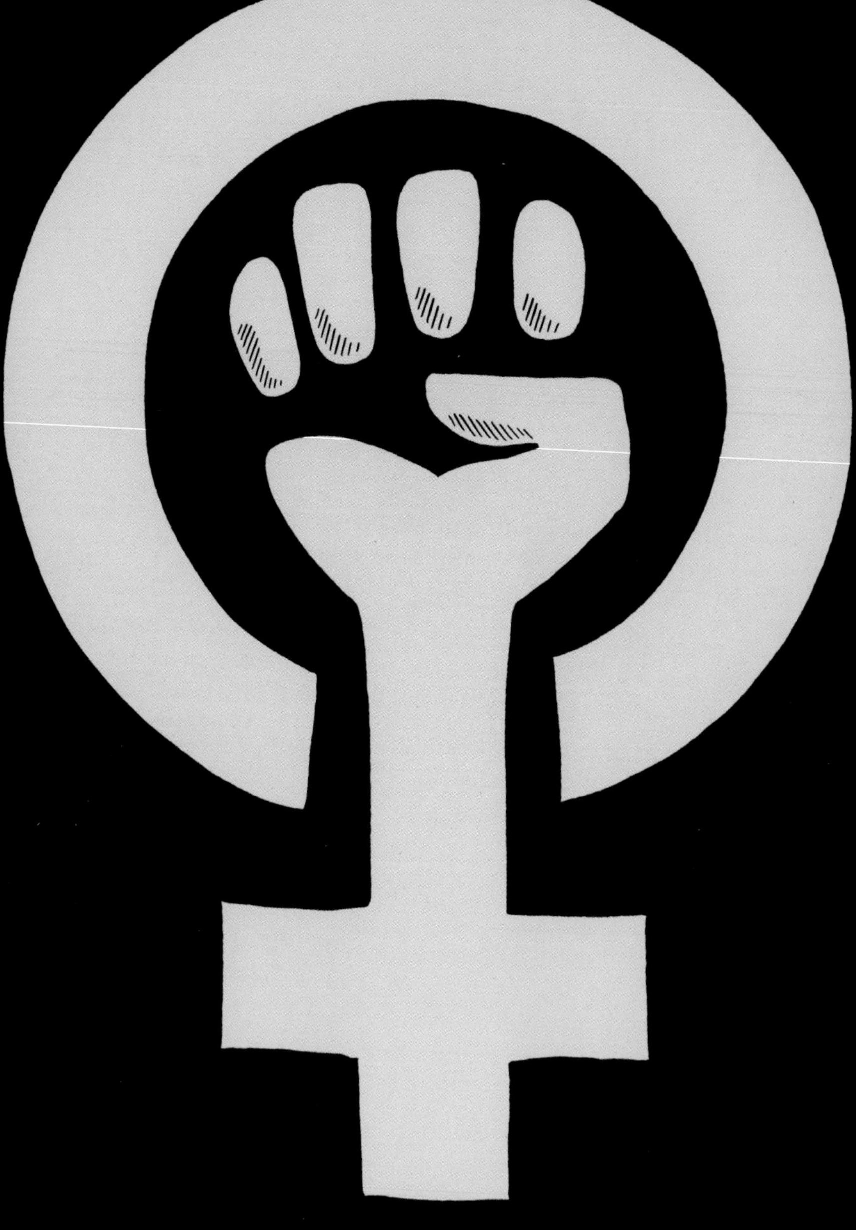

THE VENUS SYMBOL—WITH A CLENCHED FIST IN THE MIDDLE—BECAME THE SYMBOL OF THE WOMEN'S MOVEMENT DURING THE 1970s.

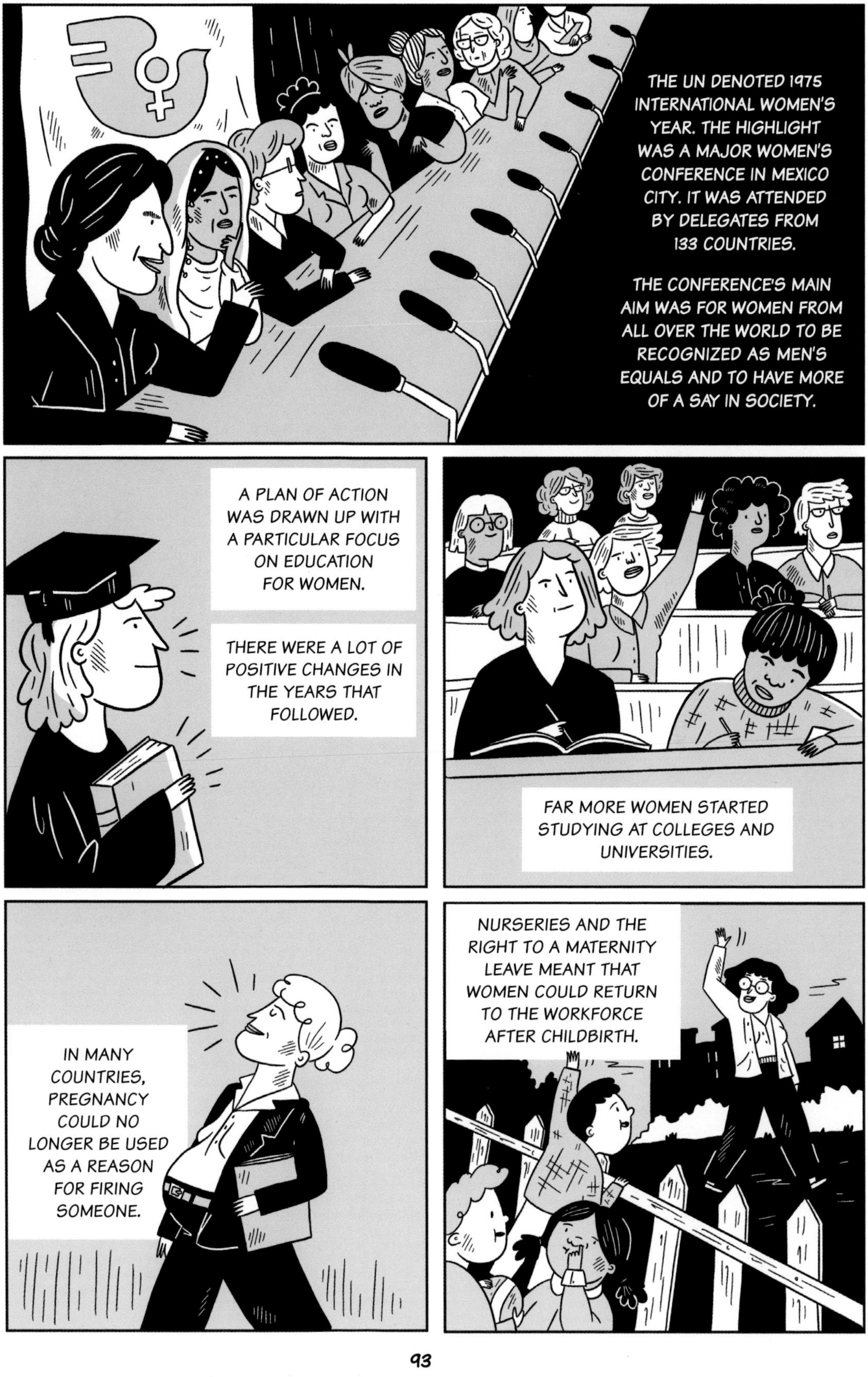

THE UN DENOTED 1975 INTERNATIONAL WOMEN'S YEAR. THE HIGHLIGHT WAS A MAJOR WOMEN'S CONFERENCE IN MEXICO CITY. IT WAS ATTENDED BY DELEGATES FROM 133 COUNTRIES.
THE CONFERENCE'S MAIN AIM WAS FOR WOMEN FROM ALL OVER THE WORLD TO BE RECOGNIZED AS MEN'S EQUALS AND TO HAVE MORE OF A SAY IN SOCIETY.
A PLAN OF ACTION WAS DRAWN UP WITH A PARTICULAR FOCUS ON EDUCATION FOR WOMEN.
THERE WERE A LOT OF POSITIVE CHANGES IN THE YEARS THAT FOLLOWED.
FAR MORE WOMEN STARTED STUDYING AT COLLEGES AND UNIVERSITIES.
IN MANY COUNTRIES, PREGNANCY COULD NO LONGER BE USED AS A REASON FOR FIRING SOMEONE.
NURSERIES AND THE RIGHT TO A MATERNITY LEAVE MEANT THAT WOMEN COULD RETURN TO THE WORKFORCE AFTER CHILDBIRTH.

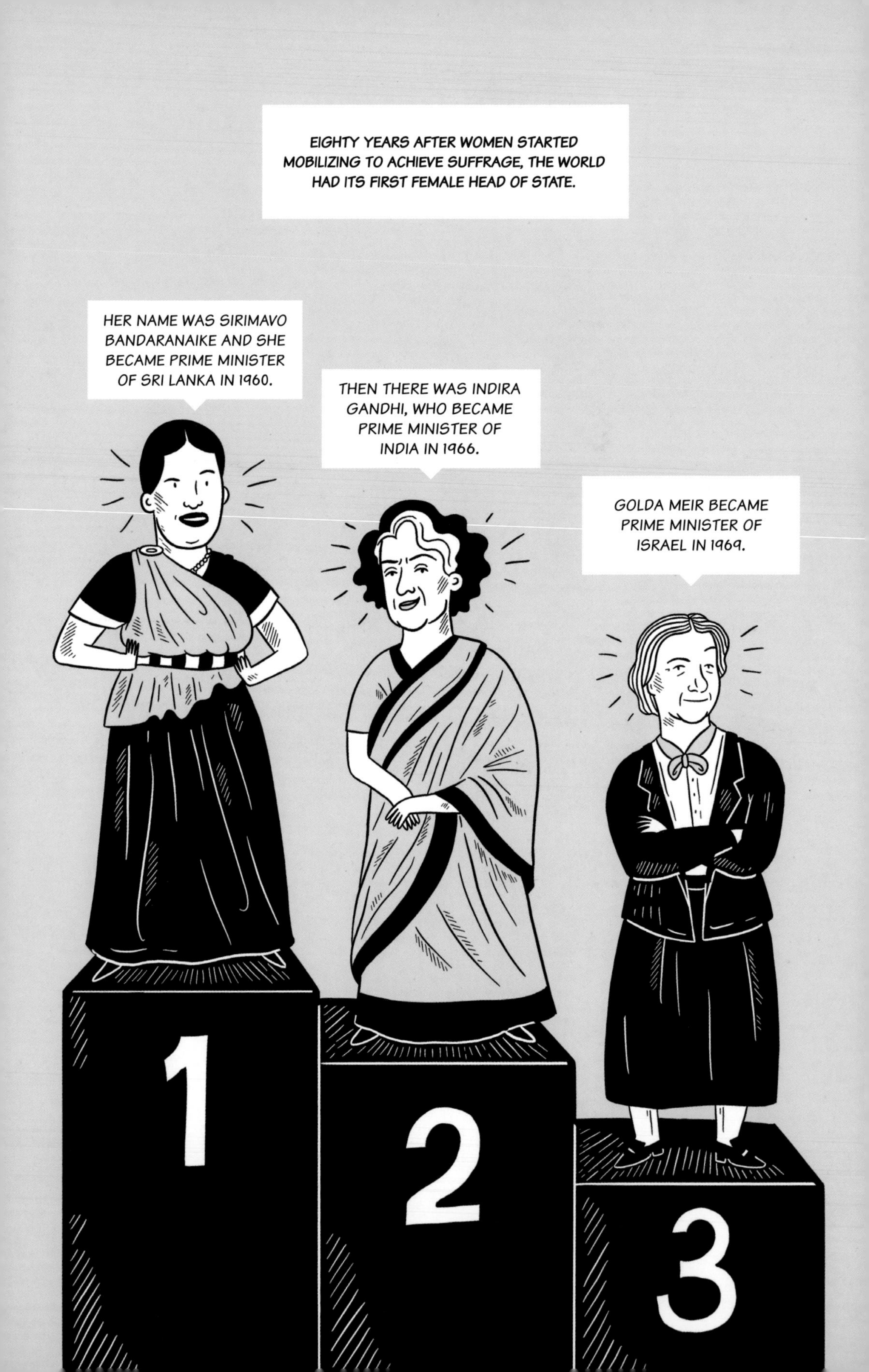
EIGHTY YEARS AFTER WOMEN STARTED MOBILIZING TO ACHIEVE SUFFRAGE, THE WORLD HAD ITS FIRST FEMALE HEAD OF STATE.
HER NAME WAS SIRIMAVO BANDARANAIKE AND SHE BECAME PRIME MINISTER OF SRI LANKA IN 1960.
THEN THERE WAS INDIRA GANDHI, WHO BECAME PRIME MINISTER OF INDIA IN 1966.
GOLDA MEIR BECAME PRIME MINISTER OF ISRAEL IN 1969.
1
2
3

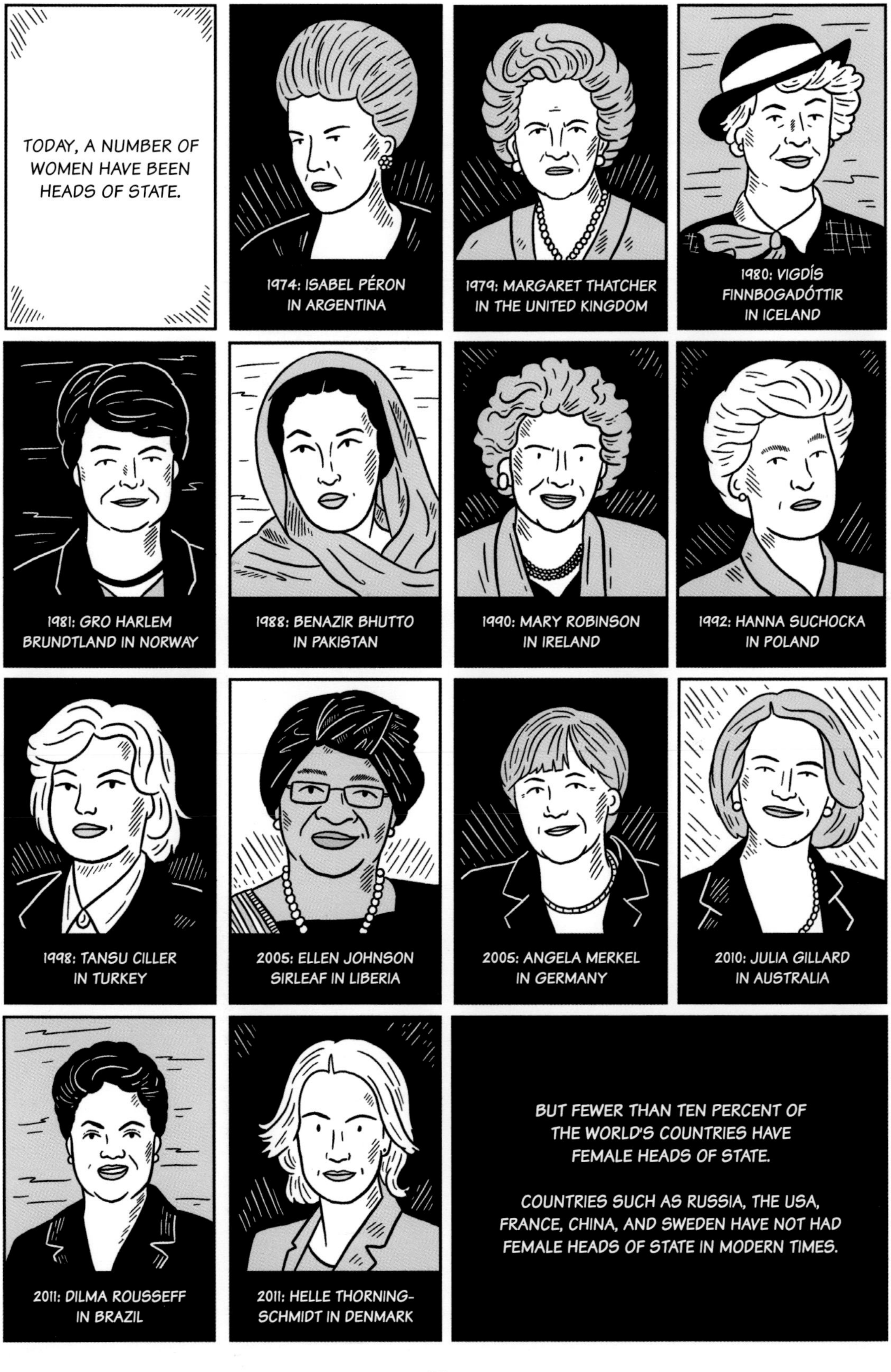
TODAY, A NUMBER OF WOMEN HAVE BEEN HEADS OF STATE.
1974: ISABEL PÉRON IN ARGENTINA
1979: MARGARET THATCHER IN THE UNITED KINGDOM
1980: VIGDÍS FINNBOGADÓTTIR IN ICELAND
1981: GRO HARLEM BRUNDTLAND IN NORWAY
1988: BENAZIR BHUTTO IN PAKISTAN
1990: MARY ROBINSON IN IRELAND
1992: HANNA SUCHOCKA IN POLAND
1998: TANSU CILLER IN TURKEY
2005: ELLEN JOHNSON SIRLEAF IN LIBERIA
2005: ANGELA MERKEL IN GERMANY
2010: JULIA GILLARD IN AUSTRALIA
2011: DILMA ROUSSEFF IN BRAZIL
2011: HELLE THORNING-SCHMIDT IN DENMARK
BUT FEWER THAN TEN PERCENT OF THE WORLD'S COUNTRIES HAVE FEMALE HEADS OF STATE.
COUNTRIES SUCH AS RUSSIA, THE USA, FRANCE, CHINA, AND SWEDEN HAVE NOT HAD FEMALE HEADS OF STATE IN MODERN TIMES.

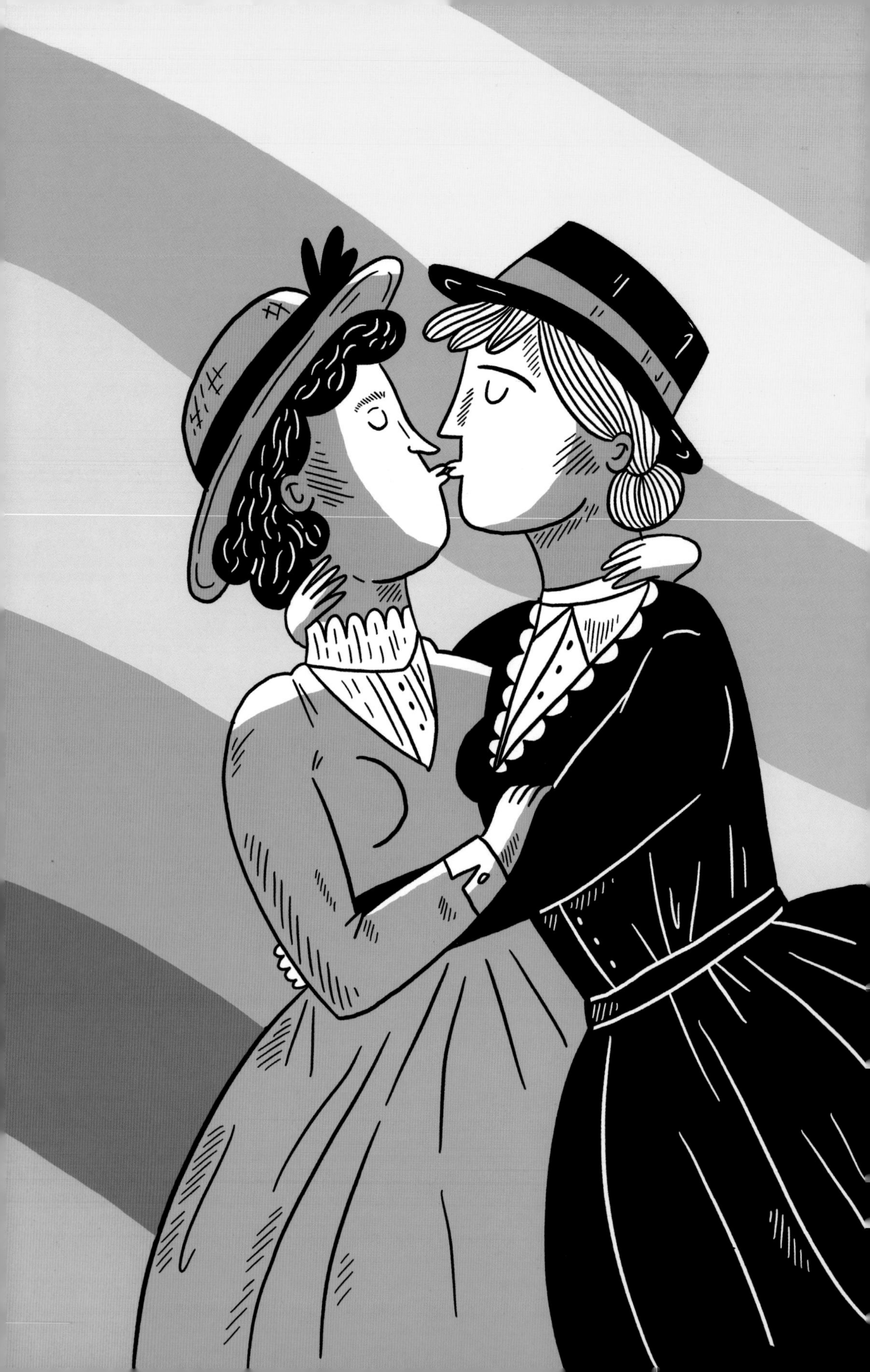

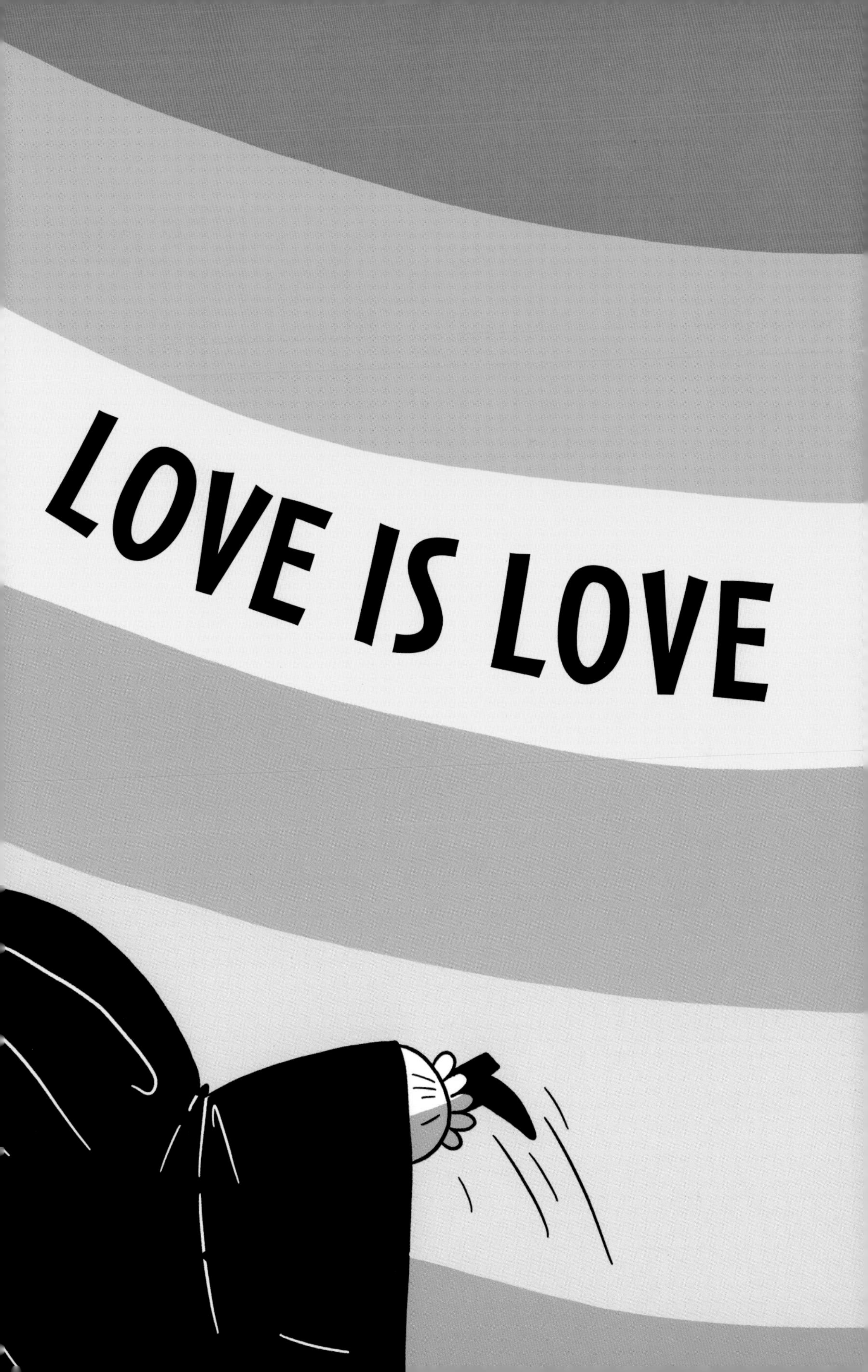
LOVE IS LOVE

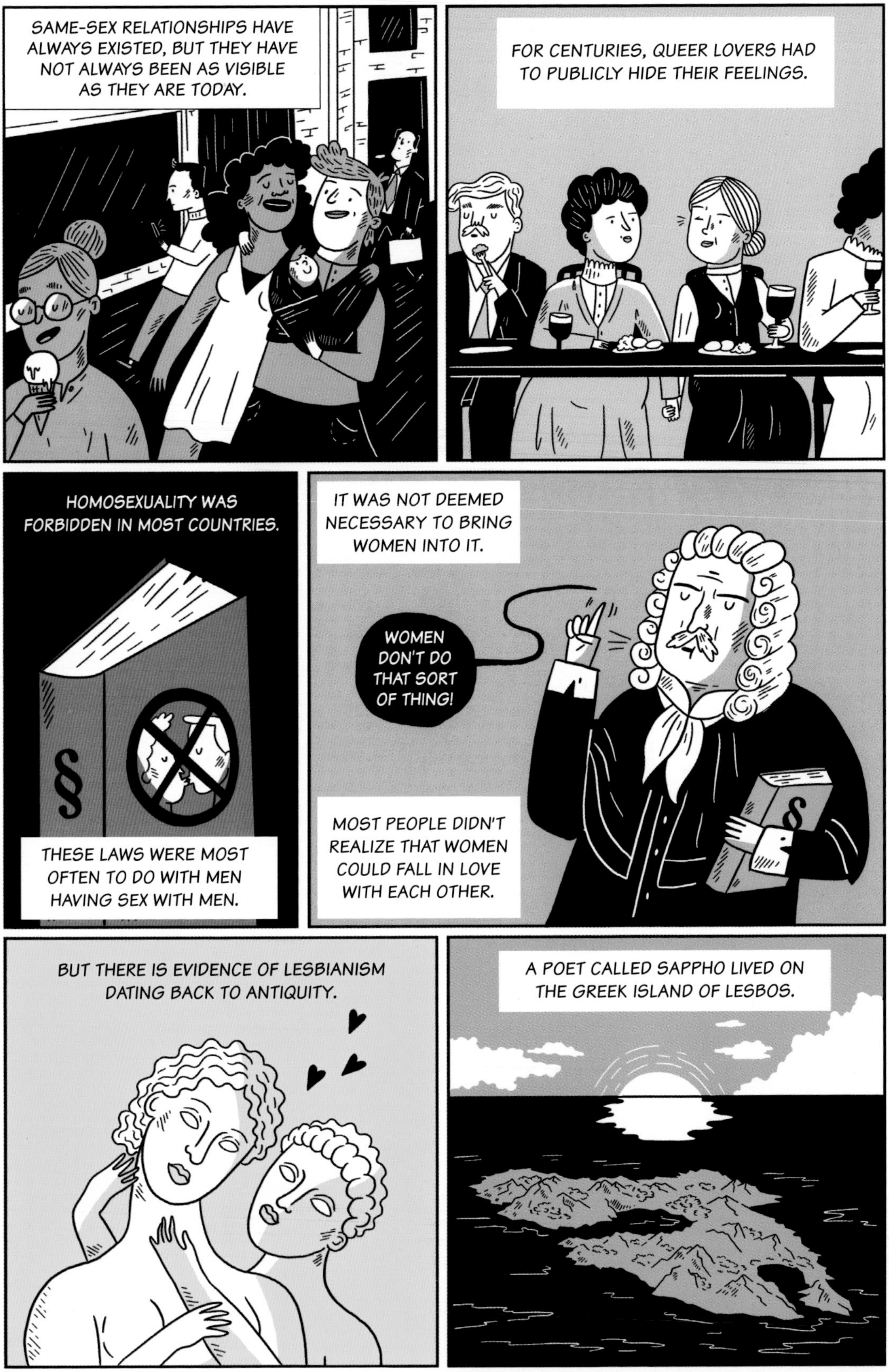
SAME-SEX RELATIONSHIPS HAVE ALWAYS EXISTED, BUT THEY HAVE NOT ALWAYS BEEN AS VISIBLE AS THEY ARE TODAY.
FOR CENTURIES, QUEER LOVERS HAD TO PUBLICLY HIDE THEIR FEELINGS.
HOMOSEXUALITY WAS FORBIDDEN IN MOST COUNTRIES.
§
THESE LAWS WERE MOST OFTEN TO DO WITH MEN HAVING SEX WITH MEN.
IT WAS NOT DEEMED NECESSARY TO BRING WOMEN INTO IT.
WOMEN DON'T DO THAT SORT OF THING!
§
MOST PEOPLE DIDN'T REALIZE THAT WOMEN COULD FALL IN LOVE WITH EACH OTHER.
BUT THERE IS EVIDENCE OF LESBIANISM DATING BACK TO ANTIQUITY.
A POET CALLED SAPPHO LIVED ON THE GREEK ISLAND OF LESBOS.

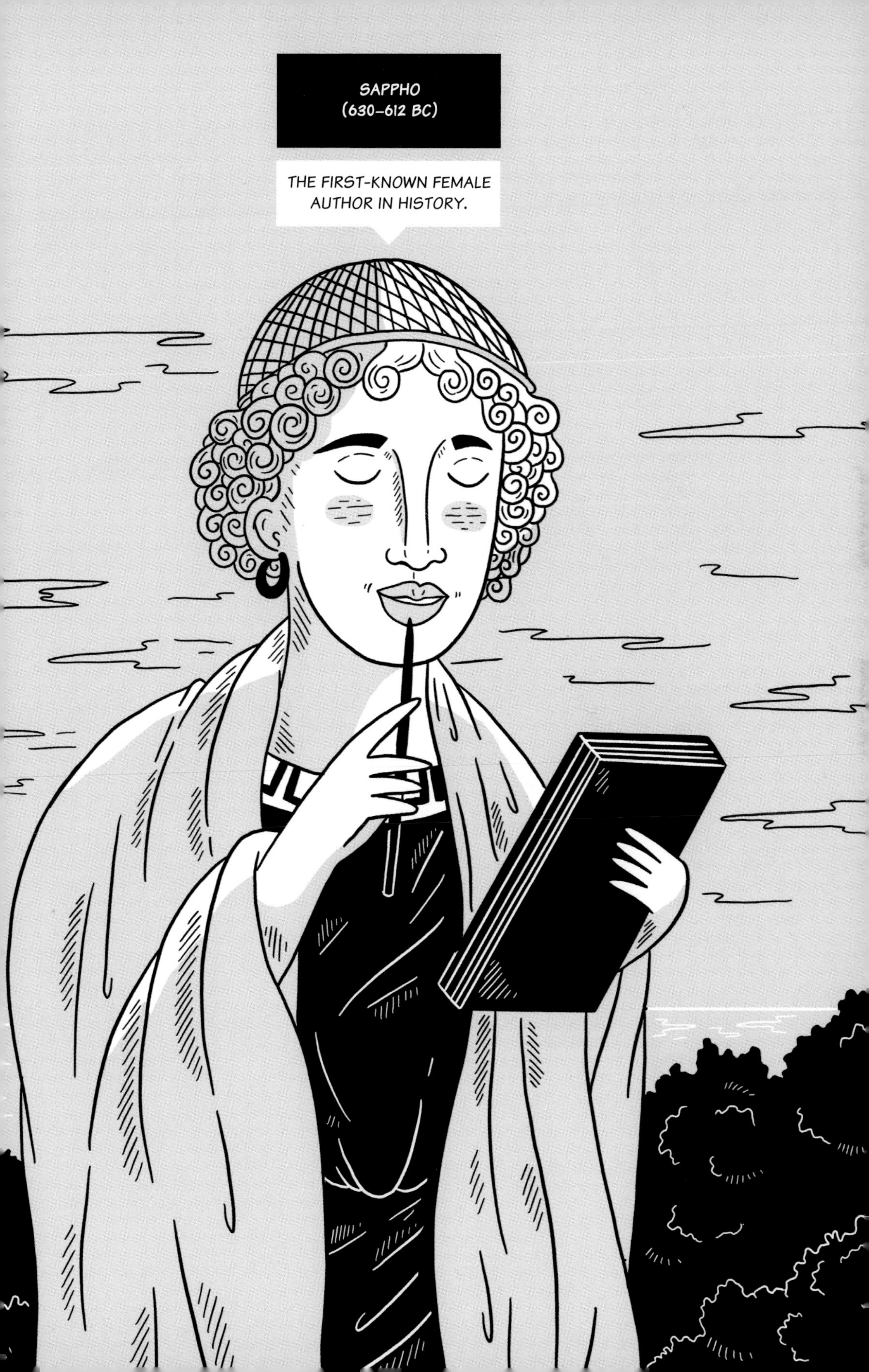
SAPPHO
(630–612 BC)
THE FIRST-KNOWN FEMALE AUTHOR IN HISTORY.

SHE RAN A SCHOOL FOR GIRLS.

EVERY TIME ONE OF HER STUDENTS LEFT THE ISLAND, SAPPHO WOULD WRITE HER A BEAUTIFUL LOVE POEM.

YOU CAME AND I WAS CRAZY FOR YOU

AND YOU COOLED MY MIND THAT BURNED WITH LONGING.

HER POEMS WERE SO INTENSE THAT THE NAME OF THE ISLAND, LESBOS, IS THE ORIGIN OF THE WORD "LESBIAN."

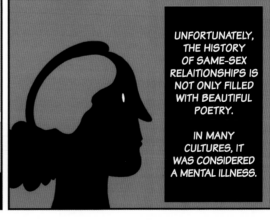

UNFORTUNATELY, THE HISTORY OF SAME-SEX RELAITIONSHIPS IS NOT ONLY FILLED WITH BEAUTIFUL POETRY.

IN MANY CULTURES, IT WAS CONSIDERED A MENTAL ILLNESS.

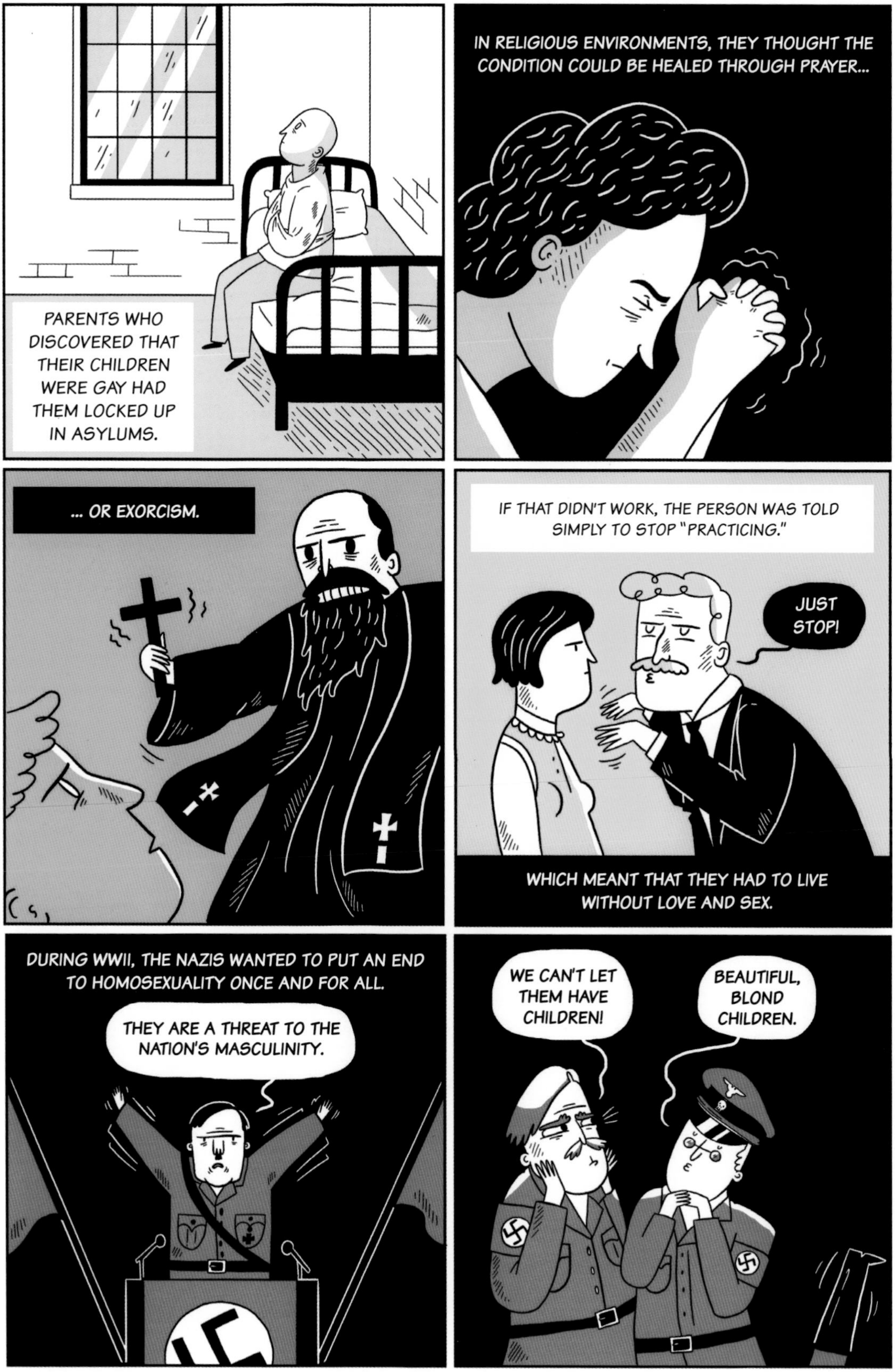
PARENTS WHO DISCOVERED THAT THEIR CHILDREN WERE GAY HAD THEM LOCKED UP IN ASYLUMS.
IN RELIGIOUS ENVIRONMENTS, THEY THOUGHT THE CONDITION COULD BE HEALED THROUGH PRAYER...
... OR EXORCISM.
IF THAT DIDN'T WORK, THE PERSON WAS TOLD SIMPLY TO STOP "PRACTICING."
JUST STOP!
WHICH MEANT THAT THEY HAD TO LIVE WITHOUT LOVE AND SEX.
DURING WWII, THE NAZIS WANTED TO PUT AN END TO HOMOSEXUALITY ONCE AND FOR ALL.
THEY ARE A THREAT TO THE NATION'S MASCULINITY.
WE CAN'T LET THEM HAVE CHILDREN!
BEAUTIFUL, BLOND CHILDREN.

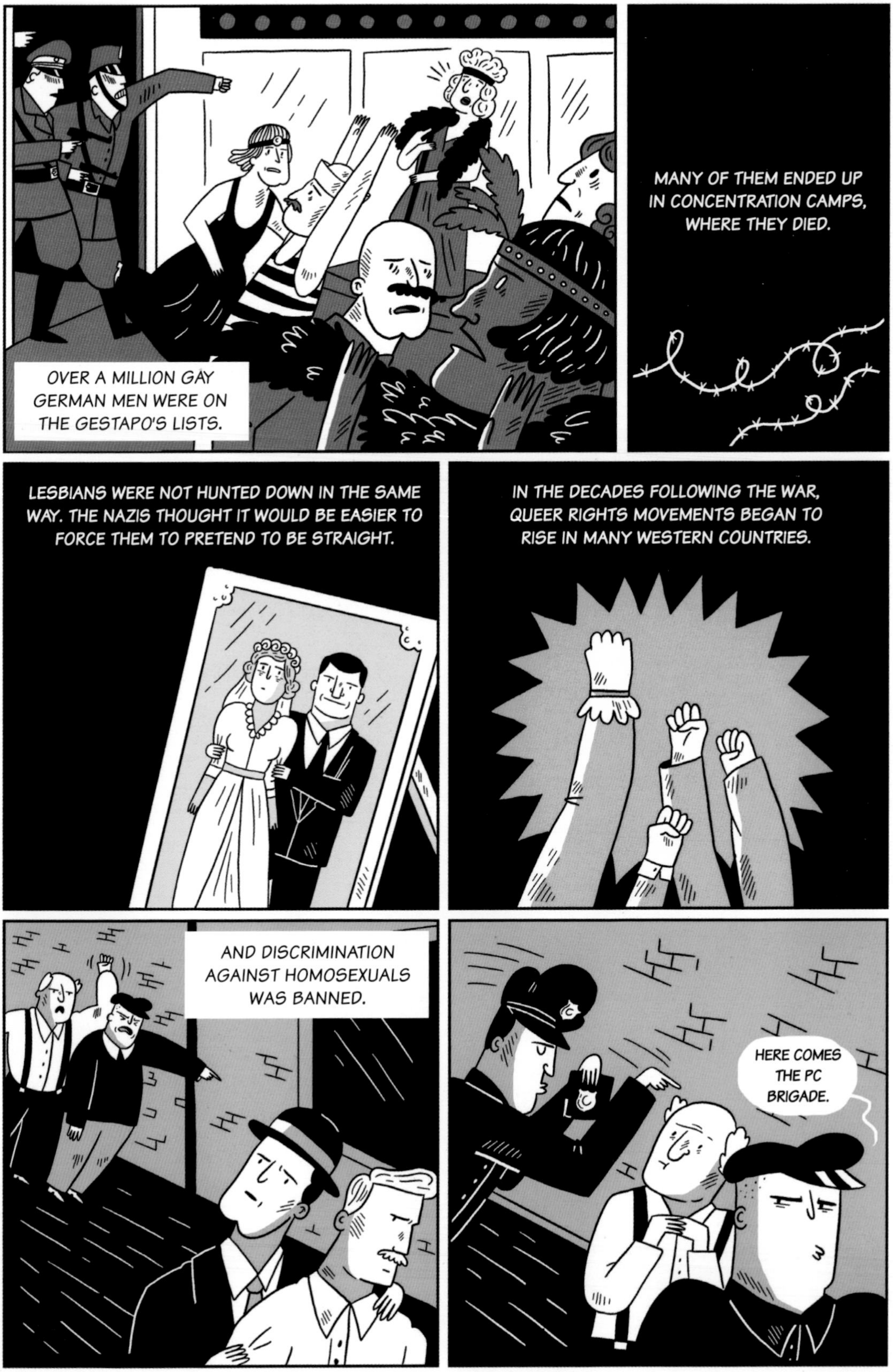
OVER A MILLION GAY GERMAN MEN WERE ON THE GESTAPO'S LISTS.
MANY OF THEM ENDED UP IN CONCENTRATION CAMPS, WHERE THEY DIED.
LESBIANS WERE NOT HUNTED DOWN IN THE SAME WAY. THE NAZIS THOUGHT IT WOULD BE EASIER TO FORCE THEM TO PRETEND TO BE STRAIGHT.
IN THE DECADES FOLLOWING THE WAR, QUEER RIGHTS MOVEMENTS BEGAN TO RISE IN MANY WESTERN COUNTRIES.
AND DISCRIMINATION AGAINST HOMOSEXUALS WAS BANNED.
HERE COMES THE PC BRIGADE.

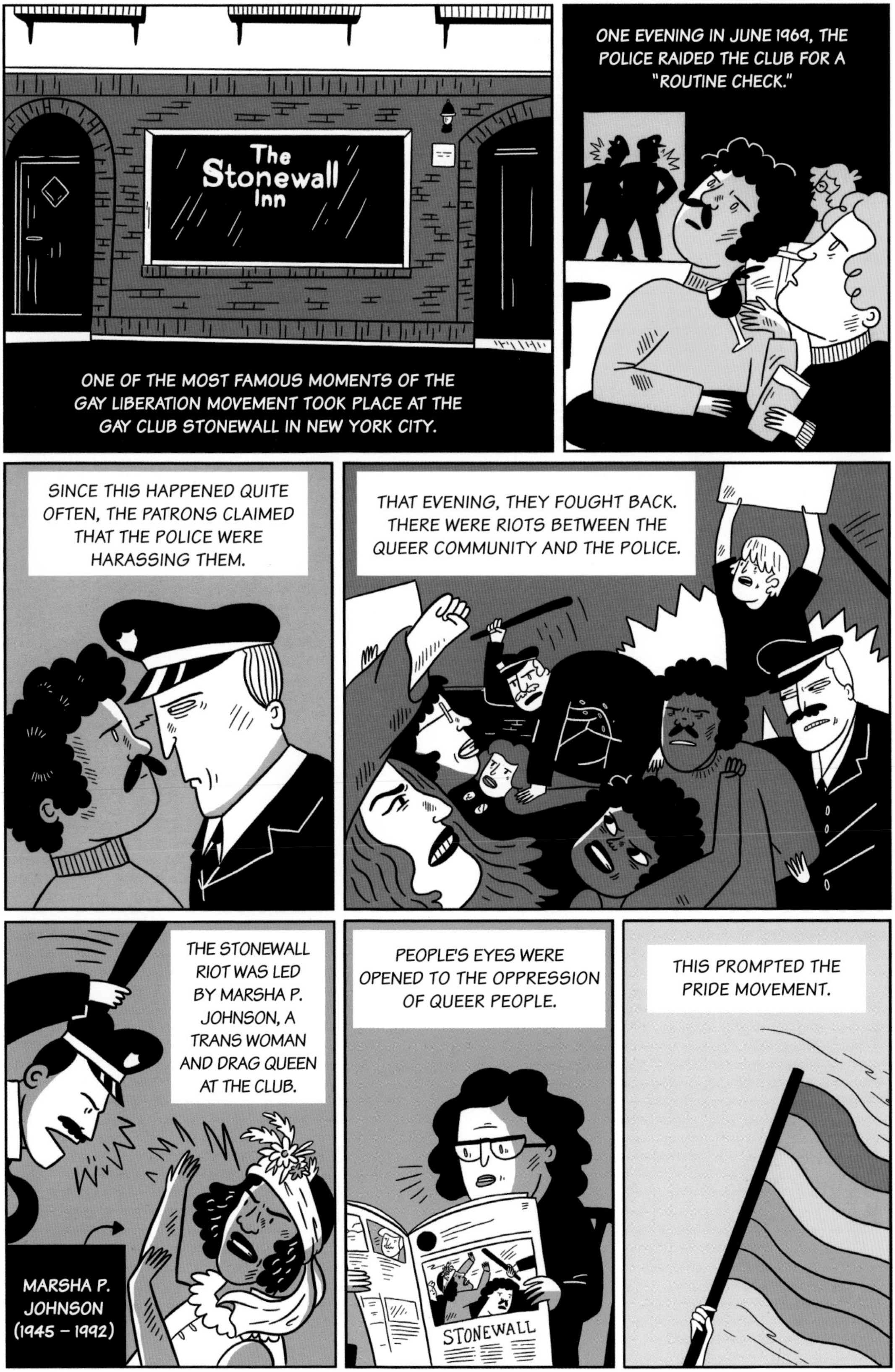

The Stonewall Inn
ONE OF THE MOST FAMOUS MOMENTS OF THE GAY LIBERATION MOVEMENT TOOK PLACE AT THE GAY CLUB STONEWALL IN NEW YORK CITY.
ONE EVENING IN JUNE 1969, THE POLICE RAIDED THE CLUB FOR A "ROUTINE CHECK."
SINCE THIS HAPPENED QUITE OFTEN, THE PATRONS CLAIMED THAT THE POLICE WERE HARASSING THEM.
THAT EVENING, THEY FOUGHT BACK. THERE WERE RIOTS BETWEEN THE QUEER COMMUNITY AND THE POLICE.
THE STONEWALL RIOT WAS LED BY MARSHA P. JOHNSON, A TRANS WOMAN AND DRAG QUEEN AT THE CLUB.
MARSHA P. JOHNSON (1945 – 1992)
PEOPLE'S EYES WERE OPENED TO THE OPPRESSION OF QUEER PEOPLE.
STONEWALL
THIS PROMPTED THE PRIDE MOVEMENT.

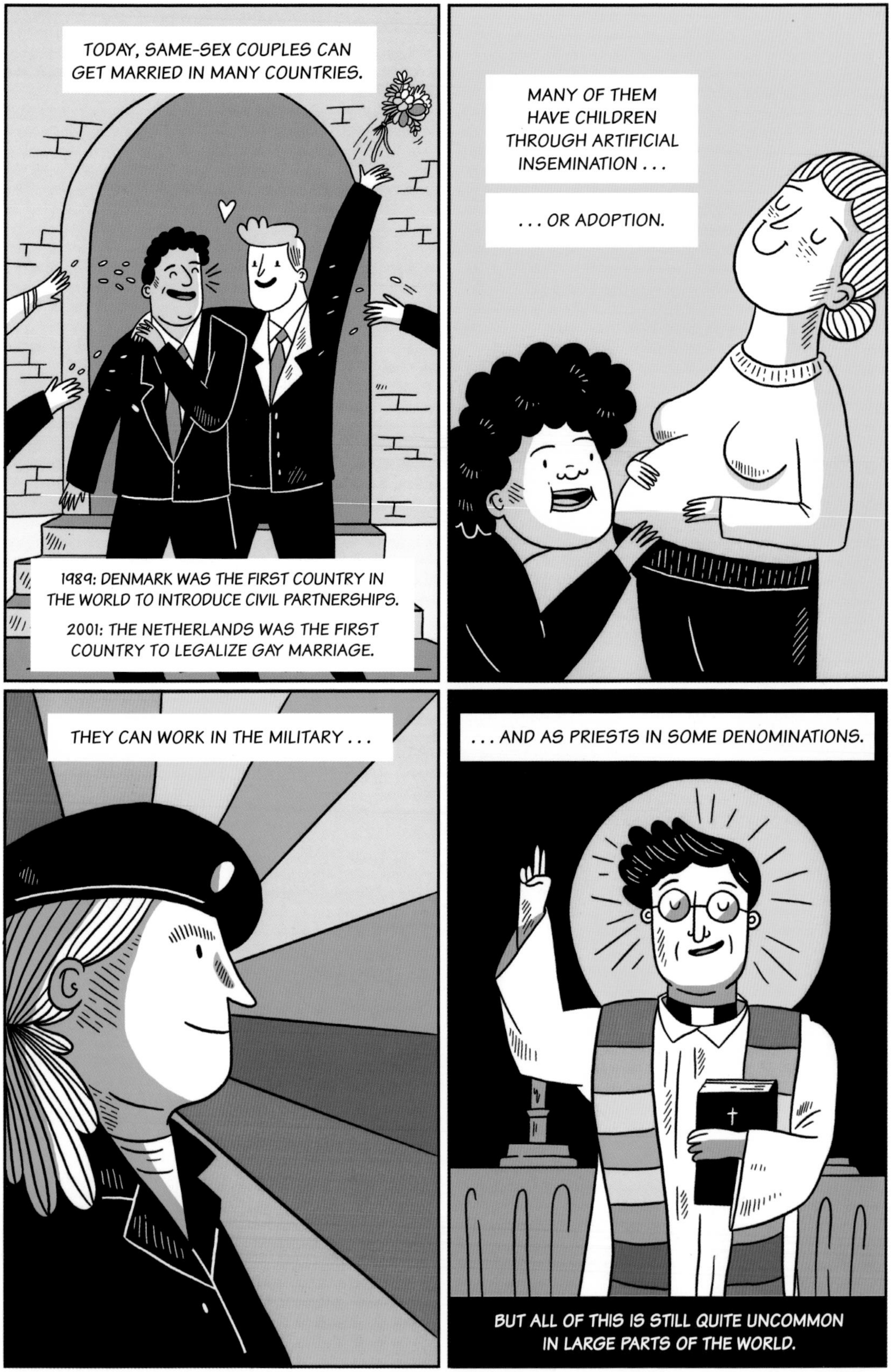
TODAY, SAME-SEX COUPLES CAN GET MARRIED IN MANY COUNTRIES.
1989: DENMARK WAS THE FIRST COUNTRY IN THE WORLD TO INTRODUCE CIVIL PARTNERSHIPS.
2001: THE NETHERLANDS WAS THE FIRST COUNTRY TO LEGALIZE GAY MARRIAGE.
MANY OF THEM HAVE CHILDREN THROUGH ARTIFICIAL INSEMINATION . . .
. . . OR ADOPTION.
THEY CAN WORK IN THE MILITARY . . .
. . . AND AS PRIESTS IN SOME DENOMINATIONS.
BUT ALL OF THIS IS STILL QUITE UNCOMMON IN LARGE PARTS OF THE WORLD.

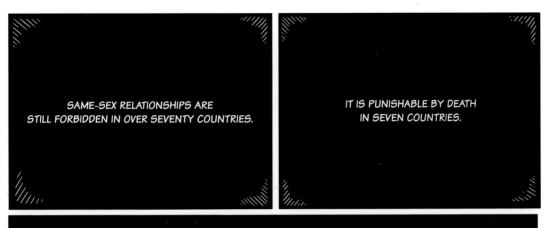

SAME-SEX RELATIONSHIPS ARE
STILL FORBIDDEN IN OVER SEVENTY COUNTRIES.

IT IS PUNISHABLE BY DEATH
IN SEVEN COUNTRIES.

THE LGBTQ+ COMMUNITY IS
STILL SUBJECT TO HATE CRIMES.

IN 2016, THE GAY NIGHTCLUB PULSE
IN ORLANDO, FLORIDA, WAS
ATTACKED. FORTY-NINE PEOPLE
WERE KILLED.

WHICH ONE OF YOU IS MALALA?

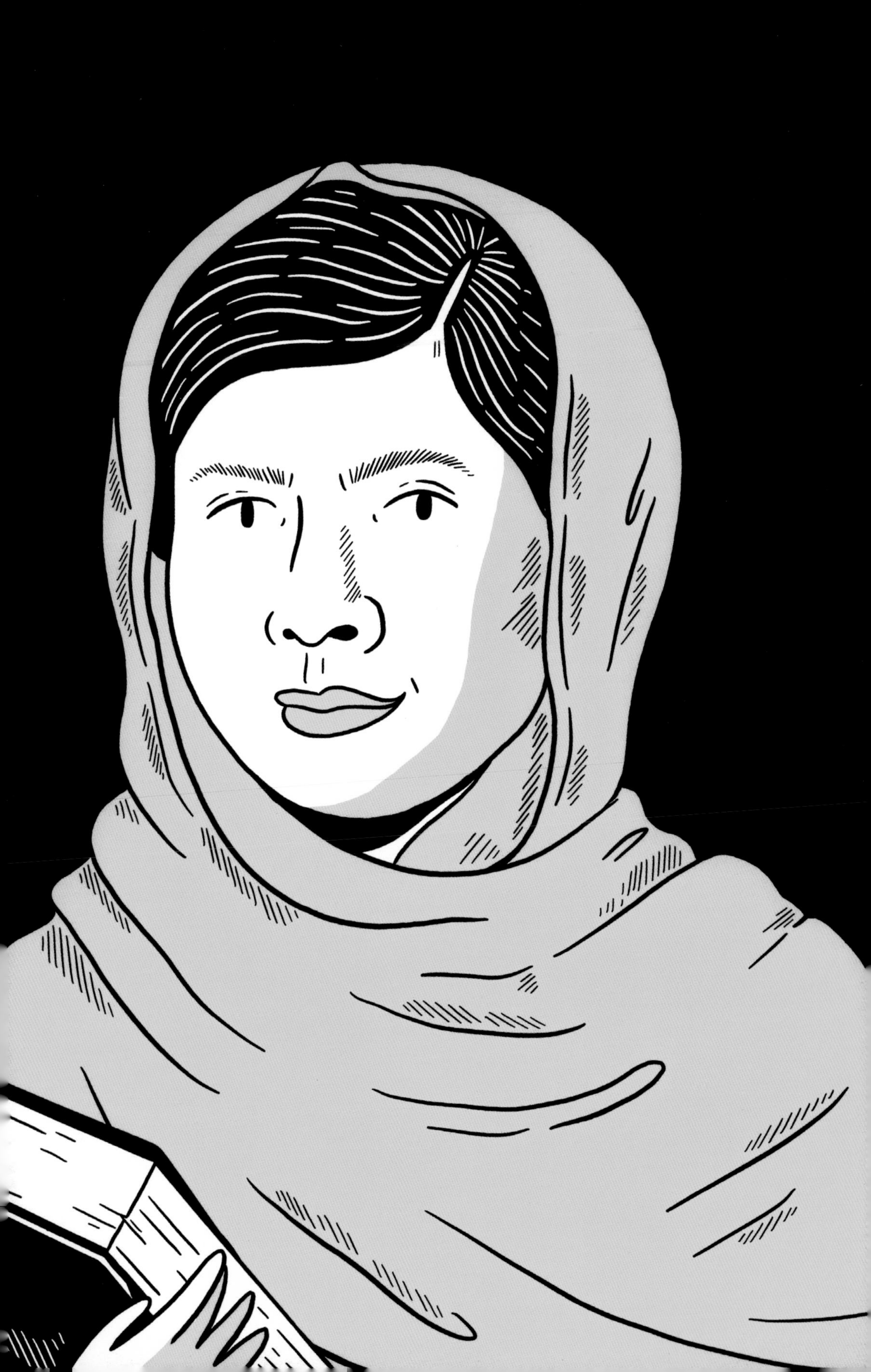

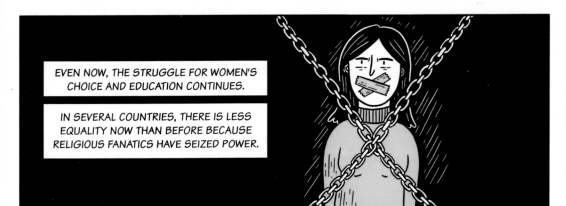

EVEN NOW, THE STRUGGLE FOR WOMEN'S CHOICE AND EDUCATION CONTINUES.

IN SEVERAL COUNTRIES, THERE IS LESS EQUALITY NOW THAN BEFORE BECAUSE RELIGIOUS FANATICS HAVE SEIZED POWER.

AFGHANISTAN, 1965

AFGHANISTAN, 2015

FAR MORE GIRLS GO TO SCHOOL NOW THAN TEN YEARS AGO, BUT MANY STILL NEED TO FIGHT FOR THEIR RIGHT TO AN EDUCATION.

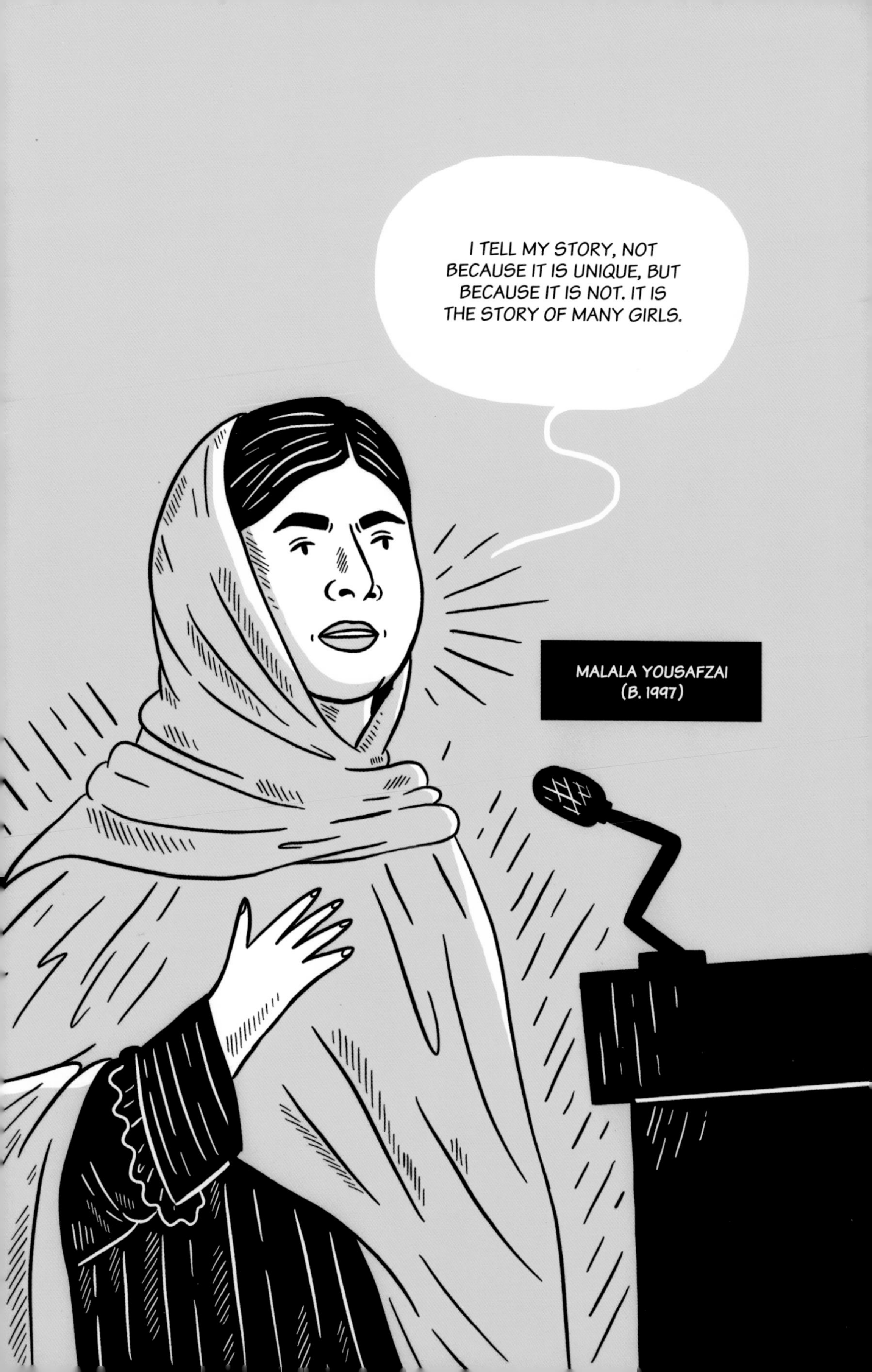
I TELL MY STORY, NOT BECAUSE IT IS UNIQUE, BUT BECAUSE IT IS NOT. IT IS THE STORY OF MANY GIRLS.
MALALA YOUSAFZAI (B. 1997)

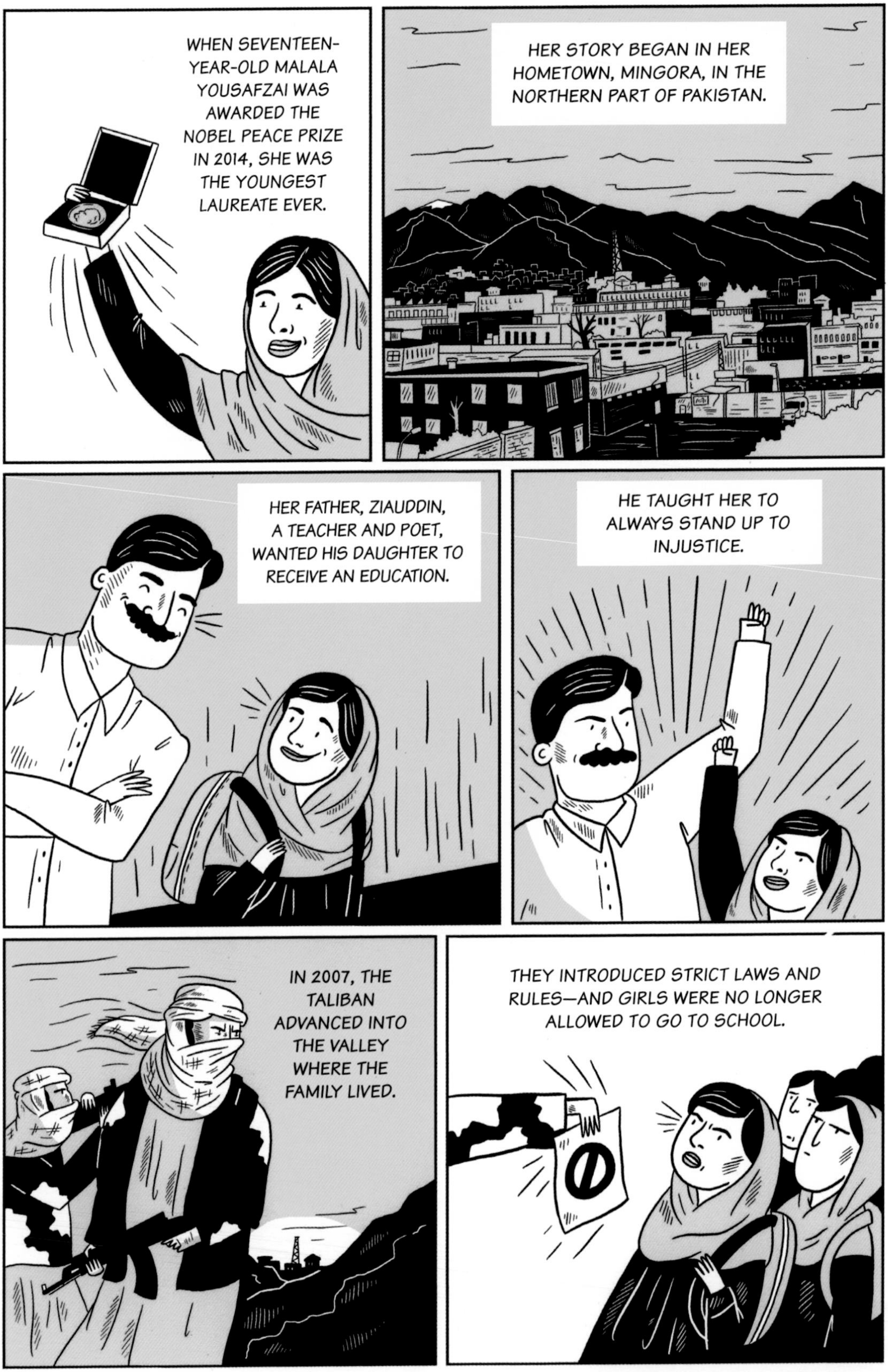
WHEN SEVENTEEN-YEAR-OLD MALALA YOUSAFZAI WAS AWARDED THE NOBEL PEACE PRIZE IN 2014, SHE WAS THE YOUNGEST LAUREATE EVER.
HER STORY BEGAN IN HER HOMETOWN, MINGORA, IN THE NORTHERN PART OF PAKISTAN.
HER FATHER, ZIAUDDIN, A TEACHER AND POET, WANTED HIS DAUGHTER TO RECEIVE AN EDUCATION.
HE TAUGHT HER TO ALWAYS STAND UP TO INJUSTICE.
IN 2007, THE TALIBAN ADVANCED INTO THE VALLEY WHERE THE FAMILY LIVED.
THEY INTRODUCED STRICT LAWS AND RULES—AND GIRLS WERE NO LONGER ALLOWED TO GO TO SCHOOL.

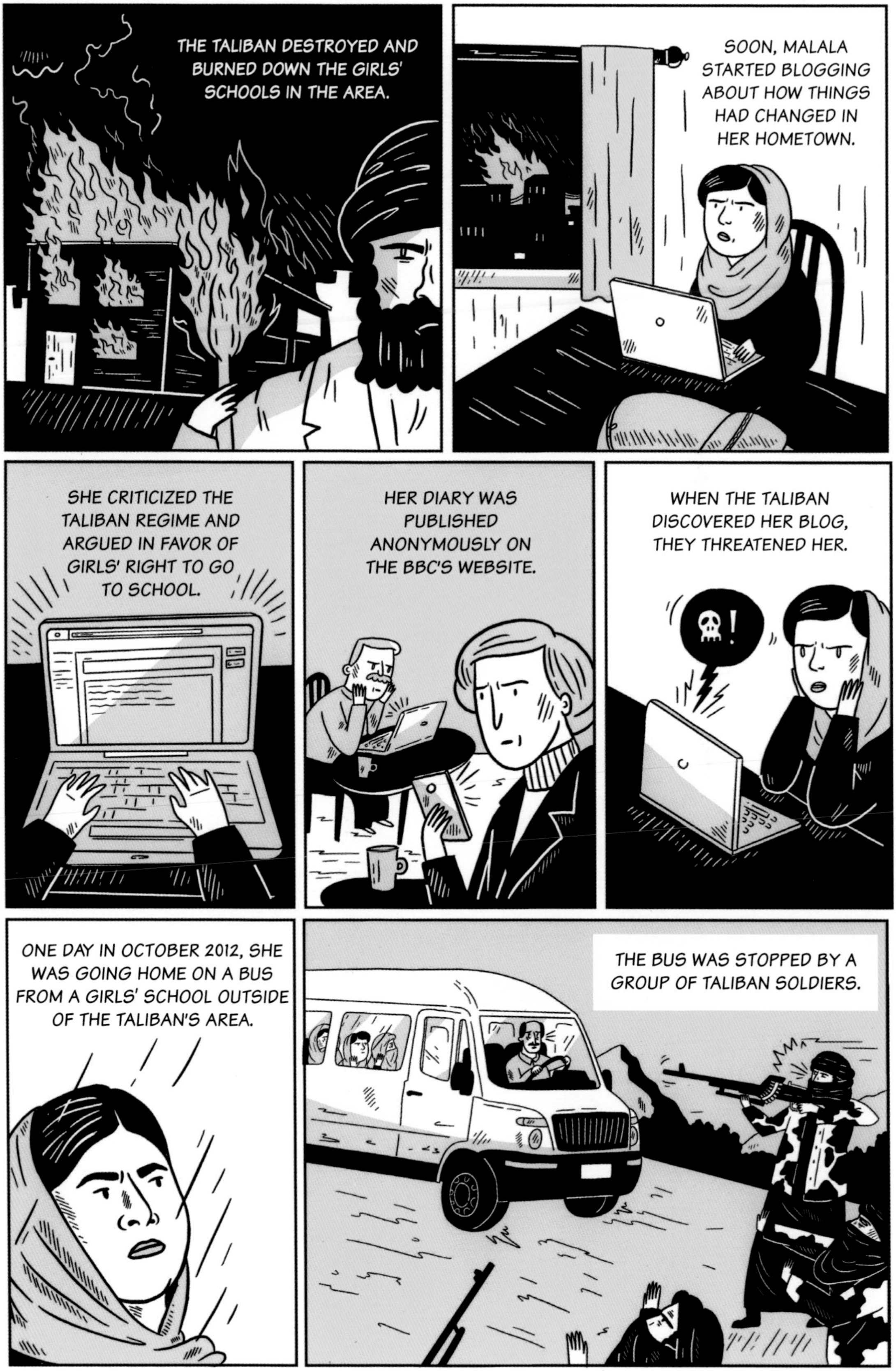
THE TALIBAN DESTROYED AND BURNED DOWN THE GIRLS' SCHOOLS IN THE AREA.
SOON, MALALA STARTED BLOGGING ABOUT HOW THINGS HAD CHANGED IN HER HOMETOWN.
SHE CRITICIZED THE TALIBAN REGIME AND ARGUED IN FAVOR OF GIRLS' RIGHT TO GO TO SCHOOL.
HER DIARY WAS PUBLISHED ANONYMOUSLY ON THE BBC'S WEBSITE.
WHEN THE TALIBAN DISCOVERED HER BLOG, THEY THREATENED HER.
!
ONE DAY IN OCTOBER 2012, SHE WAS GOING HOME ON A BUS FROM A GIRLS' SCHOOL OUTSIDE OF THE TALIBAN'S AREA.
THE BUS WAS STOPPED BY A GROUP OF TALIBAN SOLDIERS.

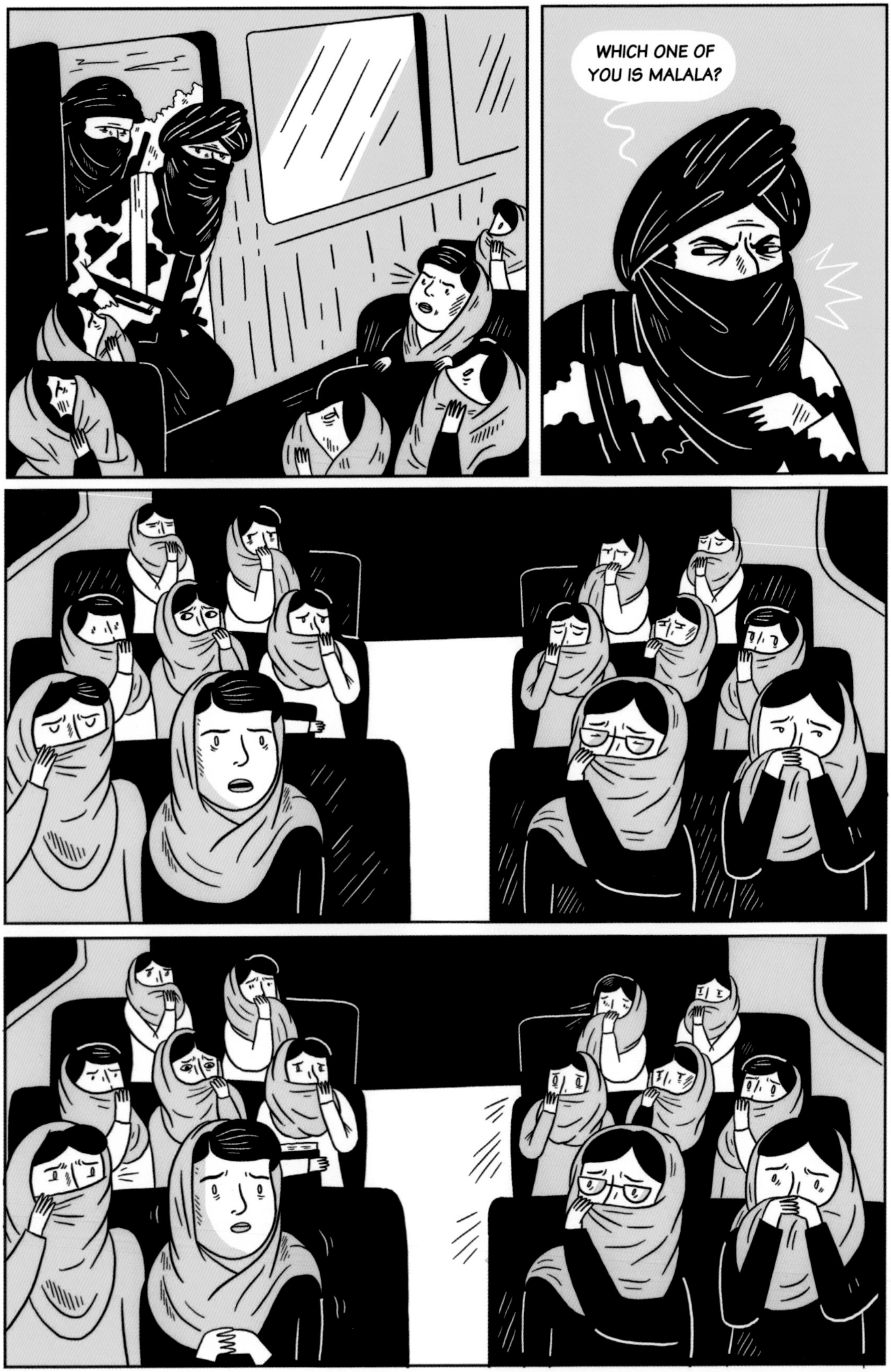
WHICH ONE OF YOU IS MALALA?

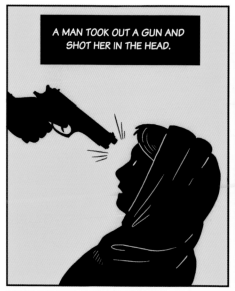

A MAN TOOK OUT A GUN AND SHOT HER IN THE HEAD.

SEVERAL OF HER SCHOOL FRIENDS WERE ALSO HURT.

WE WARNED HER SEVERAL TIMES AND SAID SHE HAD TO STOP CRITICIZING THE TALIBAN.

SHE HAS BEEN INFECTED BY WESTERN IDEALS. WE WILL ATTACK ANYONE DEFYING THE TALIBAN.

MALALA UNDERWENT SURGERY IN THE UNITED KINGDOM.

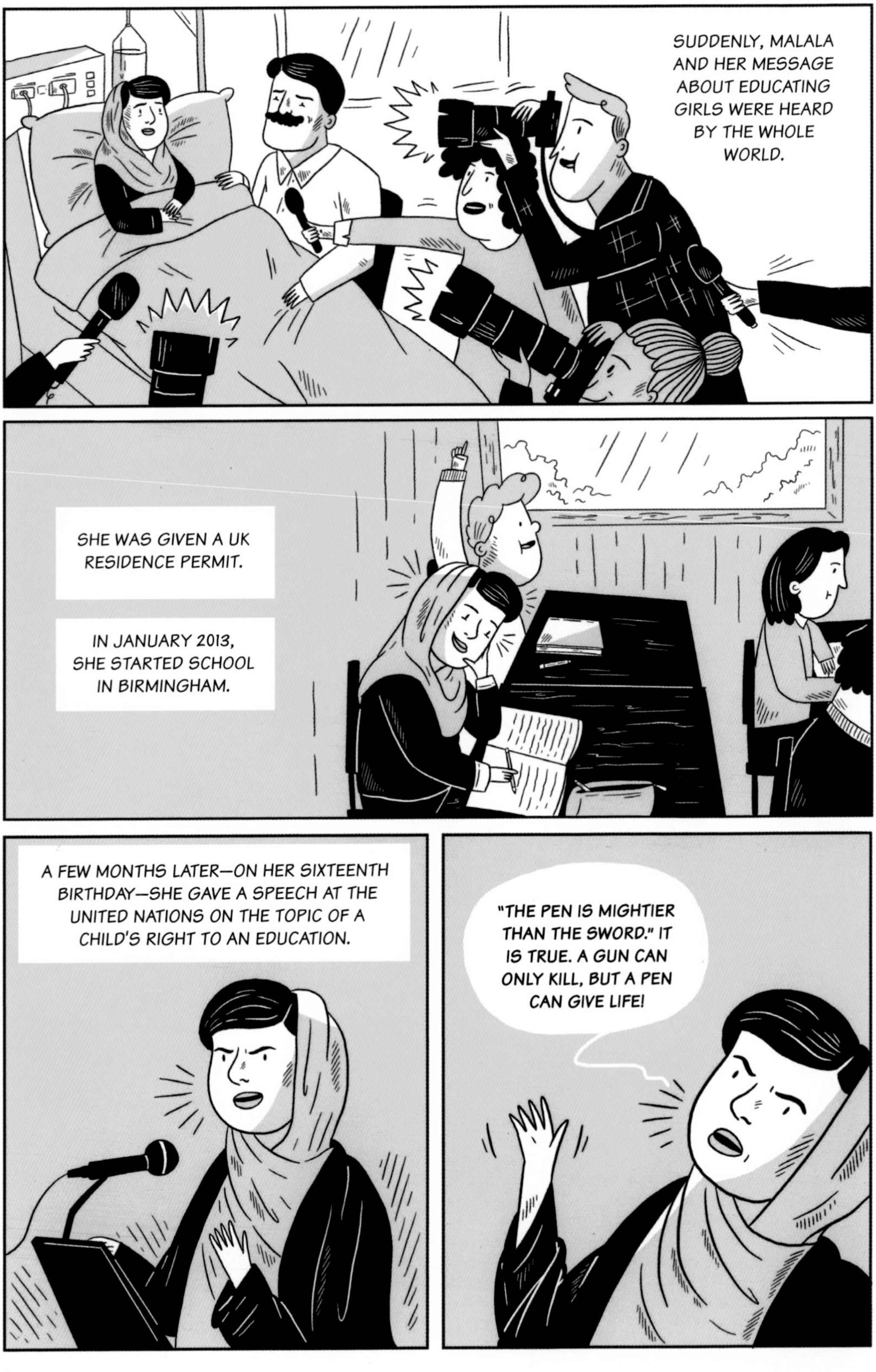
SUDDENLY, MALALA AND HER MESSAGE ABOUT EDUCATING GIRLS WERE HEARD BY THE WHOLE WORLD.
SHE WAS GIVEN A UK RESIDENCE PERMIT.
IN JANUARY 2013, SHE STARTED SCHOOL IN BIRMINGHAM.
A FEW MONTHS LATER—ON HER SIXTEENTH BIRTHDAY—SHE GAVE A SPEECH AT THE UNITED NATIONS ON THE TOPIC OF A CHILD'S RIGHT TO AN EDUCATION.
"THE PEN IS MIGHTIER THAN THE SWORD." IT IS TRUE. A GUN CAN ONLY KILL, BUT A PEN CAN GIVE LIFE!

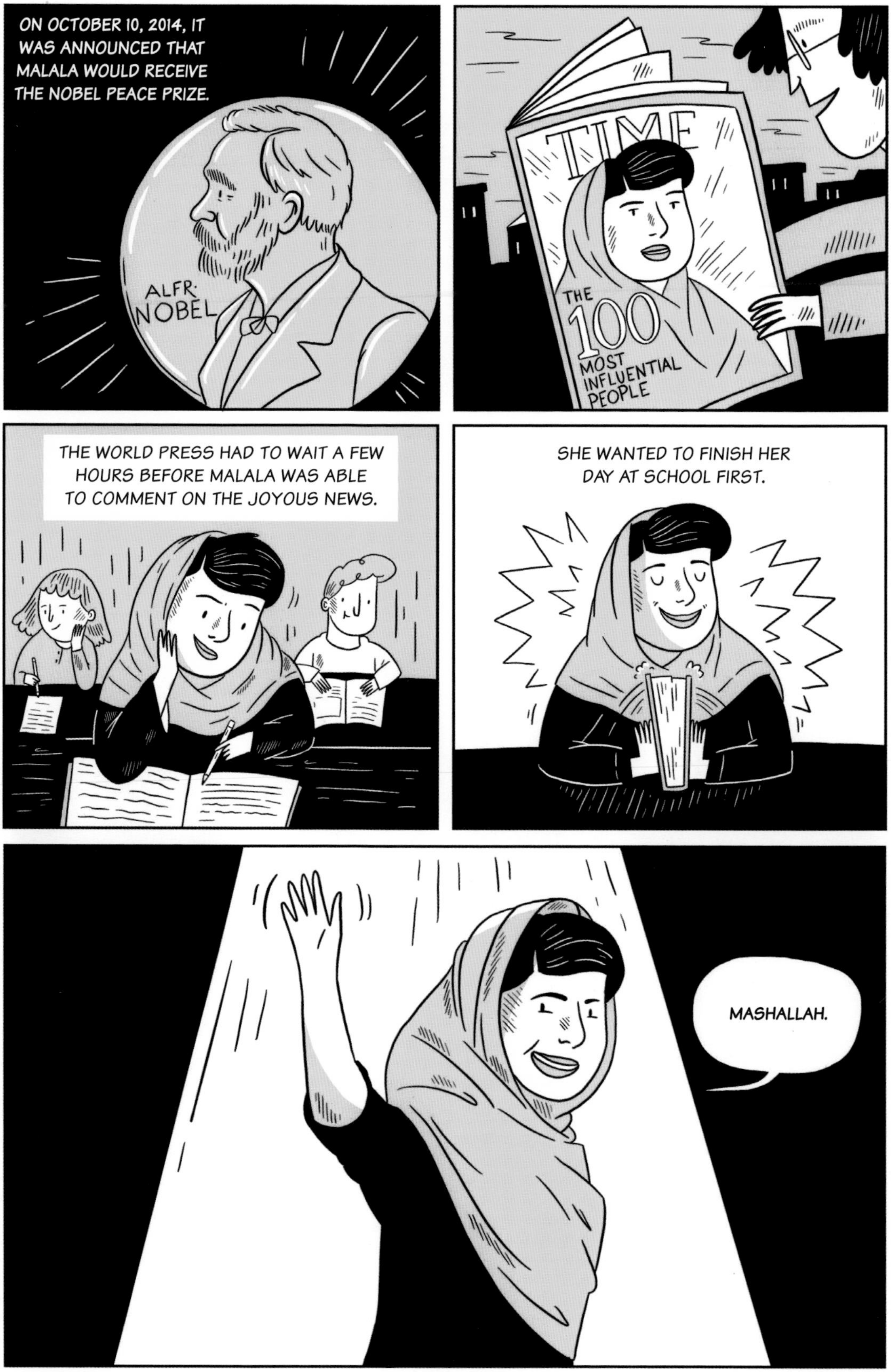
ON OCTOBER 10, 2014, IT WAS ANNOUNCED THAT MALALA WOULD RECEIVE THE NOBEL PEACE PRIZE.
ALFR· NOBEL
TIME
THE 100 MOST INFLUENTIAL PEOPLE
THE WORLD PRESS HAD TO WAIT A FEW HOURS BEFORE MALALA WAS ABLE TO COMMENT ON THE JOYOUS NEWS.
SHE WANTED TO FINISH HER DAY AT SCHOOL FIRST.
MASHALLAH.

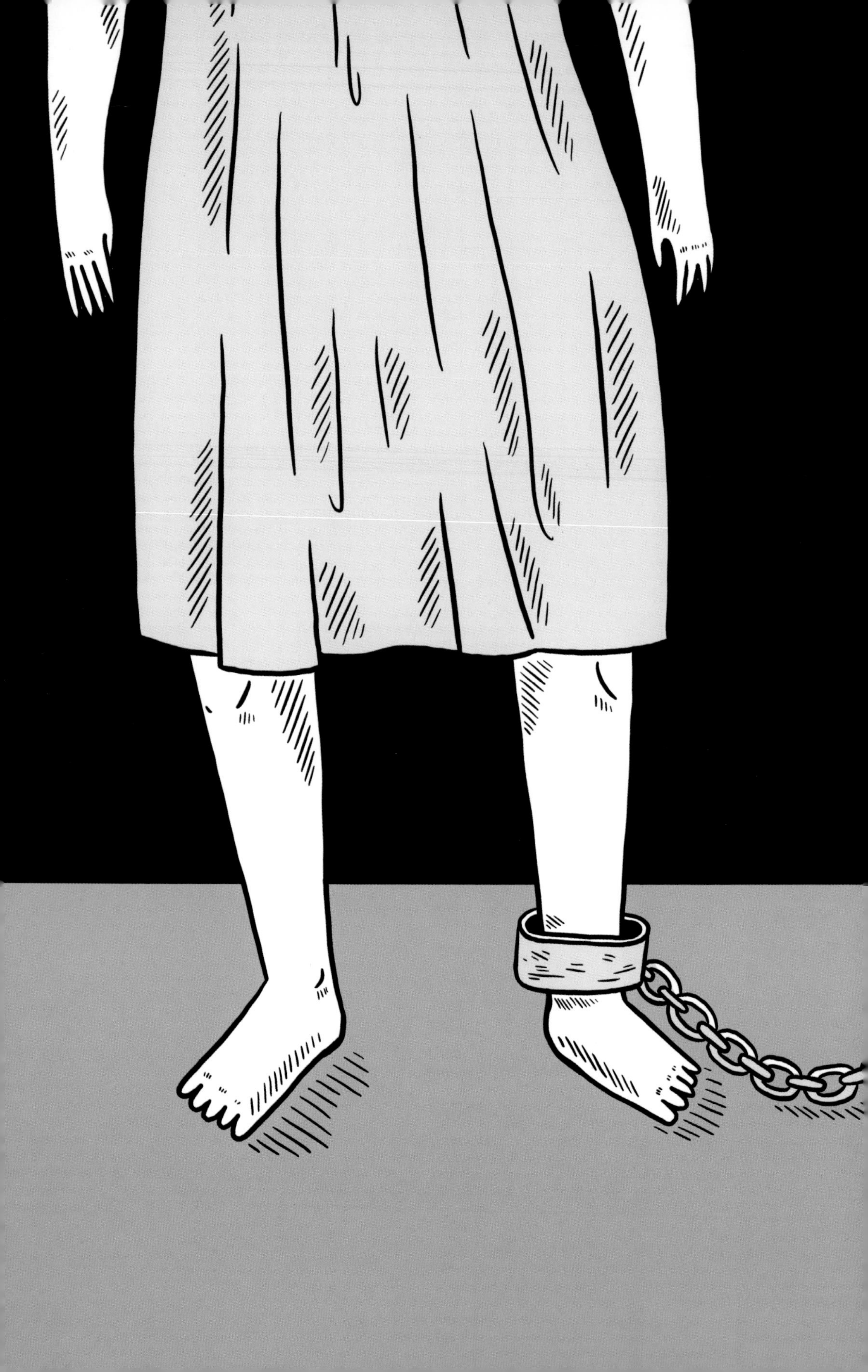

STRUGGLING TO
BREAK FREE

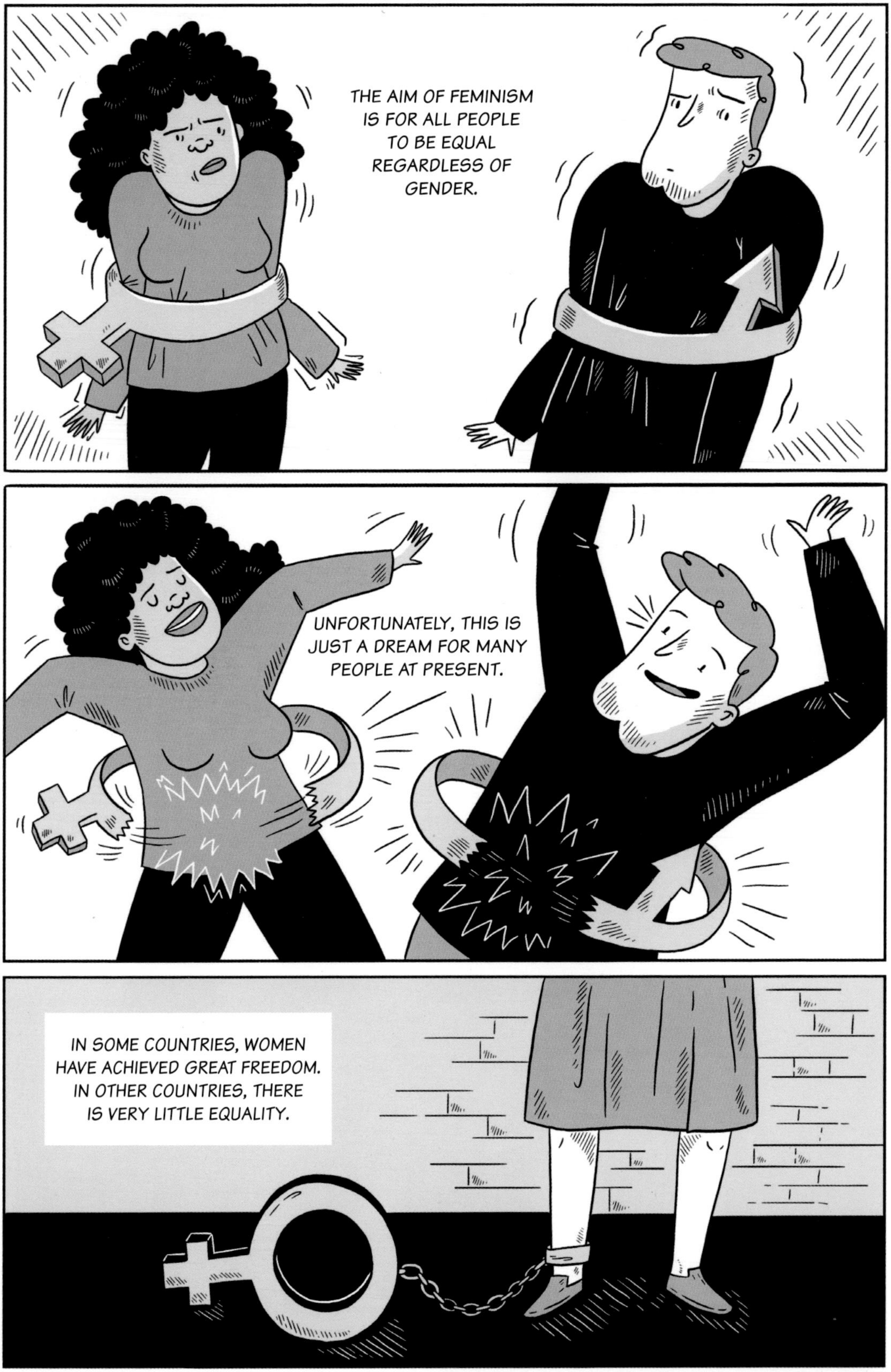
THE AIM OF FEMINISM IS FOR ALL PEOPLE TO BE EQUAL REGARDLESS OF GENDER.
UNFORTUNATELY, THIS IS JUST A DREAM FOR MANY PEOPLE AT PRESENT.
IN SOME COUNTRIES, WOMEN HAVE ACHIEVED GREAT FREEDOM. IN OTHER COUNTRIES, THERE IS VERY LITTLE EQUALITY.

IN RUSSIA, THERE IS A LIST OF OVER 400 PROFESSIONS THAT WOMEN CANNOT HAVE.

FISHERMAN
BUS DRIVER
CARPENTER
DIVER

AROUND THE WORLD, MANY GIRLS ARE MARRIED OFF AS CHILDREN.

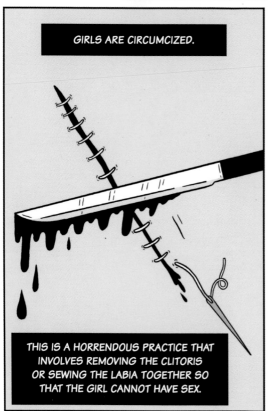

GIRLS ARE CIRCUMCIZED.

THIS IS A HORRENDOUS PRACTICE THAT INVOLVES REMOVING THE CLITORIS OR SEWING THE LABIA TOGETHER SO THAT THE GIRL CANNOT HAVE SEX.

WOMEN ARE CONSIDERED DIRTY WHEN THEY ARE MENSTRUATING. THEY ARE OFTEN LOCKED UP UNTIL THEY ARE "PURE" AGAIN.

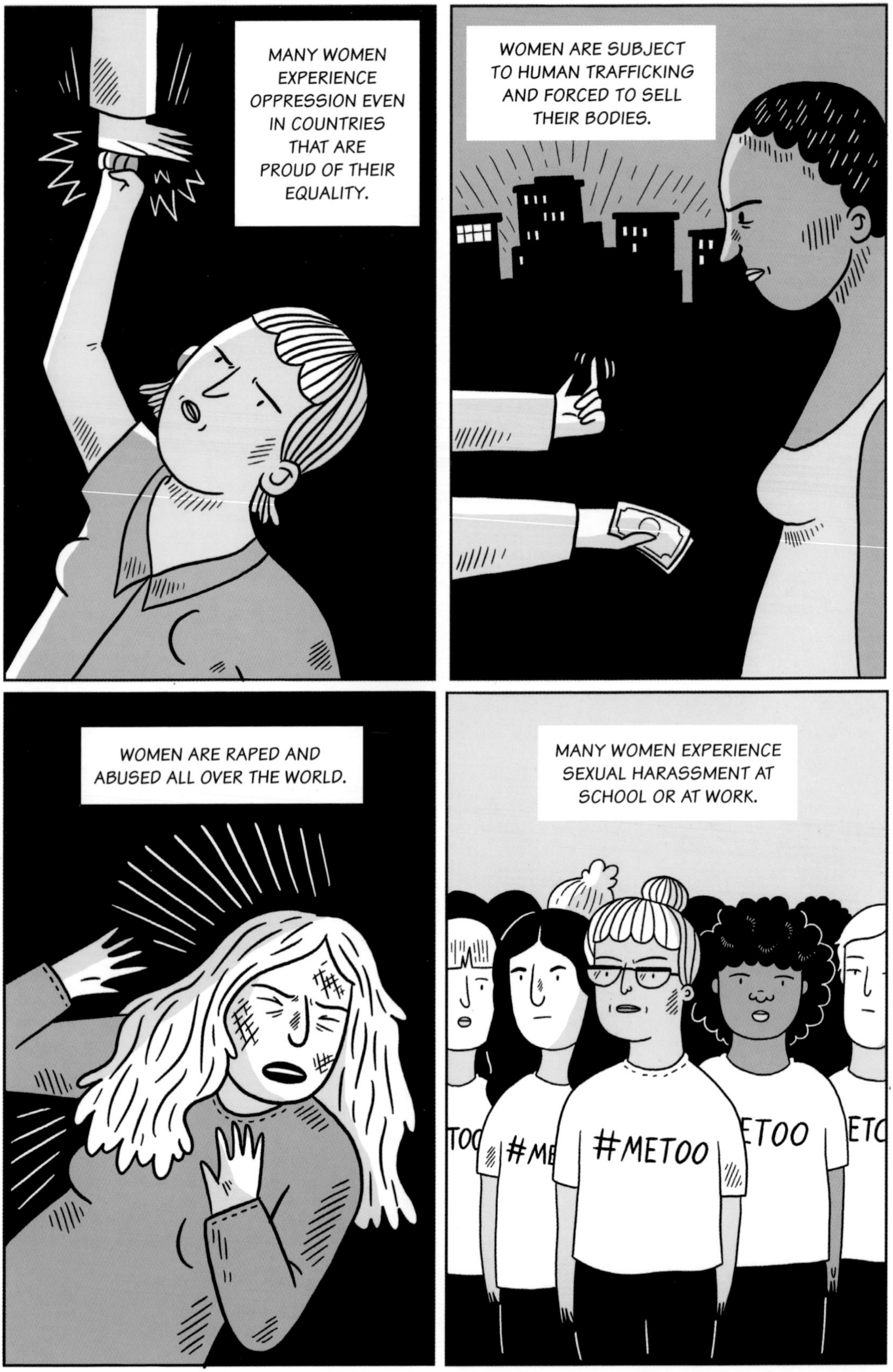
MANY WOMEN EXPERIENCE OPPRESSION EVEN IN COUNTRIES THAT ARE PROUD OF THEIR EQUALITY.
WOMEN ARE SUBJECT TO HUMAN TRAFFICKING AND FORCED TO SELL THEIR BODIES.
WOMEN ARE RAPED AND ABUSED ALL OVER THE WORLD.
MANY WOMEN EXPERIENCE SEXUAL HARASSMENT AT SCHOOL OR AT WORK.
#METOO

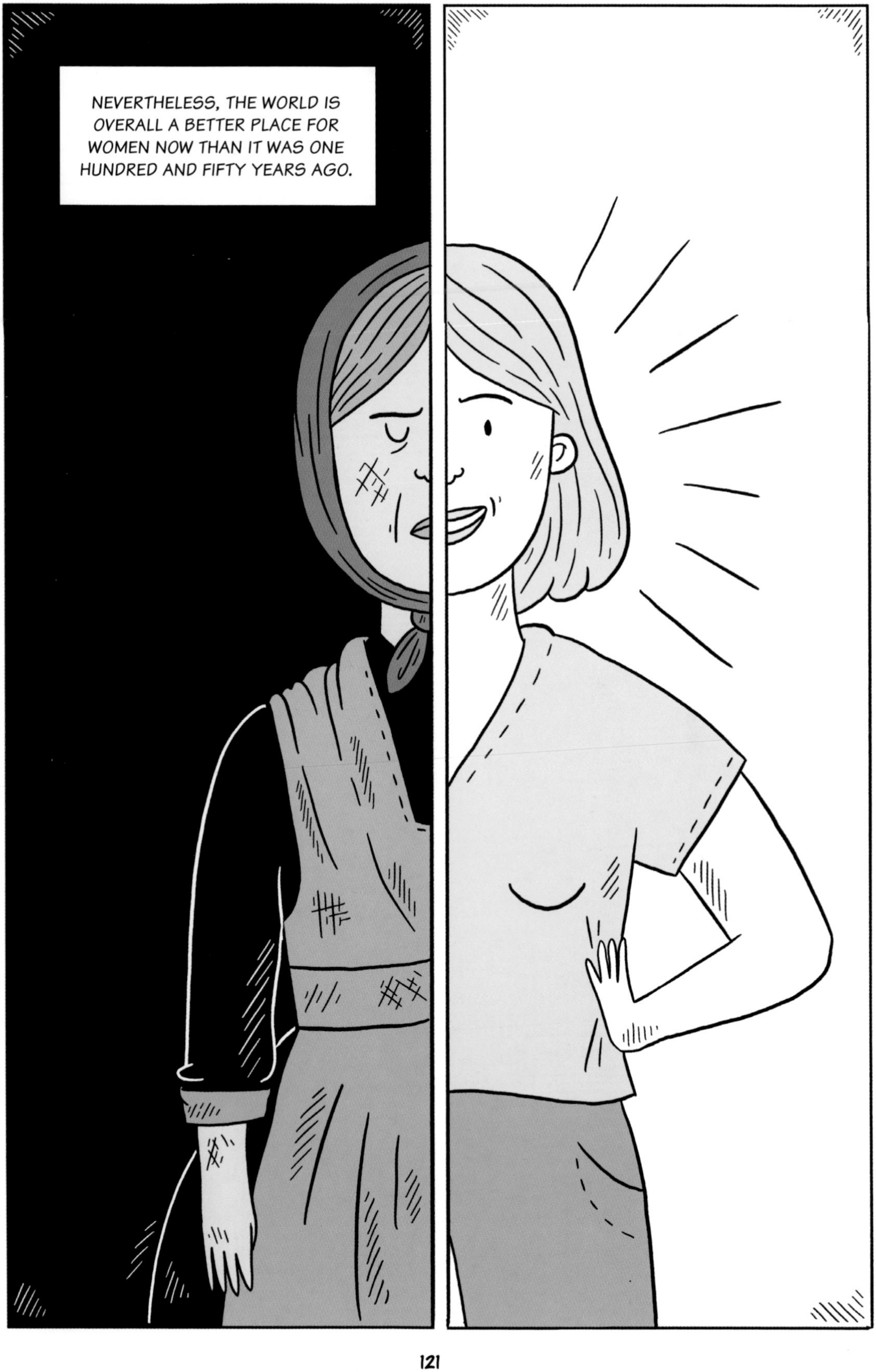
NEVERTHELESS, THE WORLD IS OVERALL A BETTER PLACE FOR WOMEN NOW THAN IT WAS ONE HUNDRED AND FIFTY YEARS AGO.

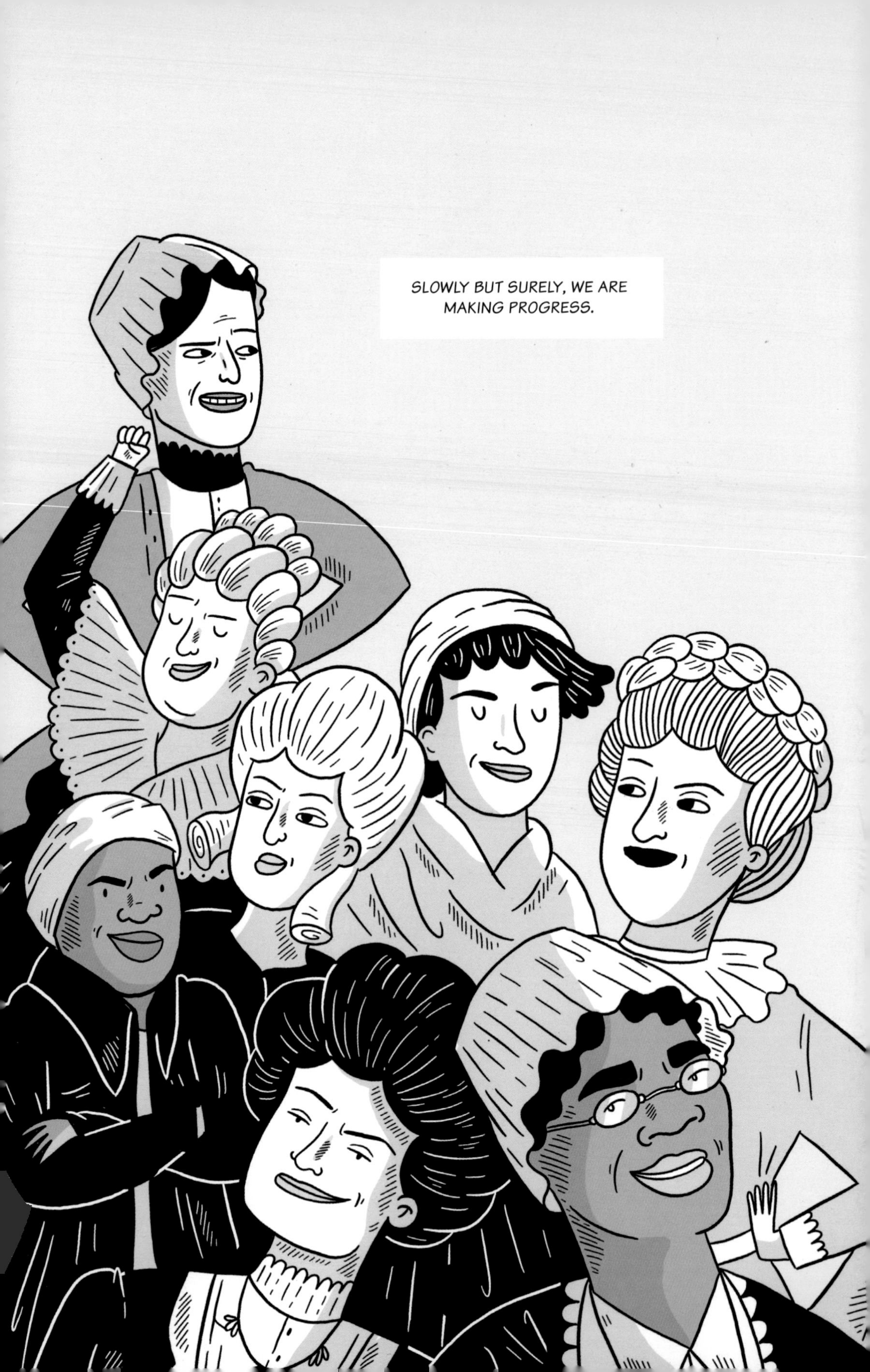
SLOWLY BUT SURELY, WE ARE MAKING PROGRESS.

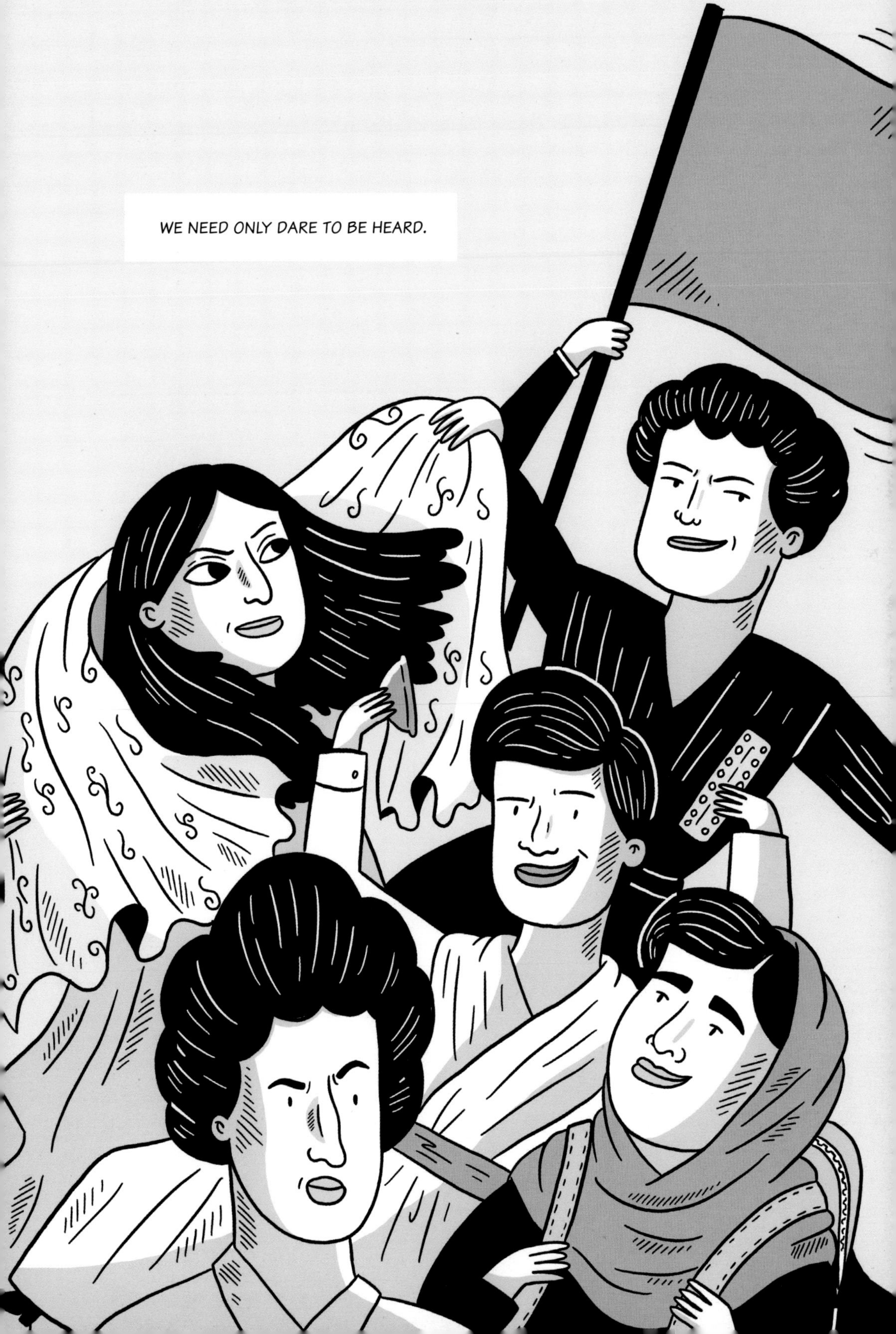
WE NEED ONLY DARE TO BE HEARD.

"IN BIG WAYS AND SMALL, THE UNFINISHED
BUSINESS OF THE TWENTY-FIRST CENTURY
IS THE FULL EQUALITY OF WOMEN."
— HILLARY CLINTON

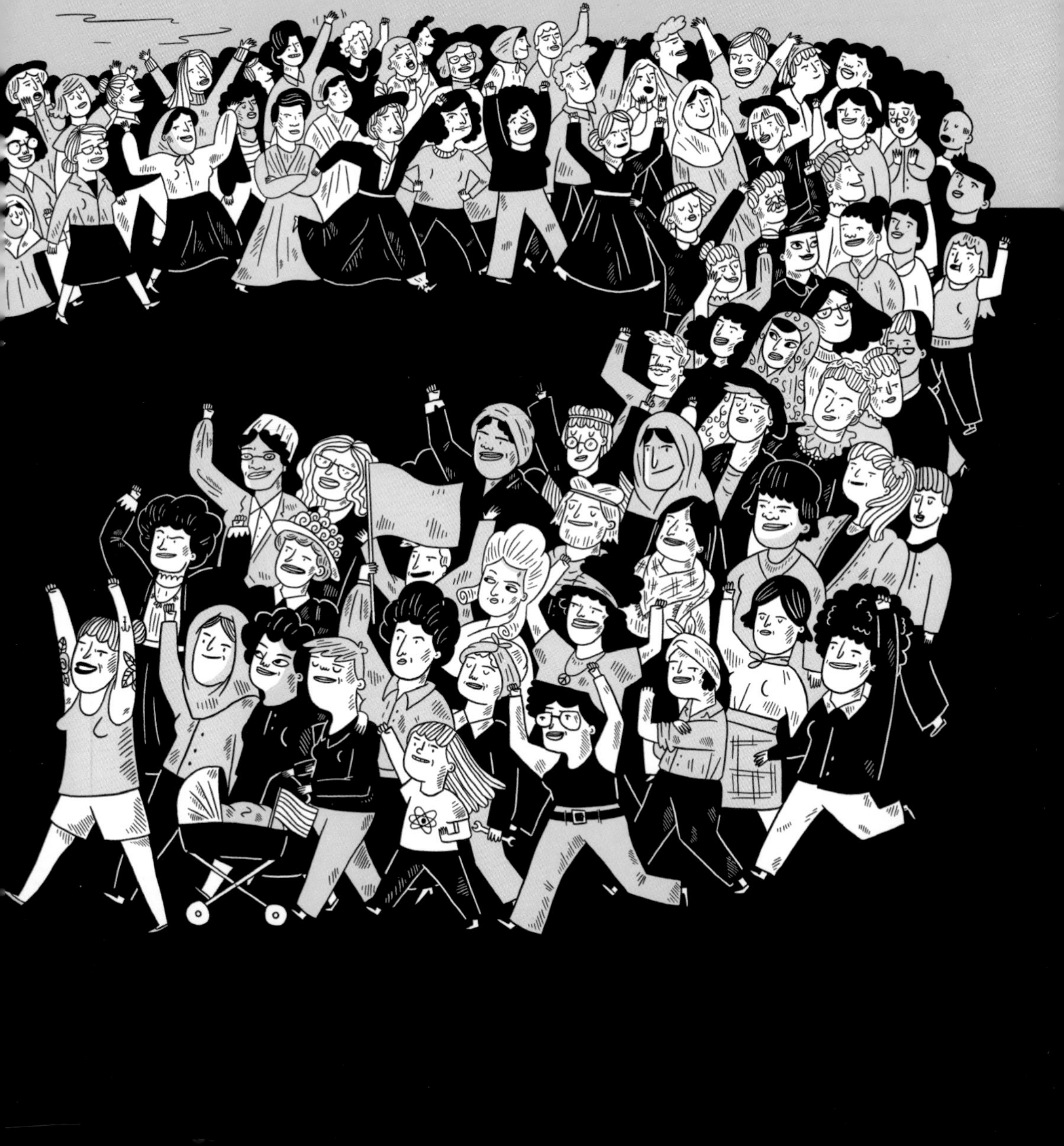

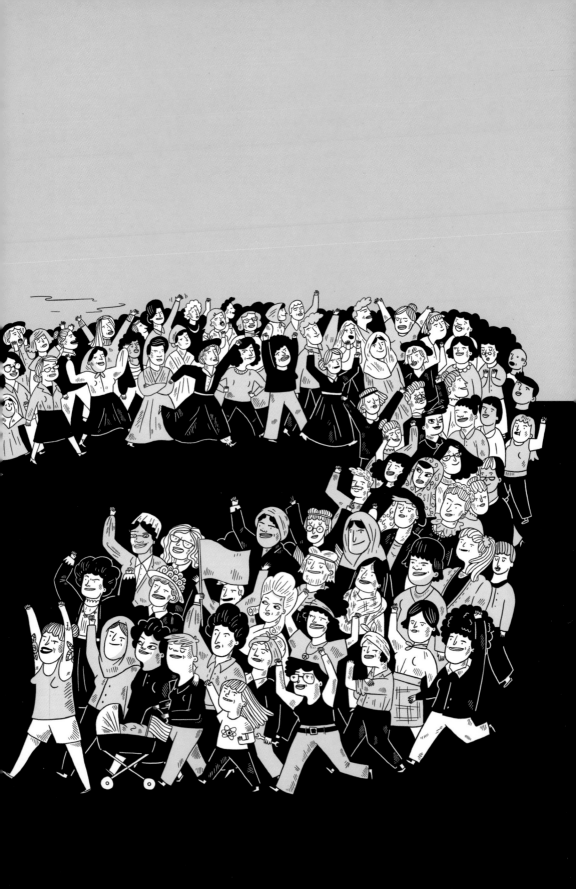

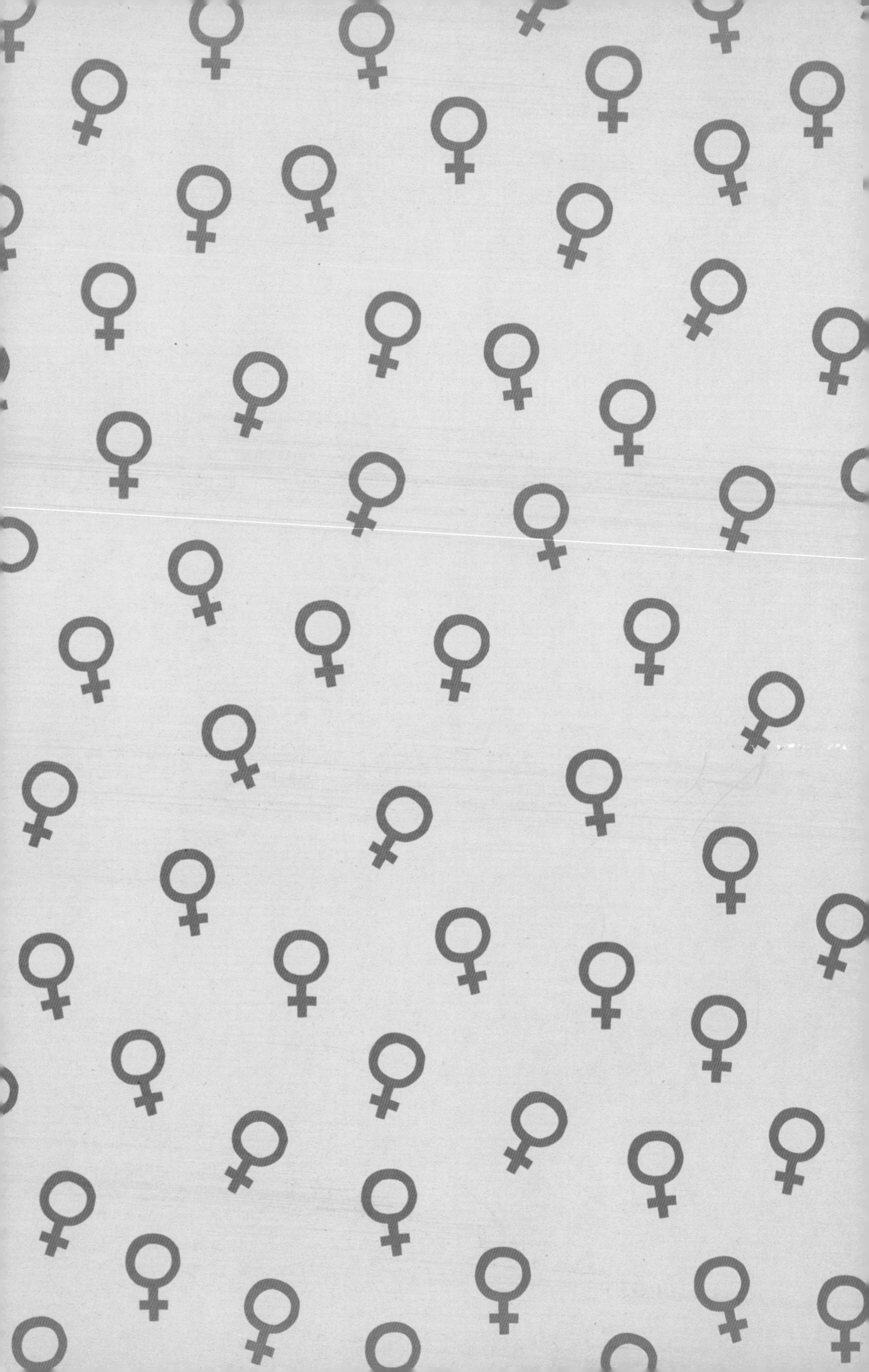